WHEN
EUROPE
WAS A
PRISON
CAMP

WHEN EUROPE WAS A PRISON CAMP

Father and Son Memoirs
1940–1941

OTTO SCHRAG and **PETER SCHRAG**

INDIANA UNIVERSITY PRESS

This book is a publication of

Indiana University Press
Office of Scholarly Publishing
Herman B Wells Library 350
1320 East 10th Street
Bloomington, Indiana 47405 USA

iupress.indiana.edu

The paper used in this publication
meets the minimum requirements of
the American National Standard for
Information Sciences—Permanence of
Paper for Printed Library Materials,
ANSI Z39.48–1992.

Manufactured in the
United States of America

*Library of Congress
Cataloging-in-Publication Data*

Schrag, Otto, 1902– author.
  When Europe was a prison camp :
father and son memoirs, 1940-1941 /
Otto Schrag and Peter Schrag.
  pages cm
  ISBN 978-0-253-01769-7 (cl : alk.
paper)—ISBN 978-0-253-01785-7 (eb)
  1. Schrag, Otto, 1902– 2. Schrag, Peter.
3. Holocaust, Jewish (1939–1945)—
Germany—Personal narratives.
4. Holocaust \ survivors—Germany—
Biography. I. Schrag, Peter, co-author.
II. Title.
  DS134.4.S38 2015
  940.53'180922—dc23

                          2015003845

1 2 3 4 5   20 19 18 17 16 15

For my mother, Judith Haas Schrag

My visions range about a dungeon cell
With Europe flung therein . . . and guarded well

WALTER MEHRING,
"Odyssey Out of Midnight
Camp St. Cyprien, September 1940"
Tr. S. A. De Witt

Map of Occupied Europe, 1940.

United States Holocaust Memorial Museum.

CONTENTS

INTRODUCTION

IN THE SUMMER AND FALL OF 1941, SHORTLY AFTER OUR arrival in New York from Europe, my father, Otto Schrag, wrote the draft of a book-length narrative about his internment in a concentration camp in southern France and our escape—his, mine, and my mother's—from Nazi occupied Europe in 1940–41. Was it to be a novel? Or was it a fictionalized memoir? After extensive research, I found the story to be so surprisingly well corroborated by the documentary record and by other accounts that it looks at heart much more like a meticulously observed personal chronicle than it does like a novel—a memoir of a harrowing year in our lives, as it was in the lives of thousands of others.

That record includes official lists of prisoners interned in the French concentration camp at Saint-Cyprien, my father's *Notice Individuelle* (his dossier), and other documents in his camp file, some now in French government archives,[1] as well as memoirs, many never published, of internment by Rabbi Jehuda Leo Ansbacher, Ernest Simon, Gerhard (later Jerry) Breuer, and others arrested in Belgium and interned in the French camps. It also includes ship manifests, interviews with survivors and their descendants, and personal visits (or post-war returns) to the places in Belgium and France in which these stories took place. It's also eerily true to what I personally recall about my own wartime experience

---

1. These are mostly notes handwritten with classic formality and sent from one official to another: "In regard to your inquiry about the subject Otto (or Othon) Schrag, I have the honor to inform you that the subject escaped on 20/8/40."

and to the history of that time.[2] My father's story was supposed to be a cautionary tale addressed, he said in so many words, to the "American reader." For any accounting of that dark period in modern history, it has to be part of the documentary record. No other memoir about the detention of Jews in Belgium and France and their internment in the French concentration camps, I believe, matches my father's.

My father died in 1971, but a smudged carbon copy of the typed manuscript, written in German, has followed me around and has been lying in one or another drawer through the seventy-plus years since he typed it. Until recently it was unread—and avoided—by me and, as far as I know, by anyone else except maybe my mother. At the urging of relatives and friends, I've now translated and edited it.

In the 1980s, I wrote my own recollections of the aborted attempt my mother, grandmother, and I made to flee Brussels ahead of the German invasion in 1940—by car, by truck, on foot—and of our days and nights huddled in a cellar as the battle for the French port city of Boulogne raged over our heads. That memoir, written for my children forty years after the fact, also covers the year after our return to Nazi-occupied Brussels in 1940–41 and our subsequent odyssey—mine and my mother's—across and around various borders, sometimes with smugglers, sometimes alone, through Belgium, occupied and "unoccupied" (Vichy) France, into Spain and Portugal and finally to New York. I was then not quite ten years old, but it wasn't until recently that I realized how small and young I was.

The rediscovery of my father's manuscript, his account of his detention in Brussels, the transport in hot airless cattle cars to the south of

2. Perhaps the most powerful corroboration comes from the concentration camp drawings and paintings of Karl Schwesig, Carl Rabus, and Felix Nussbaum, fellow prisoners at Saint-Cyprien. Nussbaum's were done after he escaped and was back in Brussels for two years before he and his wife were arrested by the Germans and sent to the death chamber at Auschwitz. Nussbaum's paintings could be illustrations for my father's story. See, e.g., "Prisoner" in Karl Georg Kaster, ed., *Felix Nussbaum: Art Defamed, Art in Exile, Art in Resistance* (Woodstock, NY: Overlook, 1990), 331. The original is in the Deutsches Historisches Museum in Berlin. Schwesig, who was not Jewish, was a political refugee; he survived four French concentration camps and a Nazi prison. He died in Düsseldorf in 1955. Most of his Saint-Cyprien paintings, many also done later, are now in Beit Lohamei Haghetaot, the Ghetto Fighters' House Museum in Israel.

France, his internment at Saint-Cyprien, one of the *camps de concentra-tion* on the Mediterranean shore near Perpignan, and his telling of my mother's and my story, put my own recollection—and the whole era—into a new perspective.

I'd read a lot about those years and thought I knew a fair amount about the Holocaust and the war. But through that rediscovered old manuscript—my own customhouse experience, though much closer to reality, and not a novelist's device as Hawthorne's was—I began to understand in new ways the fearful difficulties and terrible life-or-death choices that my parents and many thousands of their generation faced: the arbitrariness, insouciance and, at times, the sadistic cruelties of the visa bureaucracies and other officialdom; the bargaining with smug-glers and document forgers; the dreadful uncertainty about who could be trusted, who was a swindler, who was an informer, who could be safely be bribed and who not, and the terrible consequences of a wrong choice; the expropriation and outright robbery of prisoners' belongings by internment camp guards; the walks across frontiers in the middle of the night; trying to sleep in little *pensions* with the sound of boots on the pavement outside—and beyond, always the specter of the knock on the door and shipment to what would become the death camps in the East. The prospect of being sent to Dachau or to "Poland" terrorized the Jews of Europe long before the Nazis industrialized genocide. I'm not sure I knew that we might be shot on sight when we walked in across the Line of Demarcation, the widely feared and heavily guarded border between Nazi-occupied and so-called unoccupied France in the early hours of a May morning in 1941. But I assume my mother knew. Recently, when I was researching the background of our stories, I found photos of signs, in French and German, posted at the line warning that anyone crossing who disregarded an order to stop would be shot. I don't think we ever encountered such a sign, but they must have been there.

In the course of reading my father's manuscript—he called it *Helden Ohne Mut (Heroes Without Courage)*—I also gained, many years after their death, an altogether new understanding of my parents: about my mother's great strength, as well as the deep uncertainties behind her de-termination; about my father's fears and about their desperate attempts to be reunited. Despite severe restrictions and the countless chances of arrest by the SiPo (the *Sicherheitspolizei*), by the Gestapo, and by the French, my mother illegally crossed France and the Demarcation Line three times, first to help my father escape from Saint-Cyprien and to find a hiding place for him and a few friends in a small village in the Pyrenees, then to return to Brussels and get me, then again to get both of us out. Those trips, separated by false starts and failed attempts, were themselves marked by a half dozen close calls with patrols, border police, supercilious customs agents and an assortment of Nazi officials.

My father selectively used pseudonyms in his story, both for people and occasionally for places, probably in the expectation that the story would be published before the end of the war and that people, especially those who helped refugees, sometimes at great personal risk, had to be protected. He named himself Hans Licht, though he used Judith and Peter, the correct first names, for my mother and me.[3] Sometimes the changes were transparent. He talks about how after much effort he got a transit visa for the United States from a consular official in Marseille named Stanwick in 1940–41, almost certainly a pseudonym for the improbably named Myles Standish, a vice consul there who was one of the few State Department people who were sympathetic to Jewish refugees. His associate, Hiram "Harry" Bingham, the vice consul in charge of the visa section in Marseille, was another. Both would eventually be replaced by the State Department for being too generous with those visas. And while Bingham has been honored for his courage in the years since, Standish got little recognition. There are copies of a few documents issued by Standish in various archives, but a thorough search has not turned up even one photo.

Another transparent pseudonym was Löwe (Lion), the internee-physician at Saint-Cyprien who slipped out of the camp to test the blood samples that proved that there was an epidemic of typhus in the camp. The real name of that physician was Richard Baer—he later practiced medicine in New York. So the Bear became the Lion, one zoo animal for another. My father called his partner in the malt business Hirsch

---

3. He believed that the name Schrag was somehow derived from the Hebrew word meaning "the light of wisdom", which may be why he chose the name Licht, the German word for light, for himself.

(German for stag) in his story. His real name, as I recalled when I found the records from my father's internment camp, was Cerf, the French word for the same animal. The mayor of the village in the Pyrenees who helped him and his friends hide after their escape from Saint-Cyprien is Didier in my father's manuscript. My father later acknowledged his real name—it was Paul Ilhe—in an author's note in *Sons of the Morning,* a novel published at the end of the war. Fritz Lefo, his friend and business associate, who plays a large role in this story, became Lofe.

I've changed the place names back to the real names. My father called the village in the Pyrenees Lopez, an unlikely name even for a town in French Catalonia; the real name is Les Martys, located in the region called Montagne Noire—Black Mountain. Sometimes he just referred to Carcassonne as "M." But I kept his names for the people in his story, since I don't know many of the real names. Some of those people may have been merely composites or even novelistic inventions. But the events in which they took part were all too terribly real.

In combining my own memoir—written many years after the end of the war, but long before I read my father's story—with his narrative, I used my father's draft for those parts of the story that I didn't witness, and generally relied on my own memory and my shorter memoir for those in which I was present. His part is written in the third person. Mine is in the first person. I tried not to tell the same part of the story twice in two different, but often redundant, versions. This introduction, the epilogue, and all the footnotes, of course, are mine.

As in all memoirs—and all history for that matter—there are obvious problems. How much is imagined, misremembered, sheer fiction? How much has been forgotten? I also wonder, since in my own case all of it was experienced in other languages—German, French, Luxemburger Deutsch—how much was lost with the language. How much simply passed over the head of a young boy? How much has been repressed? I still read and speak some French and German—and found it surprisingly easy to translate my father's prose—but certainly not with the facility I once had.

And how much of "memory" is built subconsciously from what we get from others? In a piece in the *New York Review of Books,* the neurologist Oliver Sacks tells how when he was a boy in England during the

Blitz, "an incendiary bomb, a thermite bomb, fell behind our house and burned with a terrible, white-hot heat." Later his brother told him he couldn't possibly have seen it because he wasn't there. Sometimes, Sacks says, "we assimilate what we read, what we are told, what others say and think and write and paint as intensely and richly as if they were primary experiences." Things we recall as personal experiences we might not have witnessed at all but have seen and heard "with other eyes and ears. . . . Memory is dialogic and arises not only from direct experience but from the intercourse of many minds."[4]

There's no way to know to what extent my father got his story from his fellow-prisoners or from other refugees of the 1940s. In the spring and summer of 1940, some six to eight thousand men, the majority expatriate Germans or Austrians from Belgium, most of them Jews, were interned at Saint-Cyprien. (Tens of thousands of women refugees and children, the great majority also Jewish, were interned at Gurs, a huge camp about sixty miles from the Atlantic coast and twenty miles north of the Spanish border.)[5] Two memoirs by great writers who had been interned in French camps, Arthur Koestler's *Scum of the Earth* and Lion Feuchtwanger's *The Devil in France,* were published in 1941, and both remain powerful testaments to the pervasive horrors and venality of the times. But neither tells the story my father wrote, and since few other refugee memoirs were published, or even written, when he wrote his story in the early 1940s, it's unlikely that much of his memory—or mine, for that matter—was "dialogic." Exiles in America didn't sit around and tell war stories.[6]

---

4. Oliver Sacks, "Speak, Memory," *NYRB,* Feb. 21, 2013.

5. Later researchers estimated that a majority of German Jews from Belgium—the adult men—passed through Saint-Cyprien, though many would subsequently be moved to other camps. About 7,500 arrived there in May or early June, but roughly 2,000—many of them German Aryans—were released after the collapse of France.

6. The weekly *Aufbau,* the German language newspaper published in New York for German (mostly Jewish) refugees, occasionally found its way into our house. It carried a great deal of news and useful information for the exile community, from federal immigration requirements and news of ship arrivals to ads for Viennese pastry shops, steamship passage to Cuba and Mexico, English lessons—"speak American"—and summer (mostly Borscht circuit) resorts. It ran lists of internees in French camps, when available, and lists of Holocaust survivors at war's end, as well as articles about the war and conditions in Europe, but few detailed personal stories of internment and other wartime experiences,

In researching the background of our stories, I've found a number of personal accounts in the archives of the USC Shoah Foundation in Los Angeles and the United States Holocaust Memorial Museum in Washington and at the Center for Jewish History in New York. Jerry Breuer's—he was just seventeen when he was shipped to Saint-Cyprien—was written in Shanghai in 1941, but my father couldn't possibly have seen it. Others by former prisoners at Saint-Cyprien and other French concentration camps date from later years. There are reports based on visits like that of Rabbi René Kapel, a former French army chaplain, who described Saint-Cyprien, "a veritable desert of sand," in roughly the same terms my father did. I also found a videotaped interview with Marianne Reinemann— she was in her eighties when it was taped—who was with my mother and me when the Germans in Lille hauled us off a train in 1941.

What most struck me when I read other accounts of Saint-Cyprien internees, however, was how restrained my father's was. He mentions the sandstorm when they arrived, but doesn't say that the frequent sandstorms there made life nearly intolerable, even inside the rickety barracks. He doesn't remark on the fact that the sand outside in the daytime was almost unbearably hot underfoot and that there was no electricity in the barracks; he barely mentions the fleas, the lice, the dysentery, or (conversely) that the momentary abundance of surplus peaches, tomatoes, and other produce in the summer had a depressing effect on the lively black market of food and other goods that were smuggled (to those who had money) into the camp. The German poet Walter Mehring, who was also interned there, called it the Pyrenean Hell. The American Varian Fry called it the "pest hole of France."[7]

But I've found little in those other accounts with the richness of personal detail of my father's narrative, much less the related stories of the

---

probably because they were so common in that world and described events that most refugees preferred to forget. Founded in 1934, it ceased publication in 2004.

7. Varian Fry, *Surrender on Demand* (New York: Random House, 1945), 48. Fry's fascinating story has been told a number of times, by himself in this book, among others. More about him below. The title comes from Section XIX on the French–German armistice agreement—really the French capitulation in June 1940, which required the French to "surrender on demand" all Germans in France named by the German government. In effect, the French formally betrayed all the refugees to whom it had offered asylum.

officious consular and other state bureaucracies that made escape from the shadow of fascism and racism, and not just in Nazi Germany but in most of Europe, so nearly impossible. Several recent studies were particularly helpful, among them Marcel Bervoets's invaluable *La liste de Saint-Cyprien*, which includes the names, barracks, and other details of many of the thousands of Saint-Cyprien internees, including my father's, and Denis Peschanski's massive doctoral dissertation, *Les camps français d'internement (1938–1946)*.[8]

The horrifying accounts of the Nazi death camps, which most of the world refused to believe until the last years of the war—and which some still deny—have long overshadowed the lesser inhumanity, arbitrariness, humiliation, and malevolence of the French internment camps and the cattle cars—the forty-and-eights—in which prisoners were shipped to them.[9] There were more than one hundred of those camps, depending on what you count. The horrors of the Nazi death camps also overshadowed the willingness, often the eagerness, of the French to deliver their inmates to the Nazis for shipment east. That story has been well told by, among others, Michael R. Marrus and Robert O. Paxton in their *Vichy France and the Jews,* Julian Jackson's *France: The Dark Years, 1940-1944,* in Anne Grynberg's *Les camps de la honte,* and by Donna F. Ryan in her *Holocaust and the Jews of Marseille.* What seems to be clear now is that France's betrayal of the refugees from Nazi Germany to whom it once promised protection originated as much from the French themselves as it did from German pressure. But Anne Grynberg gives that betrayal a historical context that gets forgotten as well. The French, after the low birthrate and the terrible human and physical damage of the First World

8. Subsequently published by Gallimard in 2002 as *La France des camps: L'internement 1938–1946.* Bervoets, *La liste de Saint-Cyprien* (Brussels: Alice, 2006). I'm indebted to Bervoets for his generous help in answering my questions about the camp. His father, Hans Tragholz, and his uncle Otto Tragholz were also interned at Saint-Cyprien. After transfer to two other camps, they escaped and made their way back to Antwerp, but, like thousands of others, they were eventually arrested and shipped to a Nazi concentration camp. They died in Buchenwald in 1945. Bervoets never knew either.

9. Forty men or eight horses, "Hommes 40 ... Chevaux 8." A Société des Quarante Hommes et Huit Chevaux formed by American World War I veterans remains active to this day, but probably those cars carried more Jews to concentration camps than they moved soldiers to the front.

War, badly needed workers in the 1920s and opened their doors not only to Germans and Poles, among them many Jews, but to Greeks, Slavs, and others looking for security, bringing a sharp spike in France's immigrant population. Then, with the Depression and rising unemployment, came the backlash—the xenophobia and resurgent anti-Semitism that were linked to it and often lurked just below the French surface. The Belgian story was not all that different.

—ɯɯ—

Against that background, my father's account of existence and conditions at Saint-Cyprien, and his portrayal of the bureaucratic surrealism—the combination of bigotry, indifference, brutality, and sheer stupidity, Belgian, French, American—that drove people into the French camps and kept them there casts a powerful light on a side of the Holocaust story that's been nearly forgotten and often wasn't told. We have forgotten that the Belgians, like the French, had once promised asylum to the Jews fleeing the Nazis in the 1930s and then, when the war began, abandoned them overnight or, worse, labeled them saboteurs—the fast collapse of Belgium and France's stunning defeat were sometimes conveniently attributed to a "fifth column" of Germans—and imprisoned them as enemy aliens. The French later delivered them by the thousands—those who hadn't managed to slip away, and the many who were afraid or too sick to even try—to the enemy.

There seemed to be a time as France went down to defeat in the spring of 1940, and perhaps a little later, when discipline and order broke down, when many of the demoralized prison guards and other police simply melted away. Commanders of camps like San Nicola in Provence, where the writer Lion Feuchtwanger was briefly interned, virtually invited their prisoners to walk out. At San Nicola, a tent city surrounded by barbed wire, Feuchtwanger wrote, there were "cafés" and "restaurants" run by enterprising inmates where those who had money could get excellent meals, good wine, and almost all the culinary delights of old Vienna.[10] Most camps were not remotely like that, they were hell-holes of disease,

---

10. Lion Feuchtwanger, *The Devil in France: My Encounter with Him in the Summer of 1940* (New York: Viking, 1941), 229–230.

hunger and misery, but as my father's story indicates, there was a time even at Saint-Cyprien when it was not hard to slip away. The hard part, for those without money, visas, residence permits, identity cards and other documents, was getting any farther. For refugees—German or Polish or Romanian or Hungarian or Austrian Jews, or old labor leaders and leftists, and many others—all of France, as Feuchtwanger said at the time, was a prison camp. And since so many were stateless, or claimed to be, there was no place to which to send them back. In the view of the police and policy makers in many countries, as Hannah Arendt pointed out, the easiest thing to do, therefore, was to intern them.[11]

We have also forgotten the pictures, if we ever saw them, of the millions of forlorn refugees who crowded the roads, the train stations, the ports, the city squares of Belgium, Holland, and northern France in their desperate, usually vain, effort to escape the German invaders. In New York, there were headlines like "Witness Tells of Panic in Boulogne As Fighting Raged Amid Refugees," and "Stories of Refugees Reveal Mass Tragedy: Days and Nights on the Roads With Helpless People of All Ages Fleeing From the German Invaders." I doubt that any of us thought of it in those terms. But that was us. Nor could many who weren't there picture the surrealism of the Marseille of the early 1940s, where thousands of refugees washed up. They were people who, in the novelist Anna Segher's words, "had left behind their real lives, their lost countries. They were fleeing the barbed wire of Gurs and Vernet, Spanish battlefields, fascist prisons and the scorched cities of the North." Like them, "Hans Licht" and his friends sluiced up and down the wide Marseille thoroughfare called La Canebière in their frantic pursuit of the chain of visas and permits, legal and forged, they needed to get out. For a time, the State Department ordered the US consulate in Marseille, where thousands of refugees, my father among them, were desperately trying to secure documents, not to issue US entry visas unless they already possessed a French exit visa, which, for most, was never issued unless the applicant already had a place to go. In her novel *Transit*, first published in 1944, Seghers writes of a character, a physician, who had a contract to work in

11. Hannah Arendt, *The Origins of Totalitarianism* (Cleveland: World Publishing, 1951), 284.

Caracas, "and because of the contract, a visa, and because of the visa, a transit visa, but it took so long for the exit visa to be issued that the transit visa expired in the meantime, and after that the visa and after that the contract."[12]

As I worked on this project, I was newly moved by my recollection of my sixty-five-year-old handicapped grandmother in her struggle to keep pace with us as we lugged our suitcases on the road between La Panne and Dunkirk on the English Channel coast, and more than a little ashamed of my juvenile impatience, bordering on disdain, at the old woman's infirmities that slowed our attempt to escape. Long after my mother's death, I am newly proud of my mother's extraordinary resolve and courage, strength that I was hardly conscious of when I was with her in that year of maydays, first in the odyssey that ended in Boulogne, then in the year that followed. She disregarded the dire warnings of her friends, some of whom told her she was crazy to risk crossing the Line of Demarcation, as well at least two other sets of police and customs controls without documents—crossings that many never dared.

The terrors of the war generated a wide spectrum of responses—cowardly and courageous, self-aggrandizing and generous, honorable and shameful. Men willing to help refugees often wore the same uniforms as those who, purporting to be following official orders, stole everything the refugees had. Some took risks to help the most desperate; others betrayed them. A few did both. In the lulls between bombings during the battle of Boulogne the looters in our cellar brought back necessities—candles, tins of processed meat and sardines and chocolate, chamber pots to relieve ourselves in—and shared them with the rest of us, strangers all, who were huddled in the same cellar.

Among the first things that struck me, even at my early age, was how quickly war broke down discipline and fractured ordinary civil order. Just as quickly it confronted ordinary people with layers of moral ambivalence that they had never plumbed before. Everywhere loomed a

---

12. Seghers, *Transit* (*New York Review of Books*, 2013), 39, 99. As national boundaries shifted in Eastern Europe, people born in one country, now part of another, found it impossible even to find a bureaucracy that would issue them a birth certificate. To this day, some still do.

terrible uncertainty, both the lack of information about almost every-thing—would there be a train, how far had the Germans come, what had become of spouses and children and parents—and the epidemics of ru-mors that came with it. In every story of internment I've found, perhaps the most common affliction was not dysentery, vermin, or malnutrition but the not knowing. Each day thousands, those in concentration camps and those outside, faced life-or-death decisions affecting not only them-selves but also many others, without the least idea which road should not be taken. Sometimes, as in my father's story, a coin flip was as rational a decider as anything else.

As I indicate elsewhere in this story, I've never been sure where the necessary money came from—money to live, to hire smugglers, to pay forgers, to bribe border guards and consular officials. Some of ours must have come circuitously from my father's mother and brothers in Amer-ica. Some had been drawn from my father's business in the weeks before the war. My father's manuscript tells in some detail how my mother sold the carpets and other valuable furnishings in our apartment, and some of her clothes and jewelry, during our year under the German occupation of Brussels, and how the apartment was often full of haggling buyers. Maybe this was an unpleasantness I repressed, but I recall no such thing and wonder whether this was pure fiction—perhaps contrived to conceal some other source of money that might have been compromised had it been disclosed before the end of the war—and I've cut those parts.

But what's certain is that even in the camps people of means, and more emphatically people of established talents and with connec-tions—artists, writers, musicians, scientists, and other intellectuals—found survival and escape, no matter how risky, easier than it was for men and women without the means. There was a brisk business in black market sausage, bread, and chocolate in many camps; for inmates, hav-ing money—American dollars in particular—could be the difference between a slow death and survival. And always, of course, there was a lively market in cigarettes and, as France collapsed, in military uni-forms, blankets, boots, and other gear. For all, it took money to hire smugglers, buy documents, real or forged, bribe customs officials and prison guards. Feuchtwanger, a celebrity-writer in the Europe of the 1930s, even had his "Karl" and another inmate in the old brickworks that became the camp at Les Milles near Aix-en-Provence (he was later taken to San Nicola) who served him as quasi-valets, polishing his shoes, making his bed, and cooking a special soup for him. In some places, the old middle-European bourgeois class structure, including the familiar division between Western European Jews and Yiddish-speaking Jews from Eastern Europe, laid itself on top of the underlying misery and indignity of the camp. There are inmate paintings by Felix Nussbaum of Jewish services at Saint-Cyprien. My father, assimilated German that he was, says not a word about them. In April 1939, Jewish veterans of the Spanish Civil War—"the soldiers of liberty"—who were interned in the camp at Argelès, some four miles from Saint-Cyprien, began to publish their hand-written newsletter *Hinter Schtechel Droten* ("Behind Barbed Wire" in Yiddish). Conversely, some Jews who had fought in the German Army in World War I and were now interned by the French appealed to the victorious Germans to repatriate them. Nothing, they thought, could be worse than the rats, lice, and disease at Saint-Cyprien.

—⁓—

The great fisher of cultural celebrities in 1940–41 was Varian Fry, who was in Marseille at the same time that my father and his friends were there, in the crowds of refugees seeking the string of visas they needed to get away. Fry, a young New York editor of impeccable pedigree, who was sent to France by the New York–based Emergency Rescue Committee—in France they operated as the Centre Américain de Secours—helped secure documents, genuine and forged, for cultural celebrities, or found other means, often at great personal risk, to spirit them out of France: over Pyrenean mountain trails to Spain and then Portugal, or by ship to Martinique or across the Mediterranean to North Africa, and ultimately to the United States, Mexico, Cuba, or Shanghai. It's a distinguished list—Hannah Arendt, Andre Breton, Marc Chagall, Max Ernst, Feuchtwanger, Jacques Lipchitz, Heinrich Mann, Franz Werfel, some fifteen hundred altogether—and Fry has been justly honored for it. There was, as a US official told him, a "fire sale on brains" in Europe, and America should take advantage of it.

But his list also raises a troubling question. As the historian Donna Ryan put it, "The premise that lives of the intelligentsia were more valuable than other lives did not seem to raise moral questions for Fry, his coworkers in France, or his colleagues in New York." Paraphrasing the German-American historian Fritz Ringer: "One sees the dreadful image of somebody saying: 'Bring me your folder of art, and if I think it's good, we can save your life.'"[13] Erich Maria Remarque called them "super-refugees."

My father was never one of Fry's clients—he later wrote novels, three published in the United States, one abroad, but he was then just a bourgeois businessman, one of the last Jews to get a doctorate from Heidelberg before the war, never a cultural celebrity—and there's no sign that he ever tried to become a Fry client. But in getting his American visa from the Marseille consulate—at that time a visa only for transit to Mexico—he seems to have been a beneficiary of Bingham and Standish, the rare US Foreign Service officers of that era who disregarded their government's rigid unwillingness to admit Jews. Bingham even harbored some Jewish refugees at his house in Marseille. It was Standish—"Stanwick" in my father's story—who spirited Feuchtwanger out of San Nicola, where he was then interned. My father's description of "Frederic DeFerre," the Gaullist French agent who hid "Licht" overnight at his home in Marseille doesn't sound so different from Bingham, who did the same for various other refugees sought by the Nazis. Fry, like DeFerre and some others, worked clandestinely with the British to get skilled military personnel back to England. In his story, my father alludes to the help he got from a woman at an organization in Marseille that was helping refugees—there were a number of such organizations—but it wasn't Fry's ERC.

Yet even to me, who lived through part of it, the evocation of that era—since then overshadowed by the greater horrors of the death camps—is stunning in its terrors. How could whole nations, or at least those who purported to be their leaders, have descended into such madness? How could societies that prided themselves on their culture, their

13. Donna F. Ryan, *The Holocaust and the Jews of Marseille* (Urbana: University of Illinois Press, 1996), 145. "I wouldn't have liked to be in his shoes," wrote Lisa Fittko, who, with her husband, worked with Fry and sometimes alone to spirit people out of France. "I wouldn't like to have the power to decide which life should be saved." Fittko, *Escape through the Pyrenees* (Evanston: Northwestern University Press: 1991), 166.

respect for law, their science and their arts—sink so fast? Was it really true that people pursued by the Nazis were themselves imprisoned by countries attacked by the Nazis, and labeled "extreme suspects" and fifth columnists, as those on my father's train were? How could nations that had welcomed refugees so quickly deliver them to their enemies? How could any rational government, fighting invaders, devote precious railroad rolling stock not to transporting troops, weapons, and supplies to the front, but to the mindless shipment, often in cattle cars, of tens of thousands of aliens, some of them children, some old and crippled, to prison camps? What sense was there in policies under which thousands of men and women with essential skills—physicians, engineers, architects, chemists, accountants, pilots, seamen, tool and dye makers, mechanics, scholars—would not only be excluded from the practice of their trades and professions, but imprisoned like criminals? How could any civilized society maintain conditions in those prisons—in the shortage of food, water, medical supplies, and minimal sanitary facilities, in the infestations of fleas and lice and in the spread of fatal diseases—that were unspeakable even compared to ordinary prisons?

My own experience as a child refugee among the millions who were trapped on the roads of northern France, slept on their luggage in the train stations, and huddled in the cellars as the bombs fell and the battles raged above them almost pales next to that. Not long ago, I watched an episode of *Foyle's War,* a TV drama series about British domestic life during the war, showing a newspaper headline: "Boulogne Falls." That was three quarters of a century ago. I was there when it fell.

—P. S.
Oakland, California, 2014

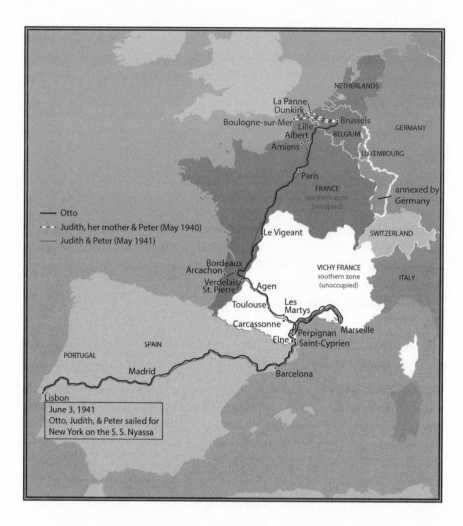

Map of Europe after the French capitulation in 1940, with the separate routes traveled by Otto (Hans), Judith, and Peter in 1940 and 1941.

Map by Darin Jensen.

A BRIEF CHRONOLOGY OF BACKGROUND EVENTS

January 30, 1933: Hitler becomes chancellor of Germany.

November 15, 1935: Promulgation of the first of Nuremberg laws stripping Jews of German citizenship. Other laws barring Jews from public office, the civil service, teaching, and other professions soon followed.

March 1936: Germany remilitarizes the Rhineland, the region along the Rhine and adjacent to the eastern borders of France, Belgium, Luxembourg, and Holland, which had been demilitarized under the terms of the Versailles Treaty. The badly divided French do not respond. It seemed likely later that if the French had responded militarily with their far greater forces, the Germans would have withdrawn. One senior German general said Hitler would have fallen.

March 1938: The Anschluss. Hitler seizes Austria.

September 30, 1938: British Prime Minister Neville Chamberlain returns from his conference with Hitler in Munich promising "peace for our time." The next day the Germans, pursuant to the so-called Munich Agreement, signed by the major European powers, occupy the strategically important Sudetenland part of Czechoslovakia. In the succeeding months, Hungary and Poland annex other parts of the country.

November 9–10, 1938: Kristallnacht, "the night of broken glass," the pogroms when Nazis looted stores and smashed the windows of German synagogues and Jewish homes and businesses.

March 1939: German troops occupy what's left of Czechoslovakia. Hitler: "Czechoslovakia has ceased to exist."

August 1939: Signing of the Molotov-Ribbentrop Pact, the nonaggression treaty under which Stalin and Hitler in effect agreed to carve up Poland and which left no doubt that there would shortly be war.

September 1, 1939: The Germans invade Poland. Within two days, pursuant to their mutual defense treaties with Poland, Britain and France declare war on Germany. Beginning of eight months of "Phoney War" in the West.

September 17, 1939: As the Poles vainly try to fight German armored divisions and aircraft with their cavalry, and with the imminent fall of Warsaw, the Russians attack the nearly defeated Poles from the East.

April 9, 1940: The Germans occupy Denmark and invade Norway.

May 10, 1940: The Germans invade Belgium, Luxembourg, and the Netherlands. All adult male German and Austrian nationals in Belgium are ordered to report to the police. The next day German paratroops capture a key Belgian stronghold, the fort at Eben Emael, anchor of the Albert Canal defenses. Churchill becomes Britain's prime minister.

May 13, 1940: Sedan, a major French defensive point on the Meuse River, falls, and Nazi armored columns pour through in unprecedented strength and with unprecedented speed, heading west for the Channel.

May 16, 1940: Churchill flies to Paris to confer with French commanders as the Germans roll through France and, when he asks where the reserves are, is told there are none. He later said it was the greatest shock in his life.

May 20, 1940: The Germans reach Abbeville at the mouth of the Somme, cutting off the French Channel coast and creating the pocket that would lead to the evacuation of some 350,000 Allied troops at Dunkirk two weeks later (May 26–June 4).

May 25, 1940: Boulogne falls to the Germans after a fierce four-day battle.

May 28, 1940: After his troops fought doggedly to help protect the Dunkirk pocket, King Leopold of Belgium surrenders his encircled forces, but defies his ministers, who have fled to Paris, and soon after to London. He chooses instead to stay in Belgium "to share the same fate as my troops," and is vilified as a traitor by the Allies.

June 10, 1940: Mussolini sends his forces to attack France in the south, but with little success.

June 14, 1940: The Germans occupy Paris, which is undefended, the French government having fled to Bordeaux and later to Vichy.

June 22, 1940: The French surrender. France is divided between a "free" zone in the southeast (Vichy France) and occupied France. The armistice agreement includes the notorious provision, Article XIX, requiring the French to "surrender on demand" any refugees that the Nazis regard as enemies of the Reich. In November 1942, after the Allied landings in North Africa, the Germans would occupy the unoccupied zone as well.

October 3, 1940: Vichy adopts the Statut des Juifs, banning Jews from high positions in the civil service, from the officer corps, and from key professions—in teaching, in the press, in radio and film—that influence public opinion. The next day Vichy adopts its law on the internment of foreign Jews.

October 28, 1940: The German occupation authorities forbid shechita, the ritual slaughter of animals for meat (meaning kosher meat) and order all Jews in Belgium to register as Jews. In the years following, increasingly harsher measures would be imposed: the exclusion of Jews from many professions. the requirement that Jews wear the yellow Star of David; the "Aryanization" of Jewish property; the exclusion of Jewish children from the public schools.

June 20, 1941: The Germans invade Russia.

July 31, 1941: Goering authorizes the preparation of plans for the "total solution of the Jewish question."

December 7, 1941: The Japanese attack Pearl Harbor. Four days later, Germany declares war on the United States, which formally brings the United States into the European war.

January 20, 1942: The Wannsee Conference, named for the Berlin suburb where it is held, in which major Nazi officials plan the systematic extermination—the industrialized genocide—of Jews in all Nazi-held territories. In the two years beginning that summer, 25,000 Jews were shipped from Belgium to the death camps in the East; 24,000 never came back.

WHEN
EUROPE
WAS A
PRISON
CAMP

The End of the Great Illusion

E ven before the previous September, when the Germans marched into Poland and he moved his family from Luxembourg to Brussels, Hans Licht had been trying to repress a growing sense of danger. The move to Brussels had been their second in four years, the first from Germany to Luxembourg in 1935, then to Belgium in 1939—yet again a new country, a new business, a new language. Despite the warnings of his brothers, who had by then all emigrated to America, and in willful disregard of the shadows to the east, he was determined not to move again. And on this spring evening, as he wound his way home past the Belgian War Ministry, he was partly reassured: there was only a single lighted window in the building, not the unusually intense level of activity behind the building's gray façade he would have expected if there was any real danger. It was only later that he recalled the date: May 9.

Everything was as silent as in peaceful times after the shops had closed for the night. For a few days now the chestnuts had been in bloom, and Licht, hands in his pockets, whistled as he walked through the streets on his somewhat crooked legs. No one seemed to notice his inner disquiet. He had brought the art of dissembling to such a point of perfection that he himself was sometimes unsure how he felt.

But now a disturbing memory troubled him. One evening a year or so before, when they were still in Luxembourg, he came home to hear the uninflected and almost inaudible voice of his mother-in-law, the elderly Mrs. Cohn,[1] who had been a widow for nearly a decade, as she talked with her daughter. He had immediately sensed an odd tension and had come to a sudden stop, holding his breath while listening for her next words. Even now he could remember almost every one of those words.

"I tell you, Judith, a sunset like this means something. It means . . ." Here she took a little breath. "War. Today the sun was completely yellow, entirely yellow, as I've seen it only once before, in July 1914. You're laughing, but you'll see that I'm right. You all will leave, will have to leave, but I don't know what will become of me."

With the German invasion of Poland, war had in fact broken out not long after. Within days, Licht moved to Belgium with Judith and his eight-year-old son Peter. A few weeks later Mrs. Cohn followed.

Despite the declared war—what would soon be called the Phoney War—their life in Brussels continued on an almost normal course. Hitler and Stalin quickly carved up Poland, but Belgium was formally neutral, and France, with its British allies, and Germany, the neighboring belligerents, were sitting behind their fortified positions along the Rhine, firing hardly a shot. So Licht left every morning for the office from which he and his partners—again buying and processing malt for breweries—ran their business, and returned every evening to his large comfortable apartment on the Avenue des Scarabées. The war itself had scarcely made its presence known. And yet it seemed to be there all around them. For the people of Belgium it was a darkening shadow, a thing some could sense only vaguely, but which others had experienced firsthand twenty-five years before in all its blood and brutality. It loomed just over the horizon to the east, half-forgotten, like a ghost, something most people tried hard not to think about.

But in the homes of Jewish refugees like Licht it was no mere shadow. For them, it was not just war itself but something even more terrible. It

---

1. Her real name was Josefine Haas. Her husband, my grandfather, had been a German officer in World War I. They were, of course, Jewish, but my father's choice of the very Jewish name Cohn still seems puzzling.

was the hard faces of men in uniforms: gray, brown, black. It was the hard sounds of hobnail boots on the paving stones and the aggressive banging on the door at night. It was the memory of Kristallnacht. It was the specter, and sometimes the personal memory, of the prison yards, the jail cells, and the concentration camps.[2]

Most knew little of the war's actual dimensions; they knew only that they stood immediately face-to-face with an unappeasable enemy, and though that enemy might choose to spare the Belgians, the French, the English, or others in its path, it was certain to root out the Jews. For them the outcome was a matter of life and death.

Licht thought of the émigrés he knew. For many years now, they had truly believed themselves to belong here as much as anyone. The hardy generations of their grandfathers and great-grandfathers, who had spent their lives tramping from one place to another with their entire livelihoods in pushcarts or in sacks on their backs, lay buried in their graves. Their weathered gravestones stood silent in the many Jewish cemeteries of Europe.

The younger generations had taken over their shops, had become lawyers, doctors, professors, artists, officials, and businessmen. And those who had emigrated to new places hoped—desperately wanted to believe—they had found a permanent new home. They thought that if it came to the worst, they had earned the protection of their new country.

There was his friend Richard Ams, who, having been one of the leading furriers in Germany, had arrived with seventeen francs in his pocket and through hard work had again become a successful man. He was invited to the homes of Belgians, played bridge with them, and came to believe he was one of them. There were Lofe and Brust and Veilchenfeld and Spatz, all with similar stories.

There was Licht himself, who had taken over his family malt processing business in Germany and, after the Nazis seized and "Aryanized" it,

---

2. Although my father never spoke of it and made no reference to it in his story, I recently learned that he may have been one of the Jews who in April 1933 had been ordered by storm troopers to wash anti-Semitic writings off walls and fences in Bruchsal, the town where we lived in southern Germany. Thomas Adam, Thomas Moos, and Rolf Schmitt, eds., *Oppenheimer: Eine Jüdische Familie aus Bruchsal* (Ubstadt-Weiher: verlag regionalkultur [*sic*], 2012), 38.

began again in Luxembourg and then again in Belgium. But were they made from the same sturdy timber as their fathers and forefathers? It was his generation that now faced the greatest savagery and unbridled ferocity that the Jews, long persecuted and oppressed, had ever confronted.

Licht walked slowly through the darkening streets. Was he wrong to stay here in Europe instead of leaving for America as his brothers had? Was he strong enough to build a new life again on another continent? There were a thousand ties binding him to Europe. He had a family to support. He had his successful malt business; his customers, who were among the best breweries of France, Belgium, Luxembourg, and Holland, respected him. So he tried to avert his eyes from all threats or danger. The many others who shared his situation were now having the same thoughts: Must I uproot myself again? Are we no longer hardy enough? Has the well of my family's energies run dry?

No, no, that's impossible, he said to himself. We've always managed to forge a new life, even under the most difficult conditions. We've started from scratch, two, even three times over; have we suddenly become weak? We cling to all the trifles that comprise one's life here. I can sit for hours at a sidewalk table in front of this café, doing nothing more than watching people go by while I slowly sip my beer; I can duck into any number of tiny bars to discuss with friends, over a bottle of the finest Burgundy, books, art, the upcoming concerts in Brussels, and talk about our families. We have the public gardens, the parks, the fountains, and God knows what other splendid spaces—all of it. Our wives are making new friends; our children are assimilating in their new languages and new schools. Must we accustom ourselves once again to some other place and give up this place where we're comfortable?

But did they truly belong? That question had never been answered. Not one person among them had a thing to complain about. Belgium was one of the richest, most welcoming, most cosmopolitan countries on earth. Everyone could live as he chose. There was no risk of being bothered by the police; people were tolerant and ready to help.

But Licht also knew that there had been no official government decision about the ultimate status of its Jewish émigrés—would the Belgians ever allow them to become secure permanent residents? He had bought five thousand dollars in American currency just in case. But I must close my eyes to this as well, he thought. I must live here and work here. I have my family, and I don't want to have to start our lives over from nothing once again.

—⁂—

The illusion ended at dawn. Judith was standing before him, saying not once, but twice or maybe dozen times as he tried to rouse himself: "Listen, there's shooting."

As he woke, he heard the sirens and the staccato thundering of anti-aircraft fire, he saw the light of a strange dawn through the window, and tried to cling to the thought that this wasn't happening, that there was nothing so terrifyingly out of the ordinary in what he was hearing, that it wasn't the outbreak of the hell that everyone had been fearing and maybe expecting for so long.

"It's the war," said Judith. "Say what you want, it's the war."

Licht turned on the radio. For a few minutes there was nothing but military marches, then a voice: "All Belgian military personnel are to report to their units immediately. Instructions concerning those on agricultural leave will follow." That was it. The music resumed. Licht had never imagined that such a stiffly bureaucratic formulation, read by some minor functionary at five on this sunny Friday morning of the tenth of May, could have such tragic resonance.

Licht and Judith began to dress. In the meantime he began slowly to grasp that something terrible had happened that night. He tried to believe that maybe this attack could be the great mistake that the entire world had been waiting for. Perhaps this time Moloch would choke on his bloody mouthful.

Then the voice on the radio was back. "Early this morning," it said, "German troops marched across the Dutch, Belgian, and Luxembourg frontiers."

—⁂—

Licht called on his friend, Van Molenbeck,[3] at the earliest possible moment. He had known Van Molenbeck even before they had moved

---

3. The mayor of Brussels in 1940 was named Joseph Van de Meulebroeck. He headed the regional conference of mayors in the fall and winter of 1940 when the Germans' first anti-Jewish decrees were issued. "Van Molenbeck" was not the same man, but the simi-

The front page of the Paris newspaper *Le Matin* of May 11, 1940.

Bibliothèque nationale de France.

The front page of the Brussels newspaper *Le Soir* of May 11, 1940.

to Brussels. They were closely attached by bonds of both business and friendship, and Van Molenbeck, a highly educated man, immediately grasped Licht's situation. But Van Molenbeck's unexpectedly cool behavior also gave Licht reason to suspect that here, too, men weren't always reliable. He found it telling that precisely this man, who had such an abundance of reserve and refined manners, who was always so attuned to the difficult questions of form and context, and from whose lips Licht first heard the word *Boches,* was now so distant.

"I've been thinking over your case," he said. "I know that you seek my advice. I believe that our army and our defensive lines are sufficiently strong to hold out for some time. If you're asking me, I say don't do anything rash, stay calm and remain where you are, keep me up to speed on everything. If you should be arrested, I'll help so far as I am able."

Licht thanked him, but without heart., "Have courage, my friend," Van Molenbeck said as they parted. "This time we'll get them." They were his last words. Licht would long remember them and his friend's accompanying handshake. It was the last that he was to receive from a Belgian.

Licht now realized that this war would become a terrible reality. The half-dazed, half-giddy state he had found himself in since early that morning gave way to frenzied activity. On the outside he remained calm, but inside a wall had just been breached. He couldn't just stand there listening and slowly processing what the external world was telling him. Somehow he had to act. This was his war, his fate and that of his family. He imagined that similar thoughts dawned on many other émigrés in Brussels. Phones rang and rumors spread, unconfirmed suspicions and vague fears inextricably tied to the few known facts. "We'll be arrested," he imagined them saying. "They're already beginning to lock us up."

At the same time, many, like Licht, must have asked themselves how it was possible. "This is where we belong. We're on their side. We fled to them precisely to get their promised protection from the Nazis. So why us?"

---

larity of names was surely no accident either. And given Van de Meulebroeck's moral and legal ambivalence in carrying out the Nazi decrees, neither was the brief characterization of Licht's one-time friend.

"Look," he heard others say. "They'll just want to keep tabs on everything. They've already started releasing some people, for in reality we all have the same enemy."

"But shouldn't we at least have our things prepared?" asked the women. "We may have to flee."

And so, in apartments scattered through the city of Brussels, and in Antwerp and in Liège and Namur, the émigrés began to pack their bags. "Like in Vienna in 1938," some thought. "Like in Prague." Like in Frankfurt, in Berlin, in Cologne.

Later in the day they got the clarity they most feared. A voice on the radio interrupted the military marches. "All German and Austrian citizens between the ages of seventeen and sixty are to report to their nearest police station within the next two hours. Anyone failing to report is subject to two years in prison."

For a moment there was a deep silence in the Licht apartment. It was now exactly 1:15 PM.

"What do you want to do?" Judith asked.

For a moment Licht's thoughts drifted to the forged Dutch passport he'd bought and stashed away for such a moment. But then his good German upbringing took over, raising his instinctive fear of doing anything illegal. "I'll report to the police as soon as possible," he said. "They'll look over our papers and then let people like me go. In any case I'll let Van Molenbeck know. He'll intervene on our behalf."

Licht's friend Lofe, who had come by, tried to say the same thing.[4] Mrs. Cohn didn't voice an opinion; long experience had taught her to let adults decide for themselves. But it was also clear that she approved of her son-in-law's decision. To her the legal way always seemed best.

Licht asked the maid, Maria, to bring him another brandy. He was no longer thinking about his family. He was preparing himself mentally for the police interrogation, considering possible questions and weighing various answers, and giving a good deal of thought about whom

---

4. As I discovered recently from French concentration camp records and ship's manifests, Lofe, who plays a large role in this story, was my father's friend Fritz Lefo, who was associated with his business. It was only when I read the name in the French documents that I recalled a name I heard at the dinner table as a boy. Of all my father's pseudonyms, this was the thinnest.

he should give as references. First in line would be Van Molenbeck, of course. But after that? Was his acquaintance Van Blatt an option? Or had he behaved somewhat flirtatiously with the Belgian Nazis? And what about the other Belgians he knew? Would they be all too glad to deny him assistance, this German Jew who might soon be in custody?

—๛—

In his autobiography, Arthur Koestler remarks that he was born "at the moment when the sun was setting on the Age of Reason." That was 1905. I was born, by the same calibration, when the last ray was vanishing from the horizon, midway between the collapse of Weimar and the election of Hitler in 1933. On the day I was born, July 24, 1931, Chancellor Heinrich Bruening, already ruling Germany by decree, had returned from London without the financial relief that "a thoroughly demoralized Germany," as the papers put it the next day, so desperately needed. The previous September the Nazis had won six and a half million votes and 107 seats in the Reichstag, an enormous gain from the previous election, and now it was only a matter of time. The lengthening shadows of that day were to pursue us across Europe for the next decade. In some ways, they would always be with us. When the Germans invaded Belgium, I was not quite nine.

Even as a young boy I had been aware of something vaguely ominous encroaching into our lives—it was like a shadow at the dinner table conversations I heard around me. But in August of 1939, in a strange mix of fairy-tale fantasy and political terror, the encroachment became palpable. A relative of my mother, Gertrude "Trudel" Lussheimer, had taken me for a vacation in Vianden, a picturesque little medieval town with a castle about an hour from the city of Luxembourg, where we then lived, and very near the German border. They've since gussied up the castle for the tourists who come to fish and walk or bike in the hills, and eat the trout, but in those days it was still just a romantic ruin of towers, turrets, and crumbling arches without gatekeepers, museum, or souvenir stand.

For two weeks that summer we walked in woods that seemed far from anything, occasionally coming to sunlit outcroppings where you could look down on the valley of the River Our below and across at the evergreen hills on the other side and see the lizards sunning themselves on the rocks along the path. Two or three times during our walks we heard men speaking German in the woods—men we could not see but whose voices frightened Trudel and therefore frightened me. Had we inadvertently strayed over the German border? Or were these German soldiers who had crossed into Luxembourg; were these the first feelers of what was soon to come?

Each time we heard them we would turn around and rush back to the village in a shared witches' tale fear that they would drag us into the woods and off to Germany. Sometimes we ran, sometimes we pretended we were just strolling. I must by then have been a little beyond Grimm, and my nightmares, those I can recall, were occupied largely by kidnappers who grabbed me and took me off in large black cars. I could recall the one movie I had seen, *Snow White,* and that might have contributed to the fear—but I can also imagine how kidnapping could have permeated the atmosphere of my childhood. The Lindbergh baby was abducted and murdered in 1932, and Bruno Richard Hauptman, who was convicted in a sensational trial, was executed in 1936. Kidnapping was in the air. Lindbergh, of course, had an ongoing love affair with the Germans, and they with him, until the war started, but I doubt that I knew that then.

We never saw the men in the woods. As I look at the map now, it seems unlikely that we could have walked far enough to stray across the border; I also assume that by then the Germans had less erratic ways of patrolling their frontier. Yet whenever I now think of the men whose voices we heard, I dress them in the uniforms of the Wehrmacht. Were they already mapping the territory for the forthcoming invasion? In the summer of 1980, when I revisited Vianden and walked in those hills with my son David, who was then just a bit older than I'd been on my first visit, it was still hard not to be haunted by the ghosts of those ghosts.

On August 25, Trudel received word from my parents to return home at once. On the previous day they had learned that the Germans and the Russians had concluded the Molotov-Ribbentrop Pact, the nonaggression agreement that almost certainly meant war not only between Germany and Poland but, because of mutual defense treaties that France and England had made with the Poles, war in the West as well. In the general expectation during the previous weeks that there would soon be hostilities, my parents had sent us to Vianden to let them prepare for their next move. One of my father's brothers, now in America, had been living in Brussels, and before the month was over—four days after Trudel and I were summoned back—we moved to Brussels. On September 1 the Germans invaded Poland. On September 17, with the Germans already on the outskirts of Warsaw, the Soviets, on the shabbiest of pretexts, fell on what was left of Poland.

There had been talk of a German invasion of Belgium, Luxembourg, and the Netherlands long before the actual event. For the previous eight months of what some called the Phoney War, the Sitzkrieg, or la drôle de guerre, the two sides had been sitting in their prepared defensive positions, the Siegfried Line and the Maginot Line, on the German-French frontier along the Rhine. Now there were rumors of German troop movements on the Dutch and Belgian frontiers, and in the evenings I overheard anxious conversations about the stories on the radio and in the newspapers. German Panzer columns had been seen moving west from Bremen and Düsseldorf and were said to be poised for a drive into Holland.

It was familiar talk: the kind of talk I had first heard in Luxembourg the year before and which, mixed with talk about passports, visas, and emigration—*Auswandern*—had become more and more commonplace in the months since. I rarely spent much time with my parents in those pre-war years; I was relegated much of the time to the care of the help—the cook and Maria the *Kindermädchen*. I ate most of my meals in the kitchen and would hear them talking about "er" and "sie"—my parents presumably—but most of those conversations went over my young head. But on those occasional evenings when I had dinner with my parents, I caught enough to begin the political orientation that I'm sure countless other children also received in those years.

My father, when I thought about him in my adult years, didn't seem to have known much about children; I think he saw them according to the patronizing stereotypes into which German culture generally cast them. But despite the emotional distance, or maybe because of it, I had grown closer to my father in those anxious pre-war months, had developed a respect for his worldliness that bordered on awe. He spoke as if he knew the political geography that fascinated me: the frontiers, the geopolitics, the military positions, the strengths of armies, the routes and ways of trains. It was not that he often discussed those things directly with me, but that in those overheard conversations with my mother and others in our house in Luxembourg, and now in our Brussels apartment, it was always he who appeared to know, who seemed to have the confidence, who explained how it all worked. The only thing that was imponderable in those overheard conversations was what *Der Roosevelt* would do. Although I didn't understand who *Der Roosevelt* was, he was obviously a monumental figure of great power upon whom all our fates seemed in part to depend. *Der Roosevelt* was the only man who seemed to leave my father uncertain.

We had sometimes taken train trips up the Rhine Valley to Switzerland, to Adelboden, where my father skied (and where I was once put in a *Kinderheim,* a sort of Magic Mountain for children who were thought to be sickly). How I loved those trains! If I had a church, it was trains: I was awed by the great high paned glass roofs of the big stations—"Were not the great glass-and-metal Victorian stations," Tony Judt asks, "the cathedrals of the age?"—loved the security of those plush train compartments; the smoke coming from a roundhouse; the roman-numeral faces of station clocks whose minute hands clicked ahead precisely one minute at a time; the beauty and power of the electric locomotives on the Swiss railroads; the symmetry of tracks and supporting structures and overhead power lines under which those Swiss trains ran; the inexpressible romance of tunnels so long and magnificent, so heroically built—the Gotthard, the Simplon, the Lötschberg—that they not only had names but a mythic dimension many times larger than their functional one. And at the end of the train trips there were often grand hotels with restaurants in which they brought your dinner on pewter plates or on dishes under pewter covers that the waiters removed with a flourish after they set them before you.

I now imagine that there had been something in my father's way of using the names of those tunnels that romanticized them—that he was, like so many others of his generation, a celebrator, maybe even a worshiper, of the great engineering works of his time. That faith, like his trust in reason and craft, was itself one of the things that made so many people so blind to what was about to happen. I cannot be sure of its effect on me or on the way I perceived those tunnels, but it would certainly not have been the first time that words and a tone casually articulated had created a love that lasted long after the words had been forgotten. It was on those trips that I most often had the attention of my parents. But it was also during those trips that I first saw the structures that had been built for the war that was to be, but that the Luftwaffe and the Panzers would quickly make irrelevant: the concrete pillboxes, the tank traps, the barbed wire and the acres of emplacements of the Maginot Line, one of the great elements in the illusion, not only of French military power, if not its invincibility, but of our own safety in Belgium.[5] Slowly I came to learn uniforms and to know from a distance the difference between the khaki of the French and that of the Belgians, to learn the silhouettes of planes, and to be familiar with the sight of convoys on the roads. The artifacts of 1930s nationhood became commonplace to me—the frosty demeanor of the douaniers, the crucial importance of passports, the colors and shapes of the gates at the borders between nations. I'd been to maybe one movie, but long before I had ever been to a play, a museum or a sporting event, I went from fairy tales and the behave-yourself teachings of children's morality tales like Struwwelpeter to the Messerschmitt and the Siegfried Line.

But how Roosevelt connected with the tank traps, the barbed wire, and the concrete pillboxes of the Maginot and Siegfried lines that I saw on those trips, and with the prospects for war, remained a mystery. Nor, to this day, do I know how aware my father was about the preparations for war, or about the preparations the Belgian government had been making for many months for the detention and internment of enemy aliens, or the fears of an enemy Fifth Column within Belgium's

---

5. It was only much later that I learned how great a strategic error the Maginot Line represented. The French, instead of developing modern air and mechanized, mobile ground forces, chose to hunker down behind their "Chinese Wall" and, even after war was declared in 1939, failed to extend that along the Belgian frontier, which was where the German attack was most likely to come.

borders that drove them. That term, Fifth Column, was itself minted during the Spanish Civil War, which had ended with Franco's victory just six months before the Germans marched into Poland.

—‰—

The first air attacks on Brussels began at sunrise. When the howling of the sirens woke me that morning I could see from my bedroom window the white vapor trails of the planes against the brilliant blue sky, and sometimes one could hear the uneven, Doppler-effect sounds of their engines as they circled in the distance. But except for an occasional flash of wing or fuselage in the morning sun, there was no way to see the planes themselves, and the explosions—bombs, antiaircraft fire?—seemed far away, were almost abstract, as if they were just an announcement, and not something that could figure seriously in the calculations of battle.

Perhaps this was not a real war, just some military exercise, and therefore not serious enough to justify my excitement. Perhaps, I felt, it was like those occasional mornings when my mother said I looked sick, but when the thermometer wouldn't rise, and I would have to go to school after all, simultaneously disappointed and relieved. War didn't frighten me; Nazis were frightening. And war promised change, another big family trip perhaps, maybe the biggest trip ever.

It was on trips that I felt closest to my father, the trips up the Rhine past those fortifications perhaps most of all. War was a boy's game played by men—and a man's game played by boys—and thus another way for me not to be a child. It promised to make me an equal. And war would certify allegiances and identities for immigrants like us in Belgium that might otherwise remain doubtful. Weren't the invaders as much our enemy as our neighbors'?

Almost since the day we moved to Brussels I had regarded myself as a Belgian, badly wanted to be one, much as I had thought of myself as a Luxemburger when we lived there in the four years before. The German attack seemed to confirm the new citizenship, the belonging, I had imagined for myself. My first language by then was French, just as it had been Luxembourgish the year before. I tried to speak as little German as I could.

Peter's maternal grandfather, Ludwig Haas, in his German officer's uniform during World War I.

Judith as a young woman in the 1920s.

Otto, Peter and Judith, shortly before the war.

Peter, aged 8, also just before the start of the war.

We had always been a more-than-comfortable middle class family. In Germany, where my father ran the family business that he'd taken over from his grandfather, my parents had a large house, the cook, the *Kindermädchen* for me, a nice car. They periodically went to one *Kurort* or another for their ailments, real or imagined. They were educated Jews steeped in the European culture of their time, assimilated Germans, they thought—Jews (they also thought), hardly at all. Ludwig Haas, my mother's father, had been a prominent German politician, a member of the Reichstag and a sub–cabinet minister before his death in 1930. He was an officer in the German army in the First World War and the army's liaison with the Jewish community in Poland. I remember seeing photos of him with his floppy mustache, his Iron Cross and his spiked army helmet. But when our war started I had never seen the inside of a synagogue, never met a rabbi, and probably never been to a Seder. Like many other Jews of our class, we celebrated Christmas with a tree and gifts, but took no notice of Jewish holidays.[6] I heard my first words of Yiddish in New York. And like many other Jews who thought themselves assimilated in Western Europe, my parents looked down on, and were probably embarrassed by, Eastern European Jews—Poles, Romanians, Russians. It was Hitler, as Sartre would say, who reminded people like us that we were Jews.

My hopes that morning for a big family trip were shattered quickly enough. Soon after I was dressed and came out to the kitchen I began to understand that while this was, indeed, war, and that we would try to flee from the invaders, my father would probably not be going with us. As the possessor of a German passport, he had been ordered to report to the Belgian police as an enemy alien, and as such would probably be interned, despite the fact that the Nazis in their drive to seize Jews' property had denaturalized all German Jews who had

---

6. Peter Feigl, who was born in Berlin in 1929, son of another Saint-Cyprien prisoner who was later murdered at Auschwitz, had moved with his parents first to Vienna and then, like us, to Brussels. He recalled in an oral interview that at Passover he and his parents had matzos with butter and ham. I don't think I had even seen a matzo until we got to New York. Feigl interview tape for the USC Shoah Foundation, April 18, 1997, published May 22, 2012, at http://www.youtube.com/watch?v=GpFARMUFntM.

emigrated—made us all stateless. In the official denaturalization documents, I recently learned, he was Otto Israel Schrag; my mother was Judith Anna Sara Schrag; I was Peter Israel Schrag. We were indifferent Jews, but the Nazis had no doubt. Overnight we ceased to be Germans and became Jews.

My parents had already started packing the few things my father would be able to take with him. "Maybe I'll be back this afternoon," he said, but from the way he said it I knew I probably wouldn't see him for a long time. He didn't try to explain; it was all very complicated—unnecessarily complicated, it seemed to me, and now that I think about it as an adult, probably very humiliating for us both: he had lost control, had diminished in status. And for the first time I began to feel that things were coming apart. It made no sense, going voluntarily to the police: why should they intern him? We were, after all, not Germans. That he should report as ordered seemed to me a sign of weakness. And with his weakness we had all become weak. Not that I expected him to resist, but I was hurt by the thought that he was in a position where he was subject to such treatment. We had not become Belgians after all; we still belonged to no one.

In the back of my mind I tried to nurture the fantasy that he was joining the army to fight the Germans, but the fantasy wouldn't grow, and I was left with the feeling that I had been betrayed. I was losing not only my father's presence, but the image of my father as a strong, confident man of the world, and all the assurance that had been so painfully constructed during the previous months. He was no longer invulnerable, was forced into an identity that I rejected. For the first time I wondered what would happen to us.

—∽∾—

Licht had left the car parked on the street near the Rue de Livourne police station. A clerk sent him down to the basement, where there were already a good many people sitting around waiting. In the half-light he could see a row of benches along each wall and a single table in the middle of the airless room. A policeman guarded the door. People were talking in hushed voices; some had tears in their eyes.

For the first time in his life Licht felt like a captive. He could no longer leave. But he did everything in his power to maintain an unconcerned look and to gather his thoughts for the interrogation that was sure to come.

More people were brought in, many of whom he knew. There was no way of having a real conversation, however. Everyone was sitting around as if caught in a fog so thick that it was difficult to breathe, let alone speak. Now and then they could hear the howl of sirens outside. After it had been determined that morning that the alarms couldn't be heard in all parts of the city, the authorities had mounted sirens on taxicabs. They had been coursing through the city streets ever since.

Around five o'clock an officer announced that all women were free to go. Licht asked a woman he knew to phone Judith and tell her that he needed her to get him some food, the clothes they'd already packed, and a blanket. By then he knew he was not going to be released soon.

A search was made of the bags the men had brought with them; scissors, straight razors, and knives were confiscated. Then they were ordered to proceed in two lines to the courtyard, where they now stood. Here was the doctor from Cologne, who had begun a new course of medical studies in Belgium; the movie actor from Berlin, now living with the support of a charitable committee; the Bavarian engineer who got smuggled over the border in a hearse—the hunted, the despised, the undying enemies of the Nazis. Slowly, flanked by gendarmes, they began a slow march on to the street. Licht, who had an uneasy sense of what was ahead, tried as much as possible to push himself into the middle of the lines. Lofe was beside him.

And now, as they marched up the street, there was a mob whistling derisively and cursing as they passed by. "Murderers!" a woman screamed. "Up against the wall with the Boches!"

Licht would have liked to sit down with the woman and tell her what it was all about, but all he could do was twist his face into a bitter smile.

As they continued their march, a taxi slowed to a stop next to the lines of marching men. It's Judith, Licht thought, and then she was standing beside him. The maid, Maria, had accompanied her and was holding a blanket and a very full backpack. But the gendarmes wouldn't allow the women to hand anything over. Judith was told to wait at the armory barracks at Etterbeek; Licht would be able to get his things there.

So Judith is on top of everything, Licht thought. She's free, which is good, and she'll be able to help me whenever she can. Yes, that's good, that's good. And for one moment he forgot his ironic look and his eyes looked up happily. But a second later, someone gave a loud shout to get back in line, and the spell was broken.

—∿—

At the entrance to the barracks, Judith was waiting for him. She gave over the backpack, but there wasn't time even for them to squeeze hands. Licht couldn't know that this exchange would be their farewell for a long time. He could only focus on what lay immediately before him.

They were led through the large rectangular yard of an armory to what seemed to have been a large industrial depot. Oil stains on the cement floor indicated that engines had once been stored here. Now hundreds of men filled the yard, assembled by the police from every part of the city. They would be there for the next night, sleeping on the floor and subsisting on the sandwiches and chocolate bars they'd brought. The Justice Ministry order applied only to men between seventeen and sixty, but many were older and a few younger, all indiscriminately swept up by the police.

"As long as we're still together, each of us is an island who has the hope that he might be able to prove that he's an exception and might still be released," Licht said to Lofe that first evening. "Once they divide us into groups that ray of hope is lost. Then one is subject to the decisions affecting the whole group."

"Don't make yourself crazy," Lofe said. "We're never going to get out of this. The only thing we can do is organize ourselves so we can have some voice in the administration of this place."

—∿—

After their first night sleeping on the floor, most already looked like they were part of the place. Only Veilchenfeld was formally dressed, as if he'd just come from a men's store, shaved, brushed, looking as if he'd only dropped in for a visit. He'd brought a suitcase on which he sat. Licht's other friends, like most of the hundreds of men around them, lay on the floor. They were all talking, but Licht heard nothing. He knew what he wanted to say, but he was seized by despair. He wanted to shout that nothing they were talking about—when they would see their wives and children again; how they could improve their situation; how they could sleep better or get food—would make any practical difference. But he said nothing. Reason told him that he was being unfair. And when the others asked him whether he agreed that Feuermann should try to get the commandant of what had become their prison to name him their inmate leader, he nodded.

And within a few hours Feuermann had indeed succeeded. He'd also gotten the commandant to declare that their conditions were unsustainable. The whole place was divided into groups, each with its leader. Licht and his friends were all assigned to the same group, under Veilchenfeld. They all had to identify themselves; lists were made. And then Licht's group was taken to a dormitory with metal beds. As they were led through the armory, Licht was struck by a depressing feeling. Where were all the troops once stationed here? The half-empty sardine tins and the pieces of worn clothing still lying about told much about the hasty departure of the men who had been bivouacked here, nearly all of whom were gone. Licht could picture the anxious faces when they learned they were being sent to the front. He could read their thoughts; they hung like old spider webs in all the rooms of the armory.

Like the others, Licht had gotten his metal bed frame—the commandant had ordered that each internee should get one, and each did. Most were now lying on the bare wire springs, their heads on whatever padding they had, staring at the white ceiling. Feuermann had also told them that that afternoon they would get something to eat, a meal that, when they got it, consisted of a broth of meat dumplings that they had to slurp out of shared bowls. Later he would tell his friends in confidence that things were going badly for the Belgian forces, that the Germans were advancing everywhere.

Licht didn't believe it. As he walked in the yard that evening, the light from the setting sun made even the bare armory look pretty. Everywhere men were gathered in little groups talking, and the crazier the rumors, the better he liked it. One was even saying that the Germans had crossed the Albert Canal, one of the keys of the defense of the whole country. That made him want to laugh. The Albert Canal? An invincible fortified line, almost comparable to the Maginot Line. What fantasies could take hold of people!

How could it be true? How could anyone who, like Licht, had been imprisoned since the day before, know any more than he did? But each time he asked, he got the same answer: they heard it from the few soldiers who still came in from the outside. As he approached one little group of inmates, they suddenly stopped talking. To him, they looked like real Nazis. The looks in their blue eyes were less hostile than they were pitying.

—⁂—

He slept soundly that night, and woke only when the others roused him at six the next morning. Again there was a line for the washbasin, but it went faster when a second faucet was connected. Thereafter there was hot coffee and a slice of dark bread, and then they tried to clean the room to make it as comfortable as possible.

At ten, a soldier brought Licht a small satchel that Judith had apparently delivered. He searched it carefully to see if she might have concealed a letter in it, but found nothing, Soon after, Ams came, his nose held high, saying, "Guys, it stinks here. You are all commanded to come to the courtyard without your baggage and line up two by two. Don't ask me what it's about. I don't know. The big military boss, who's just arrived, hasn't revealed it to me."

It was a hot morning, a Sunday, and when Licht arrived a hundred men were already standing there. Feuermann was walking around like misfortune incarnate and whispered in everyone's ear, whether they wanted to hear or not, that everything was lost. The Albert Canal had definitively been crossed and the Germans weren't all that far from Brussels.

In the middle of the area, long tables had been set up, where a commission of some twenty men was sitting, some in uniform, some in civilian clothes. According to a system Licht didn't understand, they called different groups to check each man's papers. After that they were divided into two different groupings. Those on the left, Feuermann announced, were dismissed; the others would stay.

"What criteria are they using?" Ams asked.

"First they're taking the Czechs and the Poles," Feuermann replied. "We others will come at the end, if the commission has time today." Now and then messengers arrived on motorcycles. The officers all tried to look unconcerned. Their faces said that their big moment had arrived.

As he was standing there, Licht suddenly remembered that his car must still be parked at the police station where he'd left it two days before. Judith might well need it. Licht asked Lofe, who that whole morning had been hanging around the soldiers who were guarding them, if he knew one who could be trusted to take Licht's car to Judith. Lofe disappeared into a corner and a few minutes returned to tell Licht that someone would see to it.[7]

Feuermann, surrounded by others, then came rapidly across the yard. "Go one by one into the dormitory and pack your things." He whispered. "We're leaving today, where no one knows. Tomorrow or the day after, the Germans will be here."

Licht shivered despite the heat. No one asked what had gone so wrong. Only one thought had struck them all: Where are they taking us? And suddenly they all thought they knew. One had told another, who told another: they're taking us to Mons.[8]

Licht didn't budge from the line he was standing in. He still hoped that Van Molenbeck or Hirsch, Licht's partner, a citizen of Luxembourg,[9] who had been in Paris, could arrange something special for him. Under all circumstances, he wanted to go before the commission. Ignoring

---

7. This always mystified me. How could they entrust a car in these circumstances to a stranger?

8. Mons, a city about thirty-five miles southwest of Brussels, was famous as the site in August 1914 of the first battle fought between the BEF, the British Expeditionary Force, and the invading German army in World War I. Many of them probably knew that.

9. His real name was Léon Cerf (*Hirsch*, stag, or hart, is the German for the French *cerf*), a name I vaguely recalled from my childhood when I saw it on my father's concentration camp file.

Feuermann's advice, none of the others had gone to pack either. They were still waiting their turn before the commission, each pulling documents out of his pockets and bags to make his case. But as Licht got close, the line stopped. A bicycle messenger had just arrived and the whole process came to a halt.

Then, in a moment Licht would never forget, the men at the table all pushed their chairs back, got up, stretched, and lit cigarettes. A soldier approached those still waiting and announced in French and broken German that things were finished for the day. *"Fini pour aujourd'hui."* He had to repeat it two or three times before everyone seemed to have understood.

Feuermann appeared, now completely the group leader. With his high nasal voice, he called, as loud as he could, "Report with your luggage." So it was true; they were being shipped away. Things really were going badly.

"Slowly, slowly, kids," said Ams. "Give yourselves a chance to reflect; don't make such grim faces, as if Himmler had personally marched into this courtyard. That they're shipping us away isn't a bad sign. Look happy. Our kindly hosts are trying to keep us from falling into the hands of the Huns. Pack your things, Veilchenfeld. You're going to need some time to do it."

Licht found some logic in those words.

As the three returned inside, Feuermann told them there was still bread and coffee. "Moreover," he said, "we're not going to Mons. We're going to France."

"That's what I've always wanted at this season," Ams said. "And, better, it takes me further from the shooting."

"You're really afraid of shooting?" Feuermann teased.

"Very. Despite four years in the trenches from 1914 to 1918, and despite my Iron Cross First Class, Mr. Feuermann, I've never lost it. I'm terribly afraid, and I swore to myself after 1918 that no man and no law would ever bring me again near an exploding shell."

"You know how helpless Ilena can be," Veilchenfeld was saying, half to himself, half to Ams, as he was carefully packing his things. "I know the children will help. But it will completely tear her up not knowing where I am. She'll be waiting here, and who knows what will happen if the Germans really come."

Licht thought of Judith and the wives of the others. Veilchenfeld's words were like somber background music to the images they all had before them.

Lofe came in to report that the guards had told him that, since the rumor spread that they were being shipped away, hundreds of women had gathered outside the gates.

Licht didn't expect Judith to be there. She was too reasonable. She would have decided that it had no purpose and that she would just torment herself unnecessarily. At the same time, he vaguely hoped that maybe she would come. It would do him good to see her face once more.

It was nearly seven when they lined up, three abreast, in the armory courtyard. As the doors opened, they could see the waiting women on the sidewalk opposite. Anyone falling out of line, the head of the guard detail shouted, would be shot.

Those in the front ranks had decided to move as slowly possible for the chance to see their wives—those who were there—one last time. Behind them, the whole troupe moved silently onto the street.

The dense rows of women's shapes on the curb opposite swam before Licht's eyes. Never did faces seem so forlorn; never had the world seemed so ghastly and unreal. Suddenly one of them shouted "Josef, Josef!" and began to run across the street. A guard grabbed her and pushed her back.

"*Vite!*" the commander of the guard detail shouted at the first rows, "*vite!*" And fearing what might happen if they disobeyed, they picked up the pace, which opened gaps between them and those behind. Now more women saw their husbands in those spaces. There wasn't a sound from the men. All they did was to look across at the other side as if they never wanted to forget that image. They weren't looking where they were going, as if they were wandering in a dream. Licht was as close to tears as he ever came.

The guards, holding their rifles, shouted constantly. They were dressed in worn, ragged uniforms; many were short, stumpy-legged men. For duty like this, Licht expected, they'd pick only the worst material. For once this rabble could be the master: He thought he could see how much pleasure they got from it. But this time there were no taunts from the civilian bystanders, who were deterred, it seemed, by the powerful image of the weeping women.

Some two hundred meters farther on they were led across the street to the little Etterbeek train station, where they were ordered to stop. It was now dark, but the platform was lit by brilliant arc lamps.[10] The guards stepped along the rows of prisoners, ordering the men to turn in their cigarettes, cigars, tobacco, matches, and lighters. The pathetic little satchels and bags that each brought were put on the ground and searched. Next to Licht stood Jakob Speier, a large, heavy man whose deliberate, uncoordinated movement was too slow for one of the guards. Impatiently he waited for him to open his bag. Then the guard heaved it all on the tracks, breaking bottles and scattering the contents. "I'll teach you about being slow!" he shouted. Speier, who suffered from a heart ailment, shivered anxiously. After a few minutes, they allowed him to collect his things.

Licht had nothing with him that interested the guards other than a couple of cigarettes that they took, along with the case in which he kept them. Most of those who had any items of value were robbed of whatever they had. Ams mumbled something about "nation of culture" after they took the picture of his son in its silver frame. Licht again sensed that an ironic smile had frozen on his face. This was like a grotesque scene in the theater as Speier, watched by two soldiers, whose pockets were stuffed with the loot they'd taken from the prisoners, was on his knees collecting his miserable belongings.

10. This also puzzled me. In the face of German bombing, could a train station still be brightly lit?

2

The Forty and Eights

Along train of cattle cars had come in. Soldiers had opened the doors. To Licht, it looked like a long row of dark caves. Each car was marked "40/8"—forty men or eight horses. They were ordered to step to the cars and begin boarding, sixty men to each car. In the confusion, Licht had lost his companions and now found himself among strangers. "*Vite, vite, vite!*" the guards shouted again and again. Using their rifle butts, the soldiers shoved those who weren't quick enough.

Licht, among the first in, felt his way along the walls, all his instincts suddenly alert. In the dark interior, he felt his way along the side of the car and laid himself in a corner. No sooner had the sixty been loaded than the doors were pushed shut and barred from the outside with iron bars.

There was great tumult in a darkness that was almost palpable. People elbowed and stepped on one another; no one knew where he was or who was who. Some tripped over luggage in the dark; Licht heard cursing and groaning. A man standing next to him tried to open one of the vents. He was breathing heavily, and said to someone else. "I know how these vents work. I used to be a cattleman. I've opened and shut these things a thousand times. But these swine have nailed this opening shut."

Licht didn't know who the man was—he knew no one in this car. The air was hot and sticky. The car must have been standing in the sun all day. Licht told himself not to move, use as little oxygen as possible. At the opposite end, someone in the dark began screaming. "Open, open!" Someone else shouted "Shut up!" And then, like exploding grenades, there boomed hard bangs from outside and the voices of guards, "Silence!"

At last, with a jolt, the train began to move, and from some hidden opening about twenty centimeters from the floor came a slight movement of fresh air. Licht crept slowly toward the little draft. He thought that if he could find the cracks, he might be able to widen them, but when he tried, it was impossible to do anything with just bare hands. But it was still reassuring to know that they wouldn't suffocate, and with that he began to breathe a little easier.

The next thing Licht knew, the train had stopped. He had apparently fallen asleep, despite the hard floor and the deafening noise as the car clacked over the rails. Somewhere in the car, he heard two men quietly discussing a film they'd recently seen in Brussels, and saying it had been a long time since Dietrich had been as good as she had been in some of her earlier roles. Licht had to laugh. Here in this impossibly hopeless situation people were talking earnestly about Dietrich as if they were in the dining car of the express. How strange humans are.

Once the train stopped, the air again became unbearable, and no one knew how long it would remain stopped. Licht tried to bring his nose to the little crack. His whole body was bathed in sweat and his forehead was dripping. Someone near him shouted.

"The damn Jews! It's their fault. Everything!"

"Who said that?" somebody else shouted. And then someone else, and a third and a fourth.

"Whip the Nazi, get him, get him!"

"Just try it, you rabble!" the first yelled. "I've still got my knife. Just come, if you have the guts!" Licht felt people climbing over his legs—one, then another and another. If it now came to a brawl, he thought, a lot of people would be done for.

"Where to, friend?" he asked the next one who tried to step over him, and grabbed his leg.

"I'm after that guy, the Nazi."

"Leave it already," Licht said. At that moment they began to hear the hum of approaching planes. A nearby church bell began to toll an alarm, always the same tone, high in pitch and sad. Bim, bim, bim. In the car everything became deathly still. As the planes approached, Licht sensed that they were all ducking, crouching against the walls, flattening themselves on the floor, making themselves as small as possible. A machine gun began firing. The bell tolled without interruption.

The planes came nearer—the machine gun continued to fire—then the planes passed and the sound began to fade. Only the bell still tolled.

"It's beginning to get light," someone said. Through the cracks they could see the first glow of dawn. Licht stood. In a few minutes he would be able to see the rough contours of the car. Through his private little opening, he had begun to see light.

But the train stood and the air again became unbearable. The heavy-set man next to Licht began to moan. Licht stood and asked him if he'd like to put his head by the little air hole. Like a choking animal, he crawled to the opening.

"I've got a very bad heart," he said by way of apology. "I can't stand this. I'm too old for this."

From farther away in the car, where they seemed to be lying on top of one another, came another voice. "May I briefly get at the opening, when you've had enough? I'm ailing badly. I don't want to take anything from you. I know you need oxygen. I'm a doctor . . . that is, I was a doctor."

The man with the bad heart didn't answer, but Licht answered, "Of course, Doctor."

The train began to move again. Licht laid himself on the floor next to the heavy-set man so he could get a little of the air. He also wanted to try again to enlarge the little hole. He took his house key. It had jagged teeth—and for what else was it now useful?—and started to file away at the wood, gradually enlarging the opening enough so that one could actually see the track through it. Others had managed to do the same, and they now lay tightly pressed together in threes and fours to breathe a little air. Licht called to the doctor, asking him to join them at the air hole, but got no answer.

The train now stopped at a station. "We're in Ath," somebody said.

"Then we're still not really far from Brussels," someone else said, "and we've already been under way for twelve hours."

Someone else pointed out that the train on the next track had been badly damaged. Licht, like others, pressed to see what he could. That might have been us, he thought. Only later did he learn that the train with the men who had left the Brussels armory a half hour before them had been hit by German bombs. Twenty-four, they later learned, were dead and taken off in Ath for burial. The survivors were loaded on another train.

Again there was a jerk and the train moved on. And despite the little airflow through the gaps in the sides of the train, the heat again became unbearable. In the little light that came from outside, Licht could see that the man beside him was severely ill. His eyes bulged from their sockets and he panted terribly. Sweat ran down his face; sometimes he moaned "Water," but then he could say no more.

The train stopped in an open stretch. In the next car men were shouting, *"Laissez-nous sortir; laissez-nous sortir!"* In Licht's car two were groaning; it was urgent that they get out. One said his bladder was bursting and he couldn't hold it anymore.

Like a mass psychosis, the desperate need to relieve themselves now came over them all, Licht among them. It had been eighteen hours since he'd urinated. No wonder he needed to go. They all began to bang on the walls. And the more they banged, the more furious they became. As the same concert began in the car ahead of them, Licht tried to imagine what a person outside would make of a train of cattle cars packed with sweating men, some still in their business shirts, who were banging and shouting—but he couldn't think about it anymore. Otherwise he would start to scream at the barbarity of it all.

—m—

At about three the train stopped in Tournai, where they were offloaded onto a platform lined with soldiers. No one could believe that a thousand thirsty, half-starved men could be worth all those troops. Now, as they got off, Licht sought, and quickly found, his old comrades who had been in the next car. They all looked different, except for Veilchenfeld, who looked like he'd made the trip in first class.

No sooner had they been assembled than they were marched to another armory. Every few meters along the kilometers-long march stood a guard with fixed bayonet. Marching to their right and left were more soldiers. But the worst was the local population. Hundreds of women and children, all with faces distorted by rage, had gathered along the road. They had been hit by the first German bombing raids and were told that the prisoners marching past them were German saboteurs and parachutists captured by the Belgians.

It was still hot, and the tempo their guards set was too fast for the old and the sick among them. Although most people's baggage wasn't heavy, it was often awkward. But they all knew what would happen if they lagged behind. Ams, walking next to Licht, said, "Keep your eyes open, kid. You look to the left, I'll look to the right, so we know when the rocks start flying."

But none came. Other than angry denunciations and scolding and an occasional attempt to spit at them, almost nothing happened. One old man who fell behind, a man named Mandelbaum, was beaten bloody by a couple of angry women before the guards could drive them off. A couple of gendarmes took him to the armory, where the others had already been lined up. In the middle of the hall stood Feuermann talking to the Belgian officers. The commander was a tall, desiccated man who looked like a career soldier and who made a lot of announcements, all of which ended with the words "will be shot." None of it made much difference to Licht. He just wanted rest. Like the others, he would eventually get it, sleeping on his blanket on the concrete floor of the armory.

—⚏—

When Feuermann told them the next afternoon to pack their things and report to the yard in ten minutes, they all wanted to know where they were going. What was going to happen to them? Feuermann had no answers.

Licht didn't know what to think. His greatest fear had always been that he would fall into the hands of the Nazis. All other dangers and hardships would be more tolerable than to be shipped to Germany or Poland. If they were taking him away from here, it meant that they didn't want him to fall into Nazi hands. What he couldn't understand is why the Belgians didn't just leave foreign civilians to their fate. The most plausible explanation was that in order to catch the six hundred or so who were believed to be the real Nazis living among them in Belgium, the Belgians had to intern them all. Rescuing refugees from Hitler's hordes certainly never occurred to them.

Quickly, and hardly aware of it, Licht had his rucksack packed and joined the others in the yard. He also found his little suitcase in the heap of other bags that had been left there overnight. Around them on all sides stood guards holding their rifles. In the middle stood a half dozen officers.

As they were marched out, soldiers again surrounded them. Licht and his friends had divided Mandelbaum's bags among them. They were determined not to leave him alone. And again they were taken at a quick tempo through the city. Many houses were shuttered.

It was hot and the way was long. When they got to the station, Licht was soaked in sweat. He could have drained a fountain.

And there again was a string of those damn cattle cars, which had been standing all day in the sun. Again there would be sixty men in each. But now Licht would be with his people, and when he got on, he laid himself right beside the door. It would surely not close all that tightly. Lofe had planted himself so close to him that neither could turn around. On the other side was an older man Licht didn't know. Veilchenfeld and Feuermann tried to organize things so that everyone would have a little more room. But it was impossible. No one could stretch his legs without putting them on someone else's. No one could turn without banging his neighbor in the ribs. All had stripped down to their undershirts, and most had removed those as well. Even so, the perspiration ran in great streams. The car was like an oven.

But Brust had some good news. "They forgot to nail these vents shut," he said, and started to open one.

"Get away from those things," shouted Feuermann, "Until we're out of the station."

At last the train pulled out. Brust carefully opened one of the vents and they all crowded around the wonderful opening. The light of the evening sun came through, painting their pale, sweaty faces with a rosy shine.

The train passed through a small Belgian station. Licht, who was lying on the floor, heard a horrible howling and shouting ahead, and then the train was pounded, as if by loud shots, from both sides. The farmers of the region, who had been told that the train was carrying captured parachutists, had armed themselves with rocks and now peppered the cars as they passed by. It was a fearsome, nerve-wracking din. In his panic Brust had forgotten to close the vent, and a stone the size of a fist came through the opening, although no one was hit.

Ams took charge of the vents, closing them at each station, then opening them again—and indeed the same barrage of rocks met them again and again. At almost every town rocks crashed into the train; each time they all flattened themselves on the floor; each time Licht also had the fear that somebody would take shots at the passing train. The barrages of rocks made them forget their thirst. At about seven, the train stopped at a fairly large station.

Judging from the screaming, Licht decided that there must be a great mob, and as he squinted through one of the cracks, he saw hundreds of shouting and angrily gesticulating people standing outside. A couple of gendarmes were trying to hold them back.

Ams saw it, too. The rocks, which had been lying in abundance on the adjacent roadbeds, crashed against the cars without letup. "Stand up!" he shouted. "They're going to storm the train." Ams and Licht and a couple of others jammed themselves against the doors to keep them from being opened from the outside.

Lofe looked through a hole. "They're coming nearer!" he shouted. "The cops are letting them do whatever they want. They're right in front of this car. Most of them are women."

Suddenly the train gave such a hard forward jerk that they all went flying, and then they were again on their way.

Exhausted, they crawled back to their places. Only Ams went to a vent; he wanted to see where they were going. He knew the region from an earlier trip. Soon after, he said, "Five more kilometers and we'll be in France." And by eight, when they stopped again, they were indeed at the border.

"Let's hope they'll change our escort," someone said. "Maybe we'll be rid of the Belgians." Outside, soldiers were walking up and down. Suddenly one swung his gunstock against the side of the car. "The next time anyone opens one of these air vents," came the shout, "he'll be shot."

The train stood for what seemed like hours, and once again it became unbearably hot.

"I'm not going to survive this," said Speier. "I've got open sores. I can't lie down."

They gave him a couple of blankets to lie on, which calmed him.

When the train started again, Licht tried to sleep. For a time, there was a pleasant flow of air through the cracks around the door. But people kept climbing over him, trying to find a place to lie down, then standing, then trying to lie down again. The train stopped at various stations. At one station as dawn was breaking, men in the next car banged on the sides of the next car. "Open the doors!" they were shouting. "We have a sick man," and then again and again, "Open, open!"

Ams carefully opened a vent door and looked out. "We still have the damned Belgians with us," he said. "The head slime is standing right in front of us. They're smoking and chatting among themselves and acting as if those cries for help don't concern them at all. If I only knew where we are." They kept shouting in the next car until the noisy clacking of the departing train overwhelmed their howls. And again there was the pressing need to relieve themselves.

Brust said that at the next station he would demand that they open the doors. One couldn't just let people choke in their own shit. An hour later, when the train stopped again, Brust opened the vent.

"*Mon officier!*" he called, "*mon officier!*" but that's all he got out. A half-drunk Belgian soldier aimed his rifle at the open vent. Ams, who saw it, slammed the vent shut. Then he said that they had no choice but to use the empty sardine cans and the few other empty containers they had and to empty them along the way. At first many hesitated in embarrassment, Licht among them, but nature soon overcame that hesitation and they all followed Ams's suggestion.

It was another hot day, and the air in the car again became unbearable. But now no one dared to open the vents, especially after they noticed that at another station, the Belgian guards had nailed down the doors of the vents of the next car, the one with the sick man. By noon, many were on the verge of dehydration. "If we don't get Speier something to drink," Brust said, "he'll die."

At the next stop, a large station, there was a Red Cross coffee canteen staffed by white-clad women in nurses' uniforms who were flirting with some soldiers and handing out sandwiches and lemonade. In his quiet child's voice Brust called one of the nurses. "Sister, we have a sick man in this car. Could you give us something to drink?"

"He should die," she replied and moved on.

Brust slammed the vent shut. "I have to record that," he said, "as the motto of the French Red Cross."

From the next car again came loud banging and then, in unison, a chorus of voices: "Attention, French Red Cross. We have a dead man in this car." Then they pounded again, then the chorus was repeated; it ended only when the train started again.

Ams, who became their de facto leader—Veilchenfeld and Feuermann were exhausted and were lying in the corners—now stood in the center of the car. "You saw," he shouted to be heard over the rattling of car, "You saw what you can expect from the French. We have nothing to eat and nothing to drink. We don't have air to breathe. But we still have willpower, the will to live. Pull yourselves together, guys. They're taking us somewhere and somewhere they're going to let us off."

In the evening, when the train stopped at another station, the chorus in the next car began again. Then they heard a door opening and after a minute being closed again. Through one of the gaps in their car, Licht saw a figure covered with a blanket being laid on the platform. Next to it stood a backpack. An unknown German emigrant was about to be buried in an unknown little French cemetery.

—☊—

Toward midnight they stopped at a major station. Brust looked through a vent. A light immediately outside cast a spectral beam into the car. Brust leaned out as far as he could. A French sergeant was standing on the platform.

"Give me some francs," Brust said to Licht. Then in a lowered voice to the sergeant: "Monsieur, some water please." The man approached and asked for a bottle.

Brust, who already had one, gave it to the man, who sidled over to a fountain, filled it, and brought it back.

"Try it again," said Ams, who was standing by Brust. "Here's another bottle."

"Again, please sir," Brust said. "We have many sick people in this car."

"Give it to me," the sergeant said and again he filled and returned it. In the meantime, Ams had taken the water to Speier and the other sick men. He knelt by each, but held on to the bottle. He allowed each about three swallows, then returned the empty bottle to Brust.

"Keep trying it until he won't do it anymore." The sergeant shuttled back and forth again and again until they all had had three swallows of water. At that point the sergeant came and said, "There's an officer over there. I have to stop."

Brust tried to hand him the money, but he shook it off. "No, monsieur," he said. "We're human beings, too." Then he vanished.

—ɯ—

By midday the next day, they no longer seemed to care about each other; all sense of community had broken. They had become sixty ailing individuals, each lying in his own sweat with his own pain, his own thirst, and his own feverish dreams. The train had been sitting there through the night and all that morning, and it had again become unbearably hot. Then suddenly Licht became alert. In the distance he thought he heard the sound of car doors opening, and as it came closer he had no doubt.

"Everybody stand up," said Ams, "and get clear of the doors."

Each man who could still hold himself erect slowly got on his feet. The sound of doors opening came nearer and nearer until their own doors were opened.

Outside stood a cluster of soldiers as a huge guy climbed into the car. "Hand over all your bottles," he shouted.

They all rushed to comply. They were about to get water to drink, as much as they wanted. They would survive.

But then the guy dropped the bottles on the ground and the soldiers took the stocks of their rifles and smashed them. Then the doors were banged shut.

First no one said anything. Licht was dizzy. Even before that little atrocity, he'd had trouble holding himself erect. He wanted to scream.

Ams sat down next to him. "One of these days, my dear Licht, we'll pay them back," he said. "This won't be forgotten."

"So you believe in some kind of justice?"

"Stupid brutality always gets punished."

Licht didn't want to talk anymore. He could hardly move his tongue in his parched mouth. He began to count the hours they'd been under way without being allowed anything to drink. It was now two in the afternoon on Thursday, their fifth day since they were first loaded into the cattle cars. The last time he got anything, other than three little sips the night before, had been in the armory at Tournai at three in the afternoon on Tuesday where there was a huge barrel from which one could drink, drink, drink as much as one wanted. He couldn't shake the thought that he was standing before a huge bucket of water over which he was slowly bending down.

Now the hours and the stops seemed to fuse together.

When he next awoke, they were at another station. There was the same oppressive sultry air; he felt as if he had been riding with corpses—and it was certainly possible that there were dead men here among those lying crossways one on top of another. These couldn't be real humans with souls. These were cadavers.

Again came the approaching sound of doors opening. Ams sat up and then slowly got on his feet and opened the vent door and looked out— he no longer cared if they shot him—then he turned. "Look, Licht," he called to his friend. "I'm not sure I have all my wits about me. Tell me what you see."

Licht strained to step over the prone figures and reach Ams. He looked out and then said, as if it were the most ordinary thing in the world, "We're going to get water."

Down the platform, they'd connected a hose to a fire hydrant. The hose ran like a snake into a car. A group of soldiers stood outside the car. That's all Licht could see. But what could it mean other than that there'd be water?

Ams shut the vent door again. "We don't want to stir up any anger," he said.

Licht's announcement that there would be water produced a remarkable transformation in the cadavers. They pushed themselves up along the walls, they stood over one another, they stared at the door. They had become people again. But no one said a word. They were all listening to the approaching sound of doors opening. It took about three minutes between the moment a door was opened and when it was shut again, but none of them paid much attention to that.

At last their door was slammed open. Some eight or ten soldiers were standing before it while one held the fire hose and another came into the car.

"Get your hats," he yelled.

All rushed about to find their hats. Licht had hung his on one of the hooks to which cattle were usually tied. The brown felt hat was covered with dust; its old color was gone.

Licht took the brim in both hands and held it under the hose and filled it to the limit, then bent his head to it, as he had in his dream with the bucket, and, like the others, noisily slurped up the contents. At that moment none saw the others. Even the kind Brust drained his own before he refilled it and took it to the ailing Speier. For each it was as if he was standing alone at a desert oasis trying to drink as much as he could hold. None cared what was going on around him. They cared only about easing their own agony.

Licht no longer knew how many times he had drained his own hat. As the doors were shut again, most still had a hatful in hand, trying to set it on the floor in order to save a little for later.

3

La Panne, Dunkirk, and Beyond

I would be traveling with the women—my mother, my partially lame grandmother, and the eighteen-year-old maid, Maria, whom we had brought with us from Luxembourg and who successfully pleaded with my mother to take her with us again. They seemed to be a threesome of fussiness and vulnerability, none of whom could drive a car—in those days probably few European women could—and whose undertaking of such a task at a time like this struck me as doomed to failure and therefore humiliating to me.

I had lived most of my life with women—with my mother and what seemed like an endless series of cooks and maids. I had always disliked their world—looked down on their endless fussing about things I didn't care about, things of the kitchen and laundry, their little complaints, their gossip, and what in my view was their apathetic ignorance of things which interested me. I had by then learned about the separate provinces of my existence, provinces demarcated not only by gender but by what I thought were coincident degrees of worldly competence. Women could not deal with the sorts of things we were about to confront—had never dealt with them in my experience—and my father's seeming betrayal, the abandonment, was thus magnified.

They had arranged to get a chauffeur through my father's business, but they were so enmeshed in other preparatory complications that there was no chance of leaving for maybe two or three days. Our trips, probably typical of our class, had always required elaborate rituals of preparation—days of sorting clothes, of folding and washing and ironing and storing, days when trunks, suitcases, and parcels stood in bedrooms half packed, some to be stuffed with mothballs for storage, others to be repacked, sometimes two or three times, for travel.

This time the ritual seemed even more deliberate than usual. My mother was reluctant to leave until she knew where my father was. Inquiries would have to be made; perhaps he would come back after all. And the apartment would have to be closed up, perhaps for months, upholstery had to be covered so it wouldn't fade, carpets rolled up, valuables stored or packed or stuffed into money belts. They were preparing for a migration but not for an invader who would soon be sweeping through the country.

On that first day there seemed to be no hurry; the reports from the front were optimistic. The Belgians had constructed a chain of what were claimed to be impregnable forts along the Albert Canal and the banks of the Meuse, and farther south, the Ardennes Forest was regarded as virtually impassable for the German tanks. This time the country would not be overrun in a few days. ("The Belgians," the *New York Times* reported on the day of the attack, "consider themselves ten times more powerful than in 1914.")[1] There seemed to be no rush—nothing to force abandonment of the grand tour style of the haute bourgeoisie.

I spent most of that first day in the empty lot next to our apartment house, smoking. All schools in Belgium were closed, but in the confusion at home, no one had heard the announcement, and I was sent off at the usual hour. I had never particularly liked school, but I had been a dutiful student in M. Boulanger's class at the Ecole du Bois de la Cambre N° 8, which was three blocks from our apartment, and the idea of playing hooky had never crossed my mind. Now there seemed to be no reason to go; in war there was no point in children's stuff like

---

1. "Low Countries Put Faith in Defenses," *NYT*, May 10, 1940.

school. I thought I was playing hooky. And so I walked down the Avenue de l'Hippodrome to the little Tabac on the corner, bought a pack of (I think) Boules Nationales, and returned to a corner in the adjacent lot that was overgrown with tall weeds where I couldn't be seen. I had never smoked before, nor had I ever craved smoking, but now (as I recall it) it seemed rather more natural than daring. Maybe I was just being an adult.

Later that morning I got my bicycle from the garage under the building and rode around the undeveloped area of new streets that began on the other side of the Avenue de l'Hippodrome, where I had always felt freer than anywhere else. I looked for planes in the sky— the all-clear had sounded—but there were none. Somewhere there was war, but here everything was sunny and warm and still. When I returned home, my father was gone.

We left Brussels on the morning of, I think, May 13, a couple of days after my mother managed to deliver a small suitcase of clothes to my father as he was waiting to be shipped to an internment camp in an unknown location. On the previous nights there had been air raids, and most of the residents of our building had taken shelter in a storage cellar next to the underground garage, all of us sitting silently in little family groups with our candles flickering in the darkness. Again, the explosions seemed far away, but the darkness of the cellar and the wail of the sirens put fear where, on that first morning, there had been mostly excitement. We frightened ourselves in our separate little clusters of silence. My grandmother refused to take shelter—she complained about her leg or her rheumatism—and sat out the raid upstairs. Three years later we were told that an American bomb killed her as she was sitting out an Allied raid in Brussels.

The raids reinforced the urgency of what was now beginning to look like a deteriorating military situation, though we didn't come near understanding at the time how urgent it was. In the north, along the coast, where French and British troops had been moving east from the French border to the front in Belgium and Holland, the inhabitants of the towns had decorated the Allied tanks and guns with flowers as they passed through. But by May 12, the Belgian army had begun to acknowledge a disastrous break in the line. German parachutists and

glider troops had landed on top of Eben Emael, the key fortification
at the junction of the Albert Canal and the Meuse, and were tossing
explosives and firing flame throwers through ventilators and gun slits
at the helpless defenders inside. In the meantime, Holland was being
overrun, despite the breached dikes, the flooded fields, and the blown
bridges. The Luftwaffe, so far virtually unchallenged by Allied planes,
was strafing roads and railroads in the Belgian interior. The Belgian
Army, according to other official communiqués, could hold for a while,
but help was urgently needed. On May 16, Winston Churchill, who
had replaced Neville Chamberlain as prime minister on the day of the
Nazi invasion, flew to Paris. "Where is the strategic reserve?" he asked
General Maurice Gamelin, the French commander-in-chief. *"Aucune,"*
came the reply. None.

My mother had decided not to make directly for Paris—there were
rumors that the French border was closed—but northwest toward
the Channel, toward La Panne, (since renamed De Panne, its Flemish
name), where there might be a chance of getting a boat for England if
there was no way to enter France. Of course there might be problems
with documents, but just the fact that we were moving and that thousands of vehicles had been moving in the same direction seemed to
justify the decision. La Panne was the only corner of Belgium that the
Germans didn't capture in World War I; among its claims to fame is
that King Albert of Belgium made it his headquarters in the war.

There were seven of us, jammed into my father's big Renault: my
mother, grandmother, Maria, and me, and at the last moment my
mother also felt obliged to take an older couple named Oppenheimer,
who I think were relatives of one of my father's business associates. She
had also been forced to engage a third-choice chauffeur, a replacement
for another man who replaced still another man, and whom no one
knew. I have long forgotten his name, if I ever knew it, but for a time
he seemed to me to be a reassuring presence, a skilled driver, and a
man whose eagerness to get away from the Germans matched my own
and easily overruled my mother's customary concern for safety on the
road. As soon as we were outside Brussels he seemed to know that he
had become virtually indispensable.

The roads were crowded, though not as hopelessly crowded as they would become a few days later. But it was still possible here and there to pass slower vehicles moving west and north. Occasionally we would meet military convoys going in the other direction: olive-brown trucks loaded with soldiers, black-and-brown camouflage-painted vehicles towing small cannon, little Citroen staff cars, and scores of gendarmes and *gardes mobiles* on motorcycles with sidecars, black-uniformed, leather-helmeted men with rifles slung on their backs.

Somewhere my mother had obtained a small trailer for the luggage, which swung manically behind the Renault as we cut in and out of the line of traffic, passing horse-drawn wagons, trucks, bicycles, and an endless stream of cars with whole households strapped to the roof, on trunks, on running boards: mattresses, tables, chairs, strollers, bird cages, washtubs, laundry hampers, and every sort of suitcase imaginable. "All the stables, all the sheds, all the barns had vomited into the narrow streets a most extraordinary collection of contrivances," as Saint-Exupéry described it:

> There were new motor-cars and there were ancient farm carts that for a half century had stood untouched under layers of dust. There were hay wains and lorries, carry-alls and tumbrils. Every box on wheels had been dug up and was now laden with the treasures of the home . . . Together these treasures had made up that greater treasure – a home. By itself, each was valueless; yet they were objects of a private religion, a family's worship. Each filling its place, they had been made indispensable by habit and beautiful by memory, had been lent price by the sort of fatherland which, together, they constituted . . . Those treasures had been wrenched from their fireside, their table, their wall; and now that they were heaped up in disorder, they showed themselves to be the worn and torn stock of a junk-shop that they were.[2]

The shoulder was lined with disabled vehicles, old heaps with steaming radiators and flat tires, some abandoned, some being pushed

2. Antoine de Saint-Exupéry, *Flight to Arras* (London, Pan Books, 1973) p. 73.

by their passengers, some bumping along on their flats. Occasionally a car or truck would stop to pick someone up, but by late afternoon, as we approached the coast, the people on foot had begun to outnumber those in vehicles. Many of the shops in the small towns were locked and shuttered, and the towns themselves seemed half abandoned.

Along the way, and only half aware of it, I started drawing closer to my mother. Old man Oppenheimer had become increasingly hysterical, and his hysteria reinforced the chauffeur's mounting insolence. What if the border was closed? What if there were no ships? What if we were all trapped on the road? Maybe it would be better to go to Ostend, which also was a port, rather than trying to go to France. Maybe it was already too late. Through it all, my mother remained calm, speaking in a reassuring, matter-of-act way—a long-suffering nurse to a disturbed, anxious patient—seemingly drawing strength from his weakness. She tried to reassure him that everything would be all right; at the same time she successfully patronized the driver. "You're driving very well," she kept telling him. "You're driving very well."

On the main street in La Panne, the *Duinkerkelaan*—Dunkirk Avenue—the axle on the trailer broke. We had reached the town by midafternoon, had covered some two-hundred-odd kilometers in seven hours, and were now inching through a great glut of traffic moving in both directions. In peacetime, La Panne was one of a half-dozen beach resorts on the Belgian coast, places with little hotels, beachfront cafés, souvenir shops, and hundreds of novelty bikes—two wheelers, three-wheelers, four wheelers—which the tourists could rent to ride on the boardwalk. Only a month before, on a chilly April weekend, we had spent a few days at Knokke, another of those resorts, where, with great delight, I had ridden an oversized tricycle along the beach. Now the tourist bikes were gone, the postcard racks boarded up, and there was a different kind of crowd. When the axle broke we pulled off into a side street.

"It can't be fixed," the driver announced.

"We can get another wheel," my mother replied.

"It's not the wheel," he said in exasperation. "It's the axle; it's the whole thing." My grandmother and Mrs. Oppenheimer were still sitting in the car. The rest of us were standing on the sidewalk looking at the crippled trailer. I knew the solution for it: leave the luggage behind and abandon the trailer. Our grand style of travel, it seemed to me, had quickly become a handicap.

"Maybe we can find another one," my mother said, though it was not clear whether she meant a trailer or an axle or if she knew herself. Standing on the sidewalk, the driver looked much smaller than he had in the car, a little man with a gray cap and graying head.

"We're not going on?" he said sullenly. It was more a challenge than a question, but he was speaking for me as well as himself.

"Tomorrow," my mother said. "Tomorrow, I hope." We would have to find out about the border, and the roads, and the war. Not much seemed to be moving on the *Duinkerkelaan* anyhow, we all needed rest and there was a hotel just down the street. A Belgian representative of the American Jewish Joint Distribution Committee who was there reported to his organization in New York a few months later that "more than 200,000 persons had come through this small resort in three days. The streets were so crowded that it was almost impossible to pass through. Belgians and Dutch people crossed the frontier, sometimes after a delay of 48 hours, but Poles, Russians, stateless people, etc., were only admitted as exceptions. Among the latter were large numbers of Jews. I am incapable of describing their despair, their anxiety, and their feelings of being caught in a mousetrap. A large number of them finally succeeded in crossing the frontier, just as the Allied armies were retreating toward Dunkirk."[3]

—⁓—

Late that afternoon, Maria and I went to the boardwalk. Nowadays in the spring and summer the beach is covered with umbrellas and cabanas arranged in endless, orderly rows of brightly colored canvas, and the teenagers ride their rented four-wheelers along the strip. But that spring it was bare and the hotels almost empty, despite the crowded roads and the people sitting on their luggage along the main streets. The concierge in our little hotel had explained that she could not pro-

---

3. E. L. Kowarsky, "Report on the Events from May 10 to July 30, 1940," Sept. 26, 1940, Archives of the American Jewish Joint Distribution Committee (AJJDC), AR 33/44/ 450.

vide much service—most of the men were gone; we would have to carry our own bags. There would be coffee in the morning, and if we could find some rolls at a bakery and bring them back, she would be happy to serve them to us. There was still some butter and marmalade. She hoped we would understand.

Maria and I walked past the car and the crippled trailer, across the *Duinkerkelaan* to the beach. By then most of the traffic was moving east, in the direction from which most had come; the word had come that the French border would not be open again at least until morning. Through the haze, on the horizon to the north, there were scores of small ships, a line of vessels that seemed to be steaming east, toward Ostend and Holland, and for a time we stood on the sandy edge where beach and boardwalk met and watched them. If one could get out there, I thought, one could go anywhere—to England or France, around frontiers and crowded roads and broken axles, and away from the forlorn beachfront hotels and shuttered souvenir shops that stood behind us.

A few of the cafés were still open, serving coffee, wine, and aperitifs—"Dubo, Dubon, Dubonnet," read the ubiquitous billboards—but there were almost no customers. The crowd was flowing through on the main avenue behind us, now eddying back against itself—La Panne had become a great catch basin, a channel whose currents ran in both directions—but almost none of it spilled over the edges. The few of us who were on the side streets seemed to be trapped in a crazy suspension between the vestiges of a world that had ended four days before, a collection of irrelevant beachfront artifacts, and something few of us could fully understand. I realized many years later that it was probably that day, or maybe the day before, that Winston Churchill, having become prime minister of England, had made his great "blood, toil, tears, and sweat" speech.

We were about to leave the beach, had already turned away and down the street, when we heard the planes and then saw them, almost directly overhead, six or eight circling and looping in great arcs of broken vapor trails. We ran back to the beachfront and stood against the wall of a building in a little cluster of other people who had run out from the cafés and the side streets to watch. Three or four gendarmes drove their motorcycles onto the boardwalk and stood in their black helmets, boots, and black leather jackets a few steps in front of us holding their rifles.

When the planes swooped low, their markings became visible: the red, white, and blue bull's-eye of the RAF; the black cross, edged with white, of the Luftwaffe. Occasionally someone around us would make a remark about the comparative characteristics of the planes that he believed we were watching—the Spitfire against the Messerschmitt— but for the most part we all stood in silence, watching the ballet above us, until one of the German planes was hit and began to smoke. As people watched the pilot's parachute open above them, they cheered, as if they were watching a football game, and then they fell silent again. The dogfight moved farther out, to the north and east over the sea, and the vapor trails faded, until we could see nothing but the white parachute of the German flier as he slowly floated toward the beach. The gendarmes, all standing in a row, had begun firing their rifles at him. He waved his arms in a helpless gesture of surrender but they continued shooting until he was almost on the ground. I began to feel a little sick as I watched him, suspended in his harness, hanging, hanging, as he drifted slowly down: what was it like to hang there totally exposed, while men on the ground were shooting at you? Somewhere I had learned enough to know that it was not supposed to happen this way; it was the Germans who shot helpless men trying to surrender, not the people on my side.

Maria made me turn around as they carried him up from the beach; she did not want me to see him. They had gotten a stretcher and were taking him to a military ambulance that was standing on the side street. I couldn't see much. There were people standing in front of me as they carried him past us, and I didn't want Maria to see me looking; maybe I really didn't want to see him. He was partly covered with a blanket, and all I could see was his leather jacket and the bloody stretcher.

The next morning our chauffeur and the car had vanished. He had been given some money the day before to pay for the repair or replacement of the trailer. We spent three hours searching for some sign of the car or the man, walking the streets, asking policemen and soldiers and café owners. One or two garages were still open, but no one knew anything. We were making one of thousands of futile requests, were asking questions already banal and trivial in a place that had become accustomed to lost children, separated families, broken-down cars, stolen goods, and the hysteria and chaos of war. Against all that one quickly learned the modesty that grew from the sense of one's own inconsequence.

Toward midday we gave up the search. Oppenheimer's wife found a man with a taxi who, as my mother later recalled it, was willing to take us to the frontier, a distance of some ten kilometers, in return for Mrs. Oppenheimer's gold watch. We didn't know what we would do thereafter; there were conflicting rumors about the French border, and the traffic going east towards Ostend and south toward Lille was as heavy as that going west. But the need to have a vehicle and to move—to move almost anywhere—had become ends in themselves. For three hours we had watched people pass; had seen them going in the direction we wanted to go, and every passing moment made it harder to wait. Movement had become contagious, an end in itself.

At one the taxi came to pick us up. The taxi itself was already half full—the driver had hired himself to another group for the same trip—and he had hitched a red and green wagon to the back of the car, an open trailer with benches which, in better days, had been used to shuttle tourists around town. The Oppenheimers and my grandmother sat in the taxi, the rest of us in the trailer with the luggage: leather suitcases, knapsacks, a couple of ancient straw valises, duffle bags, a half dozen gas masks, and a miscellany of parcels wrapped in brown paper. Carefully the driver maneuvered his vehicle into the stream of westbound traffic, then everything stopped. More than thirty years later, my mother sent me a letter recalling the moment:

> We were told that the frontier had again been closed and to expect a long delay. It was hot and we were thirsty and since our extension vehicle had just stopped in front of a grocery store, Maria was sent to buy some lemonade. I had provided her on the previous evening with a money belt that contained half the money from your dad's business. Oppenheimer had told me that

he heard "for a fact" that money belonging to people with German passports might be confiscated at the frontier by the French while money belonging to people with Belgian or Luxembourg identity cards like Maria would not be touched.

The moment Maria disappeared into the shop, the chauffeur suddenly broke out of the long line of waiting cars and half turned into a side street, hoping (as he explained later) to beat the traffic. My shouting to him to stop was, of course, to no avail since there was a distance between the two vehicles. A few seconds later, however, he was forced to stop because the side street was also blocked by traffic. I left the car, taking you along, but Maria, having left the shop and not seeing our car, had become panicky and run. We looked everywhere, in vain, until the old people in the taxi (especially the hysterical Oppenheimer) told me I had to board immediately. The traffic, they said, was about to move again and if I hesitated we would be left behind and I would have the lives of many people on my conscience.

The taxi, without Maria, took us to the frontier, which was open again, dropped us on the highway beyond, and we began to walk toward Dunkirk, a distance of some twenty kilometers, carrying what we could, leaving behind the gas masks and three or four suitcases. Later we left another bag by the side of the road. I was charged with a knapsack and a soft black leather valise that would follow us around Europe for more than a year, and which would develop a permanent sag from the hundreds of times one of us sat on it. It was a slow walk, extremely slow, especially because my grandmother's lameness made it very hard for her to walk at all, and we soon split up. The Oppenheimers, who were faster than the three of us, walked with another couple from the taxi; my mother, my grandmother, and I struggled on behind. We would try to meet at the Dunkirk railway station the next day.

We often stopped on the side of the road, probably spent more time stopped than walking. Sometimes I would get a little distance ahead of the two women, drop my valise on the roadside, and sit on it while they caught up. The traffic continued to go by—all of it now moving west—and sometimes other people passed us on foot. One family, bravely trying to patch a tire on the side of the road, offered us some crackers and water; six of them had been traveling in a little cardboard Citroen that would barely hold four. They had left Bruges two days before, had covered some eighty kilometers, and had spent the rest of the time repairing or pushing the car. They apologized that they were unable to take us when they got the tire fixed.

Late that afternoon we came to a little roadside café. They had nothing but beer and chicory coffee, and they were preparing to close the place, but they let us sit while the tables were being stacked around us. My grandmother never complained—she rarely spoke at all—but it was clear she would not be able to walk much farther. For a while we sat drinking our coffee—I still associate the taste of chicory with that place—and then went back to wait on the side of the road. We watched while the owner of the café locked the place up, shuttered the windows, and rode off on his bicycle: the end of civilization. In my knapsack there was still a tin of sardines, a half loaf of French bread, and a bar of chocolate, and now, sitting on our luggage, we finished them off. Toward dusk a truck of French soldiers stopped and gave us a lift.

We spent the night in a hayloft outside Dunkirk. The soldiers who picked us up were quartered at the adjacent farmhouse and would take us into the city the next morning. Now, from where we lay, we could see flashes of antiaircraft fire and the white shafts of searchlights seeking out German bombers over the city, a weird show of light and fireworks that we could barely hear, but which made the soft straw and the noise of the crickets around seem all the more assuring. That night my mother gave me a money belt with a few hundred francs. "It might be safer with you," she said, and I strapped it around my belly under my shirt. "Don't worry," I said in the darkness, "Everything will be all right." Then I fell asleep.

We found Oppenheimer the next morning in the crowd at the railway station. He stood among hundreds of people who were sprawled on the ground with their belongings waiting for a train that would never come—soldiers and old men and women, little knots of nuns, and a line of uniformed schoolchildren accompanied by a priest, who still looked as if they were on a weekend excursion—a crowd that spilled from the waiting room to the sidewalk outside and halfway down the street. (In New York, a couple of days later, the *Times* would strain for language: "There are no words to describe such a plight as that of these poor humans, driven from their homes at an instant's notice with only a few belongings, and having walked till they dropped and then suffering the terrible hazard of being machine gunned by airplanes and finally having traveled by slow stages packed in railway carriages, and some even in freight cars, halting on the way for hours at a time.")[4] It now seems overblown, but sometimes it really was like that.

Oppenheimer and his wife had found a ride for themselves—there was no room for anyone else, he said—but he had also bought a car for the three of us and found a Belgian army officer who would drive it. "God knows why a Belgian officer wanted to take off from Dunkirk at that time," my mother said later. "Everything seemed terribly confused. I think he wanted to reach his regiment." (More probably, as I thought about it as I wrote this, he just wanted to get away from it all; he was a deserter. Even then there must have been other ways for army officers to get to their units.)

Oppenheimer said he was glad to lend my mother the money for the car—we could repay him later—but it was never clear why he and his wife were now traveling without us. Certainly the car itself was no attraction, a drab khaki-colored vehicle of uncertain make and age which looked as if it might not long before have been a military staff car, and which ran best—when it ran at all—in second gear. Every few kilometers we had to stop to refill the radiator, to add oil, or simply to let the engine cool. We covered seventy-odd kilometers that day and by evening we reached Boulogne. I never saw the Oppenheimers again.

4. "Belgian Refugees Swarm Into Paris," *NYT*, May 17, 1940.

4

Le Vigeant

Many were still asleep when the train stopped again. The doors were opened and a soldier shouted, "*Descendez!*"

There was mass confusion as people scurried to get their belongings. Each wanted to get out quickly. But Licht took his time, slowly putting on his jacket, getting his rucksack on his back, and picking up his satchel. Then he climbed out of the car.

The train stood in an open field where a row of gorgeous acacia trees lined the tracks, their leaves shimmering with raindrops. The most wonderful thing was the air. Never in his life had Licht breathed anything like it. This was not ordinary air; it was an altogether unfamiliar thing, creating for him a heavenly sensation halfway between morning dew and a cool evening breeze. A great artist had lightly perfumed this intoxicating mix to further its enchantment.

Although Belgians still had the watch, French officers were about to take over. They looked puzzled as they saw their new charges, who had been described to them as dangerous prisoners.

"Look at this," Ams said to Licht. "Look at what's been written on the sides of our cars." And there, in large letters, was the word, "PARACHUTISTES."

"Now I see which way the wind is blowing," Ams said.

That's where all the bystanders' rage came from. It made Licht laugh that he had been traveling under the ensign of Germany's military elite. Things must be going really badly for Belgium if such success had to be faked. He wondered when he would ever see Judith again.

After a French officer had counted them, they were marched off. Yet they were still accompanied by the Belgians, their rifles at the ready. Behind Licht there was a man he didn't know. Suddenly one of the Belgians, a little bow-legged weasel, grabbed the golden bracelet on the man's wrist and began to yank. Licht and Ams, who both saw it, slowed their pace to draw attention to it. Still the weasel tugged. Eventually he got it and put it in his pocket.

"Report it at once," Ams said, without turning.

But the victim, an older man, said nothing. Puffing, he slowly walked on, his lower lip between his teeth. Now and then he rubbed the wrist where the bracelet had been.

When some of the old men could no longer maintain the pace, the French officer stopped the column. The man who had been robbed suddenly spoke to Licht, who was still obsessed with the theft. "Do you know," he said, "how something like this went in the German concentration camps? There they took every last thing from me. But when I got out, every last penny was there. What am I supposed to do here?" After he paused a moment, he spoke very quietly, as if to himself. "It was a keepsake that even the Germans let me keep when I emigrated; it isn't gold at all."

In the distance appeared an array of long white barracks, with windows and gray roofs.

"I see my villa ahead," Ams said.

They were taken through a barbed wire fence and stopped before one of the barracks. It had gotten dark and it was hard to get a proper impression. It was strikingly cool: they seemed to be on a high plateau. This was Le Vigeant, but none of them then knew the name of the place.[1]

---

1. This is not surprising even now; even Michelin doesn't know it. It's a hamlet of some eight hundred people halfway roughly between Poitiers and Limoges in western France.

Feuermann, whom hardly anyone had seen on the whole trip, went to a French officer who was standing near the entrance.

When he returned, they were all led into long barracks, narrow unlighted rooms that were now rather dark, but the cement floors were wonderfully covered with fresh straw. The men all sank gratefully on the soft bed.

As he lowered himself, Licht had the feeling that the worst was behind him and that he was now secure. He closed his eyes. Despite his thirst he could have fallen asleep on the spot. But there still was no rest.

Feuermann had again talked to the officer, and soon they all knew that they would get water, though it would take some doing, since there was no water in the camp. He came to Licht and told him that until that afternoon, the camp's commanding officer had no idea they were coming.

"He's a good man," Feuermann said. "When they brought us here, it scared him to death. He has no arrangements for us whatever. This is an unfinished training camp for pilots. Where exactly we are he didn't want to say. There's no connection for water. Water has to be transported here in drums from three kilometers away. And the water is unsafe since they have to throw buckets of chlorine into it. It'll make a tasty brew. The guy was also astounded that some of us are old and sick. He couldn't imagine how that fat old Speier, who they just carried by on a stretcher, was supposed to be a parachutist, and he's trying to understand what it means that the Belgians, these swine, described us on the documents accompanying us as "extreme suspects . . . *extrêmement suspects.*" That was also on the signs they'd hung on the train.[2]

Licht pictured all those who had been lined up at Etterbeek and Tournai. Some were sixty and older, decent fathers and grandfathers, most of them business people or professionals, who had fled from Germany to Belgium. Many had been in German concentration camps. Before Hitler had moved into Austria and Czechoslovakia, his Nazis had invaded the

---

2. Many different words were apparently chalked on different cars—parachutists, spies, Boches—or at least as recalled by different prisoners. See, e.g., Ernest Simon, "*Mein Weg aus Brussel nach Havanna,*" a manuscript in the archives of the Leo Baeck Institute, Center for Jewish History, New York, p. 7. But otherwise the accounts were remarkably similar to my father's; the heat, the lack of air, the thirst; the rocks that pelted the cars. And none knew where their families were.

lives of the German Jews. Those who were interned here were the natural allies of all those who had been fallen upon and plundered. And here was the government of Belgium, which had granted them its hospitality, locking them up, hanging signs around their necks labeling them "extreme suspects," and shipping them off.

From the entrance came a great hullabaloo. Incessantly a voice shouted, "Back up, back up! You'll all get your turn." The water had come, which they all had to drink out of the same beaker, the sick and the healthy. Whoever still retained some container could fill it and share the water with others. It tasted terribly of chlorine, but Licht soon got used to it. After some two hours, all had had their fill, and gradually things quieted down.

—⁂—

During the night two more trains arrived, bringing the number of those imprisoned here to about three thousand. There were some thirty or forty half-finished barracks, all solidly built, with concrete floors and slate roofs, two rows of them, surrounded by a barbed wire fence patrolled by Moroccan troops with fixed bayonets. After Licht woke from a sound sleep on the straw and went outside, he found Feuermann and some of the others, among them a man they didn't know named Bauer, talking to a French major who said again that he'd had no advance notice and had done what he could. He was about telephone Tours for further instructions.

Someone told the major that they'd gotten nothing to eat for three days.

"*C'est la guerre,*" he answered.

The first thing their guards had to do, Bauer said, is to arrange accommodations for his people. "You know that I'm one of the pure German Aryans here, and I represent their interests. We demand to be separated immediately from all the others."

"That's an excellent idea," Ams replied. "Do you know how many people you've got?"

"Yes," Bauer said. "We've formed a group of pure Germans. I've got the list in my pocket. There are 437 of us."

"You work fast," Feuermann said.

"We don't have anything to wait for. And the faster the separation occurs, the better for all involved." And so they quickly divided themselves, with the pure Germans getting two somewhat removed buildings that had not yet been fully completed.

—⚬⚬—

That night, Licht could hardly sleep. With the arrival of the new internees, space had become tight. Feuermann had recommended a "sardine system," with one man's feet beside the next man's head. Even the central passageway was occupied. And no one could take off much clothing, especially not shoes, or the odor would have become completely unbearable. If anyone moved, he would disturb his neighbor. All had accustomed themselves to hunger. Licht felt little other than a slight dizziness in his head. Now and then he had to sit down. But sleeping was something else again.

In the middle of the night, Ams said to Licht, who had long been awake, that none of them could last like this for very long. "Nothing to eat, almost nothing to drink, no chance to sleep. Not even an old nag could stand it. Feuermann has to make it clear to those people."

Licht, who was happy that he had air to breathe, tried to calm Ams. "People can stand a lot," he said. "Look at Speier, look at Mandelbaum. Yesterday I wouldn't have given five francs for either, and tonight Speier asked me if I sometimes thought about a good steak. He said he liked his a little rare. His wife, he said, does them wonderfully, and when we're in Brussels again, I have to come to dinner to taste it."

"He's crazy," Ams said. "None of us will see Brussels again. Nor do I want to. I don't like cities that I can only walk through with murderous thoughts."

"Why murderous thoughts?"

"I will never forget what these louts did to us. For me, that country has been struck from the list of civilized nations. Those guys deserve to be swallowed by the Nazis."

Licht's sense of objectivity was offended. "You're over-generalizing," he said. "You're shoving what a few people have done into a whole country's shoes."

"Licht, think of the indifference, the sloppiness—the character of these people. The Belgians are staring hypnotically at the knife that will stab them. A people that manages things as helplessly and callously as they've treated us isn't capable of heroism."

Ams's pessimism troubled Licht. He had to know what was really going on in the outside world. All their agonies—the thirst, the hunger, and all the other things they were going through—were nothing next to not knowing their common fate. He knew that for them all—both for the men and for their wives and children—it was a matter of life and death.

The next morning they found a pair of gigantic Moroccans at the surrounding fence, and between them a little French sub-lieutenant with a cigarette in his mouth.

Licht and Ams walked over and tried to open a conversation. It was a lovely day, Ams said, but the man didn't answer. Then Licht asked whether the man had a piece of bread.

"I have nothing," he said.

Then Licht went after the thing they really wanted. "You don't by chance have a newspaper? We've been imprisoned a week without any news."

"Monsieur," the sub-lieutenant said. "Don't trouble yourself. I know nothing and have no time, and even if I knew something I'm not allowed to tell you. Now back away from the fence."

"If everything were going well," Ams said, "the guy would have given a different answer."

At that moment three French officers, followed by three Africans, rifles under their arms, marched into the camp to announce that there would soon be food in the kitchen. The internees silently opened a path for them. Feuermann stepped forward to meet them. "What's going on?" he asked. "People are waiting to eat."

"If your people don't go into the barracks," one of the officers replied, "they'll be shot. Assemblies in the camp are prohibited."

Feuermann translated what the man had said. The internees scattered without a sound.

Feuermann and one of the officers, now accompanied by Bauer, who'd just appeared, went into the camp kitchen. "How should the food be served?" Feuermann asked. The officer hesitated a moment; apparently it had never occurred to him that they had no dishes or eating utensils. "That's up to you," he finally said.

"No," Bauer said. "That's your responsibility, Commander. We Germans are not here voluntarily. We were hauled here and we want to be treated like prisoners of war."

The officer turned to Feuermann and asked. "What about your people?"

For poor Feuermann, it was complicated question. The Nazis' enemies brought the enemies of the Nazis here, not to save them from the clutches of that gang, but as "extreme suspects." Where the devil did they belong? The Germans had it easy: they were the enemies of the French, who had to treat them accordingly. But what of the others, the Jewish refugees from Germany, the socialists, the Protestants and Catholics of conscience who had fled? How should they identify themselves?

Feuermann gave the only possible answer. "Commander," he said, "my comrades and I expect that France will treat us as its great tradition as a voice for human decency requires."

The officer didn't know what to say and walked off without a word. Feuermann then reported back to Licht and Ams and said, "We have to do something against the damned Nazis in this camp."

"What can we possibly do?" Ams asked. "You gave the officer the only possible correct answer—but believe me, Bauer's argument will be more effective. The Germans will intern some Frenchmen and the threat of reprisals against them will certainly help more than any talk about human decency. If you're smart, you'll let Bauer pull all our chestnuts out of the fire."

An hour later the first barracks, some 250 men, were ordered to report for their meal, and soon a long line of gray figures were waiting for a broth with a few grains of rice. Some ten men had to share each container, mostly old tin cans, and each had to wait until the man before him was done. Small sardine cans could be filled one and half times, and often the men had to use handkerchiefs to keep from burning themselves. Many who used tins put them on the ground and ate out of them like dogs.

—◊◊—

Toward midnight, a loudspeaker awakened them, barking orders. In the glow of the searchlights outside, they saw that a new trainload of inmates had been delivered.

"That will be cheerful tomorrow," Feuermann said. "Get ready for a half portion."

"What's half of nothing?" Ams asked.

There could be no thought of washing the next day, even for the earliest risers. The new arrivals had drained the water wagon to the last drop. From a few who were already walking around the camp, Ams learned that they were on the transport that the Germans had bombed. It was also they who estimated that there were twenty-four dead, because they and their comrades had to bury them. But they didn't know who the dead were. Somewhere they'd heard that everything was going badly in Belgium and that Brussels had been declared an open city. One said he was glad to be here. In the old days he was a German labor union official. The Nazis had been looking for him everywhere. If he was caught, they'd hang him.

One of the few officers who was helpful was a little French doctor. He had equipped one of the barracks as a military hospital where he provided exhausted men with coffee he brewed on a little stove. He was the only one who was aware of the sad condition that the men found themselves in. In the evening he invited Feuermann, Licht, and Ams in and told them he understood their situation exactly, but there was nothing he could do to change it. All he could do was to try to make it a little easier for them. There was no model for situations like theirs, which was totally new and had so many new problems. Solving them would take time, time they didn't have. "For the moment we have so many other worries," he told them. "More I can't tell you.... The most immediate matter," he went on, "is the business of the eating utensils. If you can provide the funds, I'll try to get some for you. But each must get the necessary nourishment on an equal basis, whether he has money or not. We also have to get buckets to carry the food from the kitchen, and finally we'll need drinking cups. Think all that over and tell me tomorrow what you propose." Then he told them what he thought it would cost.

On their way back to their barracks, Ams told Licht and Feuermann that he'd never heard of a case where prisoners had to buy their own dishes and eating utensils. He assumed that the little doctor expected to make a tidy little sum out of the deal.

"What worries me most," said Licht, "is that the French, as he put it, have worries."

As they passed the barracks of the Pure Germans, they heard them singing.

"They must think they're winning," Feuermann said. "I'm going to ask them what they're going to contribute to getting the dishes."

Ten minutes later, when he rejoined his friends, he told them that the Pure Germans would contribute nothing. "They said they were entitled to eating their food from dishes and if the French didn't provide them, they'd continue to eat out of sardine cans."

On that same evening, money was collected from the others in the camp, and two days later dishes appeared and, for each, one fork and one spoon. Each of the Pure Germans seemed to regard it as a given that he would get his utensils like everyone else. As the dishes were being distributed, Ams tried to engage the driver of the delivery truck in conversation. That they had gone without any news had become almost intolerable. The driver, who'd also been ordered to say nothing, finally let slip the observation that things weren't going well.

The driver's remark stung them all when Ams relayed it. What had sustained them was still the old hope that in invading Belgium, Hitler had made a fatal mistake and that at last the opportunity had come to get rid of him.

"What does a man like that know," Feuermann said, but that reassured no one. On top of that, there were two concerns that they would not be able to escape as long as they were interned: the rumors and the black market. They reinforced each other.

Brust had already approached Licht to ask if he'd like to buy some chocolate. It would be outrageously expensive—five American dollars a bar—but he could think it over. Very early the following morning, a Monday, Brust came to Licht again.

"The French are selling everything they have or can get hold of for dollars. You can get bread and sausage and chocolate, cigarettes, uniform pants, military blankets—if you have dollars. I'm not making anything on it, but maybe we should buy something together, chocolate for example, to regain a little of our strength."

"Talk to the others," Licht said.

But none of them wanted to pay what was asked. There was no way to know whether the dollars they saved wouldn't be needed more urgently for something else.

"That's what occurred in 1918," Ams told Brust, "You could buy everything from the troops for a few marks, including the rifle. And if this is already 1918, then the dollars will have to serve other and more urgent needs."

"Guys," said Feuermann, as he took his friends aside. "I just spoke to one of the Pure Germans, who heard from the Africans that the Germans are in Bruges, the Belgian army is melting down. Things are on the verge of collapse."

"Hold your tongue," Ams said. "Don't let them tell you tales."

"And what if it's true?" Feuermann responded.

When the commandant, an older officer with an ill-fitting uniform, personally came into the camp that afternoon, Licht approached to tell him that they were all worried by the reports of German military successes. Could he provide some sound corrective information?

A large crowd immediately surrounded them. "Don't make yourselves uneasy," the officer said. "Everything is going as it should. I can't give you details. But be assured. Keep order here and don't make our lives difficult. Then we'll also do what we can to improve your lot."

"Where are our wives and children?" came a voice from the crowd.

"Like all others," the officers said, "they've been evacuated."

"Could we volunteer for any kind of service to France?" someone else asked.

"I'm sure," the officer said, "that France will gladly accept some service, and I'm glad you asked. In any case I will seek an immediate answer."

—m—

The next day came an order from the French that each of them had to turn over all his money except for the last five hundred francs.[3] Anyone

---

3. In April 1940, French francs were trading at fifty to the US dollar. The previous September the franc was quoted at forty-five to the dollar. In April, the banks quoted Belgian francs, made "heavy" by war jitters, at thirty to the dollar. After the invasion of the Low Countries, there no longer was an official exchange rate. In 1941, a year after the French capitulated, the black market rate was 180 French francs to the dollar.

who failed to do so would be punished and the money confiscated. Those who complied would get a receipt and get their money back after the war.

Licht and his friends sat together to decide what to do. The order seemed to them to be altogether illegal, a conclusion supported by the two professors of international law who sat with them. Some thought they should turn in a portion. Veilchenfeld predicted that anyone who turned in his money would never see it again. Anyone who was left with no money would be completely helpless.

Eventually they decided that each would comply pro forma and turn over a portion of his money, but keep most of what he had .

Surprisingly, Ams disagreed. He had half of his laboriously amassed fortune with him—all told some thirty-five thousand francs. He had decided to turn over at least half of that half, an idea from which they could not dissuade him. He wouldn't need it now and this way it would be more secure than if he carried it on him.

Finally Brust proposed that they bury their money in the ground, with markers so they could later find it again. With sticks and spoons one dug little pits while others stood around him. Then the notes were counted, deposited, covered, and marked with a little stone. They wouldn't find it all, but when they later unearthed it, each would contribute part of his funds to those who had lost theirs.

The money the officers found on others, many of them poor people, which constituted a large part of the only money they had, was confiscated. That was what the guards called it. But as they suspected and confirmed later, the so-called confiscation, by which all sorts of other valuables were also taken, was nothing but outright robbery for the personal gain of the officers. None of the internees would ever see his money again.

They didn't talk much in those days. Licht was especially uncommunicative. When he could, he lay in the sun in the scattered places where there were a few grubby patches of grass. He stayed there for hours with his eyes shut and reflected on his situation. Before the war he'd had a thousand opportunities to emigrate. His mother was American and now living in America, where his brothers had also emigrated. Again and again they'd urged him to come when visas for people like him might still be had. But he'd stayed committed to Europe. He'd thought that his business success in Belgium and his firm connections with Belgians would bring a certain level of security. Until the war came he had convinced himself that what happened to them would also happen to him. Why should he have it otherwise from those he'd lived and worked with and whom he had so far regarded as his friends?

He wracked his brain to find a deeper reason for his disappointments since his arrest. There must be something about the Belgians that they themselves couldn't change, even if they wanted to. But even if he accepted as fact the quick, radical collapse, there remained an unexplained element. Why hadn't someone told their guards that ninety percent of them weren't Nazis, but poor hated, hunted, innocent people? Why had the Belgians played the gruesome trick of labeling them "extreme suspects"?

There was only one explanation. A convenient scapegoat had to be found to take the blame for the war, from whom one could get vengeance for everything that had happened. And all the better if it was a Jew, and better yet if he had once belonged to the prosperous bourgeoisie.

He tried to bring his thoughts back to what he'd discussed with Judith about what they'd do if things happened as they now apparently had. That wasn't easy, since they so often had purely theoretical conversations. He couldn't recall if they had ever drawn any definite plan. He feared that they hadn't, because it was so hard for her to reach decisions. The fear was all the greater because he knew how much Judith now needed help. The one thing that comforted him was that he had left her money enough to live on for at least two years.

If he only knew how things now stood in Belgium. What sort of government leaves us here without news? It surely couldn't hurt the French to tell us at least what things are like in Brussels. The internees had repeatedly tried to learn something; repeatedly there were the wildest rumors.

One evening, a few of them, Licht among them, met to try to sort out the rumors and paint some picture of reality. But all that emerged were contradictions. One officer had told Lofe that because of the air raids everyone in Brussels had been evacuated and that women and children had been taken to the countryside. Veilchenfeld had learned from another that all the women were in England. Maybe, they suspected, the French officers at the camp knew as little as they did—had no idea, not only about the women but about the larger war situation.

Had anyone talked to the Pure Germans? Licht asked. "They walk around here as if everything were going great."

"Nonsense," Ams said. "They know no more than we do."

"Brust spoke with one today," Licht said, "who said Hitler would be in Paris by June fifteenth."

Ams started to laugh. He said he had thought Brust to be smarter than to believe such stuff. Had Brust never heard of the Maginot Line? He asked them not to let the Nazis get the better of them.

—m—

The next days passed slowly for them all. It had begun to rain. The yard, which had been stone-hard clay, became an ankle-deep bog, making it hard go out. Instead they had to sit or lie on the worn straw. They told each other their life stories, and soon everyone knew everything about everyone else. They showed pictures of their wives and children. At night the foul smell from the ditch from the latrine that ran through the middle of the camp made it hard to sleep.

Brust rose between three and four each morning to do his black market deals. He couldn't have done much business, since people resisted spending dollars for chocolate or cigarettes. Nor were the hunger or the craving for tobacco as great as they would later become.

One evening around the twenty-fifth of May, Feuermann returned from the commandant saying that he had seen him sitting there with his head down like a beaten man. Then he banged the table so hard with his fist that his glasses flew off. The commandant then screamed at him for the shameless effrontery of coming there. What was going on?

"My little finger tells me," Ams said, turning to Licht, "that something big is going on. Way back there at the corner there's a couple of bread trucks. Why are they bringing two truckloads of bread here? Why would they, after we nearly died of hunger, suddenly want to feed us?"

"We're being taken away," Licht said.

"Good guess," Ams said. "And in those trucks are our travel provisions." It was as if the beleaguered French had nothing better to do than to ship a few thousand German, Polish, and Austrian Jews from camp to camp to keep them from falling into the hands of the Boches.

5

Another Cattle Train

The next day, when trucks holding both bread and cans of liver paste came into the yard, the men knew they were being shipped off again. Everybody was packing.

"What would you think," asked Veilchenfeld, who was clean and groomed, as always, "if we all wrote our names on the walls? Who knows, maybe they'll bring our wives here?" And so they all wrote their names and addresses and the names of their wives. Licht used a broad-pointed fountain pen, so that all future inhabitants of Barracks 14 could read, in French: "Judith Licht, sought by her husband, former address Avenue des Scarabées, Brussels."[1]

That afternoon, after having packed their food and standing for hours in the yard, they were marched back to the railway station, now looking grayer and uglier than in the bright sunshine at their arrival. The air was like nothing they'd breathed before. Today a depressing sense of not knowing hung on them. Even before they were marched off they'd talked about whether they'd again be loaded into cattle cars. Brust thought that

1. My father here used the fictional address, Avenue de l'Université, in the part of Brussels called Ixelles, which was not far away in the same neighborhood. I changed it back.

was out of the question—or if they were, at least they'd leave the vents open. After all, the Belgians were gone.

But at the next bend in the road, there they were—the same cattle cars in which they had been transported before, and again sixty men in each.

After a few minutes, the doors were shut, but the vents were open. They hoped that they would be allowed now and then to get off, and that they'd get water. By the time the train began to move, they knew from experience how to arrange themselves. They put all their baggage into the middle of the car. Licht again took a spot near the door. But most stood at the open vents and took in the beautiful French countryside. Those who knew geography began to debate where they were being taken. When night came, they all tried to sleep. They weren't allowed to get off at the stops, and so they had again to return to the tin can method to relieve themselves. But they were given a couple of buckets of water.

The next morning at about ten they reached a station, where they expected to be off-loaded. But then the train started again, now going in the opposite direction, leading them to fear that they would again be confined for days in a meandering train. After some hours, snow-capped mountains, the Pyrenees, appeared in the distance on their right. Then the train stopped again; outside, French soldiers walked along the train ordering that the vents be shut, and it again became hot. But they had the feeling they were getting to where they were being ultimately shipped. They knew they were near the Spanish frontier. Then they came to a large station, where they heard loudspeakers announcing departures. Through a crack in the door Licht saw a sign on the wall: Toulouse. He also saw what appeared to be a great crowd of women and children with luggage and backpacks. Scattered about the platform there were also all sorts of household goods, among them a birdcage with a canary.

"What do you see?" Ams asked.

"People in flight," Licht answered.

"Why did they come to Toulouse?" Feuermann asked.

"Presumably they're evacuees from Alsace," said the ever-optimistic Brust.[2]

---

2. Alsace-Lorraine, on the Rhine border between eastern France and Germany, had long been disputed territory and militarily vulnerable. In 1871, after the Franco-Prussian War, it was annexed by Germany. After World War I, it became French again.

The image of this exhausted crowd of careworn women lugging their motley assortments of belongings with them depressed them all. What could they make of it? Was Brust right?

Again and again, the loudspeaker squawked with announcements, presumably intended for the people on the platform.

Then their train started and they reopened the vents. As they came closer to the mountains, Licht spotted a road sign for Perpignan.

"That's interesting," said someone who had been lying in a far corner and whom they were hardly aware of. "I was there once. We're near the Pyrenees. Somewhere around here there's supposedly an internment camp for Spanish loyalist fighters. I've never been there, although I also fought in Spain. There were thousands of us, thirsty, hungry, exhausted, some of us wounded, thousands. . . . My name, by the way, is Ritter. "

"Go on," said Ams.

"You probably know all this from the newspapers," Ritter said. "I really don't like to talk about it."

Ams and Licht looked at one another. The man had a unique effect. His staccato manner of speaking—the broken phrases—left them tensely waiting for the next word. They all wanted to know more.

"If you don't want to tell more about yourself," Licht said, "tell us at least what you know about the camp."

"Not much, almost nothing. They never caught me. But tens of thousands died there and are buried in the sand by the sea. . . . No, I can't tell you much. But if it's Saint-Cyprien, then God help us." The last words came almost in a whisper. Then he went back into his corner.

—∞—

As they arrived in Perpignan, Ritter's words hung like dark clouds in the car. Ams didn't dare open vents on the platform side, but he looked out on the opposite side where a train crowded with women and children had just pulled in on the next track. Many were looking through their open train windows at the faces peering at them through the cattle car vents.

"Who are you?" one of the women asked.

"Belgian refugees," Ams replied. "And you?"

"We are too," she said. "Evacuated from Bruges."

"Do you have cigarettes or newspapers?" Brust asked.

They had both and threw a few across. Just then a French sergeant came walking between the trains.

"Shut them," he shouted from a distance.

"Why?" the woman asked.

"Because they're Boches," the soldier answered, which prompted an angry outburst from the women who began to shout curses at the now-locked cattle cars.

But Ams had a paper, and all crowded around him trying to see it. At last they'd know something. But the train remained standing in the station and the vents were shut, making it too dark to read. Outside, the scolding from the next train continued.

At last they began to move. Ams went to the vent and Feuermann opened it.

"Leopold the Traitor," said the headline. Below it was a terse, persuasive report, dated May 28, about the capitulation of the Belgian army.[3] They had now been under way for more than two weeks.

Feuermann took the paper and stood on a suitcase and began to read as loud as he could. Because some didn't know French, he had to stop often to translate the most important things into German. For Ams and the others, one thing was clear. Belgium was lost. The army had surrendered. Brussels was in German hands. Antwerp, Bruges, everything, even the little places that in 1914 had held out and were never occupied—all was gone.

"What about Holland?" someone asked.

"There's nothing here about Holland," Ams said. "But isn't what you heard enough? Do you think Holland survives when all of Belgium has been taken?"

Licht was calm. He saw the men before him with absolute clarity, as if they were subjects of a scientific study. It was striking how these specimens reacted to outside impulses, how they tried to look impassive. A couple swallowed hard, some bit their lips. Brust was left breathless. He was leaning against the wall with an open mouth, as if incessantly saying "Oh." Ritter, the Spanish war veteran, stood alone with his eyes closed.

---

3. The Belgian army had fought doggedly against overwhelming forces and German air power until surrounded.

And then there emerged two thoughts that must have been shared by all. One came in Ams's terse sentence: "We just barely escaped the shit." The other came from Veilchenfeld: "Our poor wives."

So through an open vent in this locked train car, sixty men suddenly got news of a historic catastrophe. It made Licht, who still felt as if he didn't belong here, think that when major events occurred, people who talk so much about politics don't think of the impact on the larger community or of the broader historical consequences, but just about themselves and their families. And, damn it all, he concluded, that is the most relevant thing. Still he couldn't detach himself from asking the broader questions of what they'd just read. He thought about Judith, but he couldn't hold back the thought that their fate was a tiny speck against what was happening in all of Europe and much of the entire world.

As Feuermann read more details, and as they sought to mine those details, there arose the familiar debates about what was said between the lines. Having come from countries with heavy censorship, many had a lot of practice, and with it a certain expertise, in truth digging. Every word was laid on the scale.

Boulogne

In theory we owned the car, but our officer-driver, a tall man of patronizing dignity, treated it as if it were his, as in some practical way it was. We had become totally dependent not only on the car but on his ability to make it move. He seemed to know it intimately, understood its moods, and knew what to kick or shake or adjust to make it start after it sputtered out. He was cordial, courtly, even relaxed, but he would not let himself be rushed. "Madame must understand. . . . But Madame must surely know."

It was now my mother who was in a hurry; somewhere during one of the many repair stops on the way south into Boulogne she had heard a rumor that the bridges over the Somme, some ninety kilometers to the south, would be blown up the next day, and she wanted to drive through the night. She had a feeling, she said, that the information was correct. But he refused; he wanted to get some rest. Surely Madame must know that in wartime it is dangerous to drive at night.

By the time we reached Boulogne, the city and its port had been subject to intermittent German bombardment for a week. In peacetime it had been a fishing port and a major embarkation point for Channel traffic to Dover and Folkestone and, like Calais, a landing

place for British tourists headed south. In 1804, Napoleon had assembled his *grande armée* there—some 200,000 men—for an invasion
of England, but the plan was so ill-conceived that it was aborted even
before Nelson's defeat of the French at Trafalgar guaranteed the British
control of the Channel. Many years later, I learned that its casino had
once made it also a major destination for French vacationers.

Now the British were using Boulogne to supply the Royal Army
and Air Force in France, and the German attacks were becoming increasingly frequent and heavy. When we arrived, there were barrage
balloons over the harbor and city with cables strung between them to
reduce the effectiveness of the German dive-bombers, but the blimps
had begun to leak and sag—had taken on the limp look of defeat. More
important, though we didn't know it then, on May 13, even as we left
Brussels, Gen. Heinz Guderian's German Panzers had breached a key
line of defense when they crossed the Meuse near Sedan, a place with
its own bloody history in two prior wars, and were now sweeping west
through northern France, beginning the great encirclement that would
end with the evacuation at Dunkirk three weeks later. Within a week
they would reach the coast near Abbeville, cutting off the British Expeditionary Force and other Allied forces in the north from the main
body of the French Army in the south. In London, the government was
already talking about using the Port of Boulogne as one of the escape
routes for Allied troops in France.

We slept that night on the tile floor of the glass-roofed palm court
of what I think was called (maybe appropriately for those there that
night) the Hotel Terminus. Most of the furniture had been removed
and the floor was covered with refugees, each of us rolled in a blanket
provided by the hotel. Boulogne had by then become a city of refugees,
people from the south hoping to get a boat to England, people from
the East like us, including tens of thousands of Hollanders and Belgians, hoping to go south or maybe by ship to England. Among them
was a growing accumulation of military personnel—French, Belgian,
and British—who had become separated from their units. It was later
estimated that there were two million refugees in the pocket that the
Germans cut off in northern France.

Several times during the night we were woken by sirens and the
sound of antiaircraft fire, but no one took shelter, despite the hazardous glass roof under which we were lying. By then people had begun
to learn to gauge the severity and proximity of the raids, to distinguish
danger from nuisance. Were the bombs coming closer, or were they too
distant to worry about? There was more talk about the Somme bridges,
inconsistent stories that they had already been blown, that they would
be blown that night, that they would be blown next morning. It was
only many years later, when I saw the military situation maps for those
weeks, that I understood what had been going on. We were about to be
cut off by the encircling German divisions south of us, or had been already been. That night it made no sense. Why, I wondered, would anyone be blowing up bridges ahead of us? The Germans were supposed to
be behind us.

The next morning, a few kilometers south of the city, we reached the
end of the line. For half an hour our ailing vehicle had sputtered along
a stretch of country road that seemed unnaturally calm and empty.
Then we started encountering traffic coming the other way, a proces-
sion of vehicles approaching like a parade along the highway—actually a two-lane road. They had been stopped at a military checkpoint
a little farther south—had been kept waiting for a while, and had then
been sent back. The bridges had been blown. Our officer-driver said he
would help us get a ride back into the city; we would have to abandon
the car, which was now almost useless, and he would try to make his
way south cross-country on foot through the lines toward Rouen. Then
he took our luggage from the car, put it on the road, and waited until a
truck picked us up.

We now became part of the crowd, three of tens of thousands of
refugees waiting around the harbor in Boulogne for transportation,
standing in bakery lines for bread, sleeping in schoolhouses, and chas-
ing rumors about ships to England that never sailed and train service
to Paris that had ceased to function. We spent that night at Le Cygne,
a small hotel across the street from a firehouse—tried to sleep through
the almost incessant wail of the sirens of the overburdened *pompi-
ers*—then returned again to the port to sit on our luggage and wait for
news of a ship, ducking into nearby buildings when the bombs came

too close. Around us, as the bombing increased, the city was slowly beginning to die, was turning to rubble and broken glass and shuttered windows. We were forced to spend increasing lengths of time waiting in cellars for the bombing to end.

We started to celebrate the small victories of survival—success in finding an open bakery or a grocery store with a few tins of processed Spam-like meat, an encounter with a schoolmistress who still had beds available in her school, a rumor that the Germans had been stopped in a great battle somewhere to the east. Motion, though always painful and halting, especially for my grandmother, itself became an object and a victory, though the circle in which we moved rapidly became smaller and the objectives less certain.

Boulogne, a crucial Channel port, was almost totally destroyed in World War II, much of it during the battle and bombardment now beginning around us when the Germans captured it, some in intermittent Allied bombing in the years of the German occupation, the rest in September 1944, when it was recaptured by units of the Canadian army. I have since looked for the house with our cellar—the shelter where we would sit out most of the battle. There is such a house still standing in the Rue Victor Hugo, but there had been hundreds like it, French row houses of three or four stories with heavy double doors and a carriageway leading from the street, under the building, to an interior court.

Next door, to the right as one faced the row house with the basement where we finally took shelter, there was a shoe store; at the rear of the interior court, which was paved with cobblestones, were two symmetrical curving flights of stairs leading to the door of an adjoining house. A car was parked in the carriageway, a Fiat, and under the Fiat someone had shoved dozens of shoes from the smashed shoe store window next door, all of them for the left foot.

Almost all my life I have assumed they were stuffed there by a looter—maybe one of the people who shared the cellar with us, and therefore someone on "my" side of the war—who only belatedly discovered that what he had taken was all for the left foot and therefore useless. Now I am no longer sure: perhaps someone, even the owner, having discovered the shrapnel-smashed window, had hidden the shoes under the Fiat to keep them from being looted. But in the final analysis it didn't matter: the fragility and the terror would be with us either way. War, I learned then, brings disorder of all sorts not caused by the fighting. And whose car was it? Why hadn't the owner taken it south long ago?

At the side of the carriageway was a door that led to the cellar. We never learned who owned the car or the building, or who lived there.

We had to run at the start of a heavy raid, half dragging our luggage along the street, half carrying my hobbling grandmother, and followed a couple of other people into the courtyard. By then the planes were so close that I could see the Luftwaffe fliers, a pilot and a rear gunner, through the Plexiglas cockpit windows of the diving Stukas, could hear the sirens the Germans had installed on their planes for their intimidating effect and the whistling of the bombs as they fell. Someone helped lead us down the cellar steps, and through the darkness to a vacant corner near a small pile of coal. Slowly, in the candlelight, my eyes adapted to the darkness.

"This time it's a big one," someone said. "They're coming closer." It was said as if the dive-bombers were trying to find us. The door upstairs had been shut, and the deep cellar helped muffle the sound, but we could still feel the tremors and hear the whistles and the sharp crack of the explosions.

"The little ones are worse," came a reply. "They're incendiaries."

"They're all the same to me. The bastards are trying to kill everybody." Much later, there would be intense debates about whether the millions of refugees that were driven to the roads were part of a calculated tactic to impede the movement of Allied troops and materiel—even perhaps the work of a German fifth column—but there was no question that the sirens and whistles on the bombers and their bombs were meant to terrorize the human targets, civilian and military, below.[1]

---

1. Nicole Dombrowski Risser, *France Under Fire: German Invasion, Civilian Flight and Family Survival During World War II* (Cambridge: Cambridge University Press, 2012).

There were maybe fifteen or twenty of us in a long cellar space, though I couldn't see those who were sitting on the other side of the stairway. Among those I recall were three Hasidic Jews in their black hats, their dark frocks, their *payos* and beards. My mother, a true product of bourgeois German Jewry, always called them "the Polish Jews"—*Ostjuden*—though we never learned where they were from. There was a Belgian couple with a little girl about my age; a group of three men, French or Belgian, in their fifties; a young woman of maybe twenty who was sitting next to the bicycle she had been traveling on; and two or three clusters of people at the far end of the room who remained shadows and silhouettes.

Most of us were still sitting on our luggage, but some had already laid out makeshift beds of clothes and blankets. My mother told me to try to sleep; it was only midafternoon, but we'd been up since five, and she hoped to start walking again. This had been the day we were going to try to get to the country, away from the embattled city, perhaps even find a way to go south. For a while I dozed with my head on my Loden jacket and the jacket on a heap of coal. The floor was hard and the coal crunched under me.

Around six there was a lull in the bombing, and we began to file cautiously up the stairs, past the Fiat in the carriageway, and into the street. No one had heard the all-clear—we had only heard the silence—and most of us left our belongings in the cellar. There was traffic again—perhaps it had never really stopped: British army trucks moving south, a couple of men in berets trying to zigzag their bicycles around the broken glass on the street, an old woman with a shopping basket filled with empty mineral water bottles. For a few minutes we stood hesitantly on the sidewalk watching them, like bathers on a beach where the water is too cold. The British soldiers in their flat soup-plate helmets provided a touch of assurance, a small earnest of remaining strength and of connections across the Channel. I desperately wanted to be with them, wanted to share the security of their trucks with their heavy-treaded tires and their powerful engines. I waved—of course—to establish my own connection, and a few waved back from the shadows under the canvas that covered the trucks.

Witness Tells of Panic in Boulogne As Fighting Raged Amid Refugees

Briton Who Escaped on Destroyer Says Port Was Thronged With Civilians When the Germans Stormed Their Way In

LONDON, May 25 (*P*)—A Briton, who witnessed this week's fighting at Boulogne, told tonight of being taken aboard a British destroyer while its guns thundered parting defiance to German troops swarming into the French city.

The witness, Frederick Brinjes, a business man, said the ancient, sunny city across the Channel had become a shell-rocked, bomb-spattered trap for thousands of refugees.

Mr. Brinjes told of spending two nights at the maritime station in Boulogne, where thousands of hysterical men, women and children waited to get out of the city. They were without water. There were no sanitary facilities. Machine-gun bullets rattled in the streets.

"There must have been many killed," he said. "I don't know how many. I know there were hundreds wounded and I saw many going mad."

Street Black With People

Mr. Brinjes reached Boulogne Wednesday afternoon.

"The street to the station was black with people," he said. "It took me two hours to fight my way through the crowd. Every time a bomb went off the women would scream. No one tried to stop them." British soldiers distributed food.

By Thursday afternoon, he recalled, German troops had penetrated the town and captured guns on a hill near the Continental Hotel.

"At 7 that night," he continued, "three destroyers alongside the jetty opened fire on German gun emplacements on the hill. The German fire was far from accurate, but one destroyer finally was struck amidships. I learned later it reached a British port safely.

"The remaining two destroyers put the German guns out of action. Many buildings along the seafront, including the Hotel de Folkestone, were shelled. The hotel was the first German headquarters.

"By 9 o'clock the Germans were coming toward the station. The British and French were fighting back, firing from under railway carriages and from behind sandbag defenses. German tanks began to appear. At the moment I got aboard the destroyer it was still firing. We made a top-speed dash across the Channel."

Wounded Britons Return

LONDON, May 25 (UP)—Hundreds of wounded British soldiers, many on stretchers, poured into England from Flanders' fields tonight and told how it felt to be in the path of the onrushing German war machine. They arrived at an undisclosed port aboard a hospital ship and passed through cheering throngs.

The casualties described hand-to-hand fighting in Belgium and their first-hand experience with Nazi parachute troops, who, they said, dropped from everywhere, "in clouds." German planes, the British soldiers said, machine-gunned screaming, fleeing children, destroyed villages and bombed hospital trains in the drive through Belgium and France.

Private Edward Horn, with a bayonet wound in his knee from fighting in Louvain, said:

"I saw the German parachutists coming down armed with tommy-guns. It was exciting to see them run away from our fire. We ourselves were bombed out of several hospitals. We saw the wreckage of a hospital train the Germans had bombed.

"That was bad enough, but my blood boiled when I saw the German planes diving over ruined houses in Belgian villages, turning machine guns on terrified children, who ran screaming for shelter."

"We gave Jerry something to think about," Corporal Fred Slater said. "It was pretty tough going during hand-to-hand fighting on the Belgian frontier, with the enemy in front of us and planes dropping clouds of parachutists behind us.

"We turned a gun on one cluster of parachutists and killed a score of them before they touched the ground. I saw at least a dozen of them dressed as women, all carrying tommy-guns, which they used on every one in sight. We got them, all right."

One Scottish soldier summed up the fighting by describing it from his stretcher as "a devil's paradise."

The New York Times
Published: May 26, 1940
Copyright © The New York Times

I wanted to go once more to look for a ship—it had become a habit by then—but there were black clouds of smoke rising from the harbor that blocked out the evening sun. "I don't think there are going to be any more ships," my mother said. We would go back to the cellar, get my grandmother and find a more comfortable place for the night. The schoolhouse where we'd slept the night before was only six or eight blocks away. There had been a mattress there for my grandmother, and there had been hot soup to eat with our bread.

But the shrinking circle around Boulogne had tightened. By the time we had gotten our things from the cellar, the raids resumed, and we rushed back down to reclaim our corner. A few of the people who had been there earlier in the day had left and a few others had replaced them: the woman with the mineral water bottles we had seen on the street, and a trio of German Jews—a Professor Pinkus and his mother and sister. The Hassidim, who apparently had never left the cellar, and whom I don't ever recall seeing in daylight, seemed to be washing their faces and beards with something I took to be whiskey or cognac.

There now seemed to be more candles illuminating the figures around the room, and more supplies for makeshift residences: newspapers to spread on the ground, more blankets, more coats and rags for bedding, welcome fruits of the looting. It was as if people had used the intervening time to look not for escape but for ways to survive a siege. Under me, next to a little pile of papers, I found a flier with a drawing of a boy running toward a couple of police officers and pointing to the sky: "If you see parcels or leaflets falling from the sky," the flier said, "or if you see parachutists coming down, notify the authorities immediately." But we were well past that.

The bombing continued intermittently into the night, and night flowed into day. We began to mark time more by the ferocity of the attacks and by the lulls between than by the clock or the calendar. "The next time it stops," my mother would say, "we'll go look for bread." Or

Facing.
New York Times story from the AP about
"panic" in Boulogne, May 26, 1940.

"When this is over we must get you some shoes." Someone in the cellar who had a notebook and pencil taught me to play *bataille navale*—battleship—and I played game after game, sometimes with my mother but more often with a young Belgian girl whom my mother much admired for her ability to stay clean despite the coal, the soot, and the shortage of water. During the lulls we would go out and look for food; once we found an open bakery where, miraculously, we managed to get to the front of the line before the bread ran out and the bombing started again; another time we found some cans of processed meat in an *épicerie*; a third time a man on the street gave us a box of crackers. I don't recall that we were reduced to begging, but we must have come close.

By the second or third day, looting had become widespread, and people started returning to the cellar with crazy collections of odd items most of which they couldn't possibly use: boxes of buttons and ribbons, a stack of cheap china plates, lamp shades, vases, ornamental brass fixtures, pencils, rolls of butcher paper, and, of course, the collection of left shoes from the smashed shoe store window next door. At the same time, we began sharing our possessions—food, blankets, candles, eau de cologne for washing—and slowly there grew a crude sort of tribal courtesy.

Not that we developed any sense of community or that we organized ourselves. Even the sharing was impulsive and haphazard, almost furtive, as if acts of generosity were as hazardous as theft. The Hassidim refused to eat anything that wasn't kosher—and thus ate almost nothing—and remained aloof, and the figures at the other end of the room, the people behind the stairs, remained nothing but silhouettes. But on our side little groups began to cluster; the three of us with the Belgian family and the Pinkuses; the three men with the girl with the bicycle.

Soon it became impossible even to go outside. We started to use the chamber pots that now became a useful part of someone's loot, and emptied them, when we could, into a drain in the courtyard upstairs. Through that day and into the night the explosions became more frequent and intense, crashing and tearing through the buildings around us and sometimes shaking the ground on which we sat. In the short intervals between explosions I could hear the chanting of the Hassidim, and sometimes someone would ask what time it was—for the reminder of ordinary times, maybe, some link to the world we'd left, though hardly for its utilitarian value. Otherwise we rarely spoke.

Slowly the sounds above were changing, though I'm not sure anyone else noticed, as shells replaced bombs and the rattle of machine gun fire mixed with the explosions, all the time building in intensity, and now adding the odor of smoke, dust, and gunpowder to the stench of our feces and urine. They were fighting in the streets above us. I knew I was afraid, but the fear was laced with expectation, the feeling that at last something would be resolved—there was even the desperate hope that the Allies were winning the battle and that, in any case, after all this waiting it would soon be over and there would be something else.

It was hard, despite the fear, not to become caught up in it, to derive some faint pleasure from the violence, even to welcome it as justification for the failure to escape and for one's cowering existence in a coal cellar in a doomed city. I think I knew that I was collecting sensations and sounds the way tourists collect souvenirs—the more violent the better—thereby to have something to take home from the trip to show and remember. I was becoming a survivor, which enabled me to share in this war. For a while I even slept in the warming security of the surrounding violence. I wanted everything to be over, but I also welcomed the need to stay below and the mounting, violent, sometimes deafening justification for it above.

Late during the night the battle moved away from us, like a storm passing, and in the morning everything was eerily still. After the incessant pounding, the silence itself was stunning, a shock almost as severe as the explosions that preceded it. For a time no one spoke; then the wondering and the speculation began.

"It's seven thirty," said one of the three men. "What day is it?"

"It's Saturday. May 25." Two weeks and a day after the German invasion began.

"Someone should go up," said Pinkus. The Hassidim were chanting again.

"It would be better for a woman to go," one of the men said. "It would be safer for a woman."

"Let's wait a while. What's the hurry?" The reply came from a group by the stairs.

"Marie will go," the man said. Marie was the woman with the bicycle. We were all looking at her in the candlelight as she stood at the bottom of the stairs. They had given her a flashlight, and she was shining the yellow beam at the cellar door above her. Did they really think it would be safer for a woman?

Slowly Marie climbed the stairs, opened the cellar door and stepped into the carriageway above us. The bright sunlight reflected on the stairwell from above was itself a blow, a break into our hermetic world.

She returned a minute later, leaving the cellar door open. She had seen some soldiers on the street outside and described them to the three men. Field-gray uniforms with helmets that came down over the ears and covered the back of the head.

"They're Dutch," one of the men declared.

"What do you mean, Dutch?" came a voice from the silhouettes. "There are no Dutch troops in Boulogne. They're Germans—Boches." The uniforms were similar, he explained, but (incongruously) "any fool can tell the difference."

"I know what Germans look like," the first man replied, now all offended dignity. "I am a veteran, an *ancien combatant*, from 1914. What do you know about it?"

Although others joined the debate—about insignia and uniforms and helmets—it was really a one-sided argument. The consensus was that they were Dutch; only the silhouette continued to insist that they were Germans. We must all have known better—we wouldn't still be sitting there in the darkness in fear if we really believed otherwise. Yet in our illusive collective isolation it was easy to conjure up the French tanks we had seen, the British trucks, to invoke that impregnable Maginot Line and the whole vaunted force of the French army, surely the most powerful in Europe, in support of the desperate need to believe. Around the room, people offered recollections, suppositions, anecdotes, and speculations. They heaped them on to make the case conclusive until, at last, as if to celebrate the great victory we had willed into being, the *ancien combatant* began to sing the *Marseillaise*:

> *Allons enfants de la Patrie*
> *Le jour de gloire est arrivé!*

As he sang, someone on the street began to pound on the carriage doors upstairs, an insistent pounding, and Marie was sent up again. Now there was absolute silence in the cellar. We could hear the carriage doors being unbolted, heard the boots on the cobblestones above us, then saw the men outlined against the light in the open cellar door. There were two of them, big men who looked bigger with their uniforms and equipment. Each had a gas mask canister and a pair of hand grenades hanging from his belt. Their rifles were on their backs; they were not holding them—that was confidence—and their bayonets were sheathed on their hips. For a moment I thought longingly of the too-young British soldier who had given me a chocolate bar a couple of days before—the chocolate soldier—a boy with a pale blond face and reddish hair who seemed infinitely fragile. These two by themselves wiped out the might of the whole Allied army so carefully constructed in our cellar just a few minutes before. One of them was shining a large flashlight around the room. *"Alle 'raus."*

"They want us all to come up," Marie said. They were the first German soldiers I'd seen; now they were just checking to make sure there were no troops hiding among us.

—⁓—

Portions of the city had been completely destroyed, had become heaps of brick, concrete, and wood overhung with dangling telephone wires. The streets were littered with the carcasses of disabled half-tracks and cars and trucks that were already being stripped of their headlights and tires. There was broken glass everywhere, and everywhere I found shrapnel and the brass shell casings of rifle and machine gun bullets, more souvenirs. A hole had been shot through the clock tower on the city hall; the clock, which was still there, was stopped at five after three. Many years later, reading the newspapers of that month, I learned that Boulogne had been bombed almost without interruption for four days and nights.

And yet, even on that first afternoon of occupation, portions of the city had begun to function again. When we first emerged from the cellar that morning, there were still corpses on the street and in the doorways of buildings; they were the first dead I'd ever seen. By afternoon

Above and facing.
The streets in Boulogne after four days of intensive bombardment and the fierce battle leading to the Germans' capture of the city in late May 1940.

Municipal Archives, City of Boulogne-Sur-Mer.

the dead were gone. The Germans had posted their first orders to the population: The inhabitants were to sweep their sidewalks. Anyone caught looting would be shot. Here and there, people had started going through the rubble, collecting things in baskets and carts—boots, gas masks, vehicle parts, belts—or tying them to bicycles, and children were climbing over the ruined half-tracks, replaying the battle that had ended just twelve hours before. A few stores had reopened; there was a little bread and, as before, a few tins of sardines and processed meat.

We spent those first few days in an abandoned house. My mother told me later she had found it through a cobbler to whom she had gone to get my tattered shoes repaired. The house belonged to friends of the cobbler's wife who had gone south when the bridges over the Somme were still intact; God only knew where the owners were now. Our presence there would help protect it from the looters. "We are good people here," the woman had said. "But in times like these, one never knows."

For a time our existence was a continuation of what it had been before we buried ourselves in the cellar. Each day we went looking for food and for news, standing again in breadlines outside bakeries, and sometimes we all watched sullenly as German soldiers entered the store, took large bundles of loaves, and left. Sometimes they took the entire supply and hauled it away in cars while the rest of us began looking for another line. The lines, created by scarcity, had become signs of hope.

There was still no civilian transportation, no way to get anywhere, except on foot or by bicycle, and nothing but fragile rumors about the war. To the northeast, the great evacuation had begun at Dunkirk, but we would learn little of it for more than a year. Each day we heard people speaking furtively about an Allied counterattack, and sometimes the talk was bolstered by brief Allied air raids on the city and the harbor, but otherwise we knew nothing. Our victories came in the form of bread, potatoes, and an occasional piece of hard salami. We boiled the potatoes on an old wood stove in water that we hauled in buckets and bottles from a fountain. There was no running water in the house.

We had taken the Belgian family and the Pinkuses with us, but it was my mother who functioned while the rest of them worried and argued. Pinkus's sister, despite her days in the cellar, or perhaps because of them, had developed an excessively morbid fear of bombs, and the quieter things became, the more fearful she seemed to be. I later learned that before they left Brussels, she had seen a neighbor's house destroyed, and she was certain that she herself would be killed by a bomb. The fear turned out to be prophetic. Just before they were to leave Boulogne, she walked into a store when an Allied bomb hit the place and she was killed instantly.

The Belgian couple, in the meantime, were often screaming at each other about what I took to be his role in getting them into this predicament. If he hadn't done one thing or another, she complained—hadn't waited so long—they would now be in England, would be safe and away from all this. "And what makes you think England is safe?" he would shout at her. We were all afraid, afraid of the Gestapo, afraid of concentration camps, afraid of the uncertainty. But we were also desperate—my grandmother especially—for a place to call home. The best we could hope for was to be sent back where we had come from, and that was hardly a cheerful prospect.

Still my mother continued to go out, looking for food, for information, for anything that might be helpful. The crazier things became, the more stable she was. The rest of them were almost paralyzed. They had remained calm through a violent week of bombing; now that it was over, they were coming apart. After a few days with them, we packed up and left.

—⁂—

The residence of the Sœurs de Saint Vincent de Paul was an island of order, a picture-book cliché of a convent surrounded by chaos. My mother had found it during one of her excursions; she had seen a couple of nuns and three young girls carrying a pot of geraniums on the street and had followed them to their convent on the rue Butor.[2]

For two or three weeks they took care of us. If we wanted bread we had to go out and find our own; everything else they provided. They had taken in other refugees, among them a number of children, and

2. The formal address in the archives of the Filles de la Charité de Saint Vincent de Paul was 21 boulevard Daunou. Rue Butor is immediately behind it.

each day we children were given "lessons," a couple of hours of reading, spelling, and arithmetic taught by a young nun with a singsong voice who became furious if we were late. Occasionally I would go out with my mother, doing errands for ourselves or the sisters, but I spent most of the time in the garden behind the convent, a quarter of an acre that, as my mother recalled, had been untouched by war and which was now alive with flowers and birds and blossoming fruit trees. Given its proximity to the port, it was surprising that it remained unscathed. The sisters—the order now calls itself the Filles de la Charité de Saint Vincent de Paul—had maintained an orphanage for girls there, but most of the girls had been evacuated, some to England, when there were still ships. We seemed to be the beneficiaries of the evacuation.[3]

The harbor was less than a mile away; sometimes in the garden I heard the trucks and machinery the Germans had brought in for the repair work, and now and then, I thought, the shouting voices of the Germans themselves. My mother, in the meantime, did a little needlework for the nuns. Now almost out of money, she had offered them a necklace in payment for our board, but they refused. If she wanted to help, she could do sewing and embroidery. "My work wasn't up to their standards," she said afterward. "They would have been better off taking the necklace, but that isn't what they wanted."

The Germans showed up only once at the convent—two officers looking for stocks of food. The sisters had had a room full of eggs chilling in the basement, apparently a pre-war donation from a nearby farmer. But word had come that the Germans were foraging in the city, and the nuns had quietly let it be known that any "poor person" in town could come to the convent for a "small gift." They had given the eggs away, two or three to a person, until the supply was gone. When the Germans arrived, the nuns courteously ushered them through the cellar, then ushered them out. I watched them as they left, wondering when they would be back, but they never returned.

3. I owe this background to information generously provided in 2013 by Sœurs Fromaget and Annie of the Services des Archives of the Compagnie des Filles de la Charité de Saint Vincent de Paul in Paris. The orphanage and another elsewhere in Boulogne were shut down many years ago.

I began to feel secure there. The streets outside were often crowded with German military traffic—trucks and armored vehicles crunching over the broken glass on the cobblestones. At first, people would stand in silence, sullenly watching them as they passed, perhaps still not quite believing it, but after a few days they seemed no longer to notice. Almost every day there was an air raid; sometimes I was awakened by the sound of bombs and antiaircraft fire, but that, too, was becoming peripheral to our lives.

Within, the convent remained a world unto itself whose bell-tolled schedule followed its own rhythm. I knew I didn't understand that rhythm, but I also felt I didn't have to, that this world was safe precisely because it would neither make demands of us nor attack us. I shared a room with a couple of other boys, and each morning we would go to breakfast together, and then to our lessons. We were required to help in cleaning up our room and in clearing the refectory, where we all ate together, and sometimes we were reprimanded for kicking a ball into the flower beds, but otherwise little was asked. Even our occasional trips to the cellar during air raids seemed to have more to do with the rhythms of the convent than with the harsh necessities of war. Much later I wondered how we had been so lucky. Why hadn't the thousands of other homeless refugees in Boulogne found their way to the convent's sheltering door?

Toward the middle of June, the Wehrmacht ordered us back to where we'd come from, Brussels in our case. The edict, on fliers posted around the city, had come directly from the military authorities: all refugees were to be repatriated. Most had to find their own transportation, and for many of the hundreds of thousands of refugees in northern France—altogether an estimated eight million, Belgian, Dutch, French, had tried to flee the German advance—that meant walking. But because my grandmother was old and infirm, we were provided for, I think, by the Red Cross. First there was a truck and then, somewhere else, a sad, old, sooty train that moved slowly, often stopped in the middle of a field or in a wood, and took almost twenty-four hours to cover a stretch that normally takes three. I recall almost nothing of that trip except the grayness of it, the grayness of the smoke, of the sooty train car windows, and of the wretched people on the roads and

the forlorn countryside through which we passed. Even a child understands enough to know that it all reeked of loss, defeat, and despair.

The city of Boulogne was almost totally rebuilt after World War II.
The ferries no longer run from Dover to Boulogne—for people without
cars, the Chunnel train is far more convenient; for those with cars, the
ferries run to Calais. But in the spring and summer, the waterfront is
crowded with tourists. At the same time, when I returned on a visit
in the 1970s I also found that the government, trying to fill a desperate post-war housing shortage, had built a complex of cheap high-rise
apartment houses on a hill in the northeast part of the city, tenements
really, in which the elevators were covered with obscene graffiti and so
pungent with the smell of urine that many inhabitants wouldn't ride in
them.

I interviewed someone in one of those apartments in the 1970s, from
which I could see the Colonne de la Grande Armée through an upper
story window, a monument to another invasion of England, Napoleon's
in 1804, which never took place. Beyond it are the British military cemeteries, acres and acres of them; then the concrete ruins of the German
bunkers and pillboxes of the Atlantic wall, another set of monuments
to stupidity and arrogance, and beyond that the coast of England. On a
clear day, one can see them all.

In the city at that time, the toy stores were full of models of tanks
and Stukas and Spitfires, and in the military cemeteries there are rows
upon rows of gravestones, all carefully maintained by the British government, each of them marked with the name, rank, unit, date of birth,
and date of death of the man buried there. Many of them were no more
than nineteen when they were killed. They are from both wars. In the
spring of 1975, I walked among them with tears in my eyes and wondered whether one of them had once met a young boy on a street in
Boulogne many years before and had given him a bar of chocolate.

7

Saint-Cyprien

The station sign said "Elne." If this is where they were going to be off-loaded, said Ritter, then they were at Saint-Cyprien. And so they were.[1]

When the doors were opened, they were loaded with their belongings on large trucks on the square opposite. Ritter sat next to Licht. "These are our good old Spanish vehicles," he said, stroking the side of the truck. Although it was a clear evening where they stood, there was a strong wind.

"Now you'll experience something that you'll never forget," Ritter said.

"What?" Licht asked.

"Sandstorms." Licht thought the man wasn't quite right in his head.

---

1. It must now have been the very end of May, or maybe very early June, although one train seemed to have arrived on May 19. Gret Arnoldsen, *Silence on Tue* (Paris: La Pensée Universelle, 1981). Arnoldsen was also interned at Saint-Cyprien, and later, after the flood that destroyed Saint-Cyprien, at Gurs. The train that was bombed by the Germans—it had been standing in a brightly lit station—did not arrive until June 3. On the way, it made several stops where the prisoners were marched into various camps. Jerry Breuer, *Mon séjour depuis mai 1940* (document on file at the Leo Baeck Institute, Center for Jewish History, New York).

The sleepy Elne train station where Otto (Hans) and thousands of
others were unloaded from the cattle cars that brought them to southern
France for transfer to internment camps. The station today is little
changed from 1940 when they arrived.

Photo by Peter Schrag.

By then, the news of the fall of Belgium, until then known only in
Licht's car, had spread to others. So now hundreds of men sat miserably
as the column drove off, moving at hellish speed through a village that
looked quite Spanish. There were many women on the street, but few
men. Here and there they passed a gendarme.

"Look out for rocks," said Ritter, crouching low behind the side of the
truck. But Licht stayed upright and looked at the eyes of those who were
standing along the street. He touched Ritter's shoulder. "They don't hate
us," he said. The faces of the women were sadder than they were hostile.
"I wouldn't be surprised to see a girl winking at me."

As they went around a bend, Ritter stood and said, "Over there, that's
the place."

"Where?" Licht asked. "Over there where there's fog?"

"That's not fog," Ritter countered. "That's sand."

The nearer they came to it, the more yellow the sun became, and the more powerful the storm, the thicker the sand. Suddenly Licht had a mouthful. He could hear nothing but the whistling of the windstorm. Then he felt a thousand pinpricks on his skin. Ritter sat with his hand covering his face, and Licht did likewise, but still trying to see between his fingers. They were now on a wide dirt track in the camp that ran between two rows of neglected wooden barracks, many half-wrecked, most without windows and with great holes in the walls, all of it surrounded by barbed wire two or three meters high. It looked like a gigantic ghost city, enveloped in a thick yellow fog, built on white sand, and totally forlorn. Ritter put his lips by Licht's ear. "Four thousand dead Spaniards," he shouted. "They lie buried everywhere around here. Men, women, and children, with their dreams."

After driving so far that Licht wondered if an end would ever come, they stopped at last and all climbed down. Holding their hands over their eyes, they were marched through a gate. Some old men had to be supported so they could stay upright against the wind.

A couple of ragged souls were standing there.

"I know that guy," Licht said to Ams. He belonged to a forced labor detail that the French had impressed at Le Vigeant when they were held there, and after being shuttled about, he had landed here the previous evening.

"How are things here?" Licht asked.

"You can see it. It's a great place to die. You're walking on graves."

"What a lovely place," Ams said. "The genius that thought of shipping us here, I'd like to get to know him."

They were led to their barracks, sixty men (again) in each. Licht was put in number 25. They were shabby wooden structures whose lower walls, buttressed from the outside, tilted outward from the ground. Inside there were compartments, separated by crossbeams, each for two men. Each side housed thirty men. There were two windows, but no floor, no straw, and few chairs, benches or tables. They had to sleep on sand, even as the wind drove more heaps of sand through the holes in the walls. Lying there for five minutes when the wind blew meant being covered with more sand: in their eyes, in their mouths, in their hair. There was no protection from it. It could make people crazy.

It was already getting dark. They all lay down wherever they were standing. The sandstorm raged with undiminished force and the barracks groaned as the men would have liked to groan. They had gotten nothing to eat. Some chewed on crusts they had saved. Then they enveloped themselves as best they could in coats and blankets and tried to sleep.

Later Spatz, a man some of them knew, appeared and said that arrangements were being made for the leadership of the camp and that he had been proposed for the job.

"And what about Feuermann?" asked Licht, who was angry that he'd been wakened just as he was falling asleep.

"The others will reject him," Spatz said. He didn't say who the "others" were.

"Then I'm for Spatz," Ams said. "It's in our interest that one of our group is part of the leadership."

For most it made too little difference who was chosen to ask questions. What was really at stake? The French would in any event do with them what they wanted. One day the devil would fetch them, the camp, and the sand anyway.

The next morning, after the wind had abated, they could look at the camp, erected by the Spanish. After standing at the border by the thousands—men, women, children, horses, wagons, some sick and dying—they were at last allowed into France, fenced in on the beach with barbed wire, and only then given lumber, tar paper, nails, and hammers. In Licht's part—Ilot[2] I—there were about sixty barracks. Many still had crude Spanish markings. Here lived block leader Ramos, there Captain Lopez.[3] Licht thought he might some day write about it, the *Retirada,* the retreat of Spanish loyalists following their defeat after three years of

---

2. Literally an islet. In this context, a block of barracks.

3. Of the thousands of Republican loyalists who fled Spain after Franco's victory in the Spanish Civil War (1936–39) and had been interned here and in the other camps hastily thrown up near the border, some had since been forcibly repatriated; some conscripted into French work battalions; others had succeeded in emigrating to Mexico and Latin America.

Mont Canigou, one of the highest peaks in the Pyrenees, viewed from Elne. On clear days it was a beacon to the prisoners who could see it from behind the barbed wire at Saint-Cyprien.

Photo by Peter Schrag.

brutal civil war by Franco's falangists in 1939, but who would then care? Who would be interested in that story?[4]

Sun-bleached animal bones lay everywhere in the sand, now looking like petrified fossils from a long-ago past. On one side, separated from them by the barbed wire, was the ocean, which on this day was a beautiful blue and adorned with little whitecaps. On the other side, more barbed wire, another Ilot of barracks, and then, seemingly within reach, the Pyrenees. Snow must have fallen during the night; quite far down, the mountains were white.[5]

After the makeshift kitchen let it be known that there would be no food until afternoon, they set out to make emergency repairs to their quarters. Since there were no other materials available, they used old pieces of wood and nails that were lying around, most probably left by the Spanish, and tore planks from unused barracks. The latrines, each a platform about two meters above the ground, with large tubs for the waste below, were ill-conceived structures erected on the side of the camp from which the wind blew. There was no toilet paper and they never got any. Soiled pieces of note paper, rags, and, when they later got newspapers, newsprint blew over the whole camp; within a few days there would be no spot where used paper wasn't lying or flying around.

Remarkably, the paper problem was among the worst they faced. Already after two days Ams told Spatz that it was intolerable. Spatz, who was now their voice, went to the camp commandant, who laughed and said he'd pass the complaint on.

When Ams asked Spatz about it in the barracks that evening, Spatz tried to assuage people, asking for patience. There were so many large problems for the French to solve concerning their internment that Ams and his friends couldn't ask for everything at once. They should trust them a couple of days.

Thereafter the internees all began to cut little pieces of cloth from shirttails and handkerchiefs with which to clean themselves and washed

4. Somewhere among my father's things, I found a few penciled pages from a little notebook in which he seemed to have begun just such a story.

5. This was—is—the nine-thousand-foot peak of Mont Canigou, about thirty-five miles to the west, one of the highest and most dramatic in the Pyrenees and a place of symbolic significance in Catalonia.

them out at the pump. Some filled sardine cans with water and used wet rags to wipe themselves. The soiled water naturally seeped into the ground and would later be pumped up as fresh water.

After two days, drinking from the pumps was prohibited. They were to be used only for washing. Drinking water was available from a purification system—and that water had the familiar taste of chlorine. But they used the pump anyway for washing their dishes and cups. The paper problem was never solved.

—⁓—

From the first day the depressing condition of the whole layout weighed heavily on them all. Some ailed terribly, both physically and in spirit. Most of them, men who had once led orderly, comfortable bourgeois lives, were now, for the most, going around in the summer heat dressed only in their undershorts. Some had simply wrapped rags or towels around their thighs. They had to forget most of their habits of cleanliness and hygiene. They had to forget about eating at tables, sitting on chairs, sleeping on beds. They had to forget about reading. Still, they tried to retain their dignity.[6]

On the evening of the first full day, they got warm pea soup and a piece of black bread to break into it, which they all ate with delight. Afterward, for the first time in a long time, they had the pleasant feeling of being satiated. Then Veilchenfeld, Ams, and Licht watched a beautiful lightshow as the sun went down over the mountains. But they were also seized with a terrible sense of loss and longing as they returned to the barracks, which had no electricity, and stared into the darkness.

6. "The living conditions at St. Cyprien," wrote the representative of the American Jewish Joint Distribution Committee, who had visited the camp, "are unbearable and almost surpass the limits of human endurance. But all these physical privations, no matter how painful, are nothing compared to the moral distress which reigns at St. Cyprien, as probably at the other camps, too." The report also makes clear that internee "leaders" like Spatz were widely distrusted. "Those whose duties put them in touch with the French administration are especially reproached that they think only of their own release and neglect the interests of the others." E. L. Kowarsky, "Report on the Events from May 10 to July 30, 1940," Sept. 26, 1940, Archives of the American Jewish Joint Distribution Committee (AJJDC), AR 33/44/: 6, 7.

Suddenly, old Speier exclaimed, "I'm a dumb old wretch and it's good that young people should be in the leadership, insofar as there's any to be had. But have any of you gentlemen ever asked the French why everything is as it is? In my whole life I've never done anything bad. For thirty-five years I've sold shoe inlays. I've never had any run-ins with the police, and I'm being treated not even like a criminal, but like a dirty animal."

"We want to know our status," someone interjected. "And before everything we want to know what's going on with our wives."

There was that word again, the word that weighed on them night and day. A man named Julius who had recently married and whom Licht had found sobbing in a corner, jumped up. "Yes, yes," he screamed, "I can't take it anymore."

Ams interrupted. "Shut your trap. Stop behaving like a hysterical female. What do you mean you can't stand it anymore?"

Now there was an uproar. Most were on their feet in the darkness, all shouting. It was a scandal, the filth, the barracks, the senselessness of it all, screamed these mature, experienced, worldly men; it was an obscenity that they weren't told what was going on with their wives, that they weren't told anything.

After some effort, Spatz finally got himself heard. "What you say is correct," he said. "Don't you believe that I've asked the officer? He answered that he didn't know anything either, even about where his own family was. It was the war."

"Does anyone out there," Licht interrupted, "even know that we're here—say, the Red Cross?"

Brust began to laugh. "You've forgotten," he said in a friendly tone, "the reception we got from the Red Cross."

Spatz continued. "For now we're not allowed to write. Not a line goes out of this camp. Nobody, dear Licht, knows where we are. It all takes time. Take it as the Pure Germans are doing, try to improve our situation: build chairs and benches and tables, improve the barracks. That's the only way we can now help ourselves. And now, good night."

But they weren't satisfied.

"Can't you learn anything about the general situation?" Feuermann asked.

"Nothing," Spatz said.

"The Pure Germans told me today," Feuermann said, "that Boulogne has been captured and there was fighting at Amiens."

"Don't let anyone tell you fairytales," Spatz said. "And if you do, don't spread them."

"Why don't we get any war news?" Licht asked. And when Spatz said he didn't know, Licht got angry. He stood up in the darkness. "Listen all," he said, his voice quivering. "Are we going to accept this? They don't give us much to eat. Fine. They don't tell us where our wives are: '*C'est la guerre,*' but that they don't tell us anything about the general military situation is unmitigated malicious chicanery."

As Licht spoke, Spatz stood again. "Is that supposed to be a criticism of me?" he asked.

"It's only a criticism if you can't unequivocally give us your word of honor that you've asked."

For a moment, there was silence. Then Spatz said, "I've tried a thousand times to hear how things stand. I never got any information."

"We're not asking that you find out, but that you ask."

"Okay," Spatz said, "I promise to ask them."

—⁂—

Some in the camp had been building little stools from wood and nails they salvaged from the derelict empty barracks. The Czechs were particularly skilled at it and were now selling them for a few francs each.

Spatz came back from the office. The commandant had seen people sitting on such stools, he said, and as of today it was forbidden to build stools and similar items. Those that had been built had to be taken apart. Only waste wood could be used, and there was none of that.

"What do you want?" Ams asked. "This is waste wood."

"Tomorrow, when they inspect, you'll get into all kinds of trouble if they say that you had things made from the wood of the barracks," Spatz said.

"By tomorrow, nobody will see anything. And by the way, what's new about the war situation?"

Spatz claimed to have asked. "The officer said he couldn't answer, but that people should have confidence."

"We've heard that before," Ams said.

—ᴍ—

The next morning Ams and Licht asked Brust: since he could get chocolate and cigarettes, could his black market connections also get him newspapers?

"I'll try," Brust said. "But there won't be anything good in it. Look at the Nazis. They've been talking about a great victory, some sort of breakthrough near Sedan."

"But how can these guys know more than we do?" Licht asked.

Brust looked at him. "Generally you don't seem so dumb. Do you seriously believe that after the collapse of the Belgians there's still any hope left?"

"That's not the question here. I want to know how the Nazis know more than we do."

"I have no idea," Brust said. "But there's one guy in that gang that I went to school with. He's no gossip and relatively decent. His name is Mützenmacher, and today he took me aside. 'France is done for,' he said. 'We've broken through at Sedan.' How did he know? I asked him. He answered that was his affair, and then said again that they would be in Paris on June fifteenth and then there would be either peace or an armistice. It was of course possible that all France would be occupied. But don't let crazy people make you crazy, he said. Nothing will happen to anyone who's done nothing against us. Those who've crossed us, those we'll get."

Brust stopped for a moment, then turned to Licht. "What do you make of that?" he asked.

"There are only two possibilities. Either what these swine say is true, in which case they have some connection that we don't know about. If so we have to do something about it. Or they're lying, in which case it's even more important to do something."

"What kind of connections could they have?" Brust asked. "Maybe they have some kind of contact with a French officer who's a Nazi. They must exist."

"Let's get a paper," Licht said, "and then we'll have some information of our own."

"I'll try," Brust said. "In the meantime, let's keep all this between us." Then he went off on his secretive ways.

What worried Licht most, other than his not knowing what was happening with Judith, was the thought that one day the Germans would be there. What should he do then? He had imagined that scene before, but on that day it made for a particularly ugly picture. He took Ams aside.

"Have you considered the possibility," Licht said, "that one day the Germans could be standing here?"

"You may be right," Ams said. "Since we're so isolated everything is possible."

"We should prepare. Up there on the ridge is the Spanish border. I assume that if the Germans were coming, the French would abandon us. Then the gates will be open for a little while and the watchword will be *sauve qui peut.*"

"We should form a small group, a select group of people who can put up with hardships. And we have to find someone who can show us the way."

They immediately thought of Ritter, who had fought in Spain. Would he do it? If Franco's police caught him, wouldn't they hang him?

When they found Ritter, he was busy making himself a knife. He had gotten a hammer somewhere and was sitting by the little track for the carts on which the tubs of waste from the latrine were hauled off every day. In his hand he held a piece of metal some ten centimeters long that he'd found lying in the sand. He'd laid it on the rail and was hammering one edge to sharpen it. Licht touched him on the shoulder.

"How's it going?" he asked.

Proudly, Ritter showed him a knife he'd already finished. It was quite sharp and useful.

"That's great," Licht said. "But listen, I have to ask you something."

"Ask away. I don't have to answer if I don't want to." And then he went back to hammering. Licht sat beside him. The smell from the nearby latrine was vile.

"Do you know the way over the Pyrenees?"

"Of course. Do you want to take a walk?"

"I would gladly do it if the Germans came."

Ritter stopped hammering. "What's up?"

"Nothing," Licht said. "Nothing at all. But I don't like the rumors in the camp and I'd like to prepare."

"Who else?" Richter asked and went back to hammering.

"Ams and Brust and Lofe and a couple of others."

"No more than five or six," Ritter said.

"So you'd do it?"

"Of course. I'll take you."

"And what if they grab you?" Licht asked.

Richter laughed. "If the Nazis find me here, I'm completely finished anyway. In Spain I've got friends. Do you think there's nothing but Francoists? I'm your man."

"Fine. Let's all of us discuss it. Tomorrow morning right after roll call, by the fence on the ocean side."

—⚍—

Licht was awakened in the middle of the night by the sounds of trucks and voices shouting orders in the distance. He woke Ams and asked if they should look.

"Anybody seen walking at night gets shot," Ams said, "But let's open the door. Searchlights were shining into the adjoining block of barracks, which had been vacant.

"New arrivals," Ams said. "Maybe there'll be a whole lot of our friends from Brussels among them; maybe they'll know something."

The next morning proved Ams right. The neighboring block now had occupants, but guards had been posted along the barbed wire between the two sections and orders issued that no one was to go within five meters of it. So now the internees stood on each side, looking at one another. Here was the father, there the son. Brothers were separated from brothers, friends from friends, all divided not only by the fence but also by five meters on each side of it.

As they all tried to be understood, there was so much yelling that no one could hear his own words. On the other side, two people brought an old man toward the fence. A man who stood near Licht grabbed him by the arm and shouted: "That's my father, see there, that's my father."

They tried to point out the son to the old man, just as the old man collapsed. Had he seen his son? Was he sick? Was he dead? The son rushed like a madman to the barbed wire and tried to climb through it. The guard, an elderly man, pulled him back by the sleeve. "No, sir," he said.

"But that's my father," the son shouted. "Dead or sick, I don't know. You understand? My father."

The guard hesitated. Then he said, "Wait here a moment." In Catalan, a language that none of them understood, he called a guard on the other side. After going to the old man, the other guard called something back.

"Your father is alive . . . not dead, not dead," he said to the young man, whom he was still holding by the sleeve and who then got up and walked back from the fence to stand silently among the other, many of whom were still shouting. A couple of hours later, when Licht passed by the spot, the young man was still standing there.

In the meantime, Licht's block had been trying to assist the new arrivals, who still had had nothing to drink or eat. There seemed to be no rule against throwing things over or through the fence: apparently that had never occurred to the commandant. Empty bottles flew across, to be filled and thrown back. Bread was thrown across. After looking for some time, Licht spotted a physician he knew from Brussels.

"Hello, Baer!" he shouted to the man, who recognized him immediately. "Is Strohmann among you?"[7]

When Baer nodded, Licht told him he'd like to speak with Strohmann, who had been their family doctor in Brussels, and that he would meet him there at five.

—ᴍ—

"What you need," said Ritter when they met at the fence by the shore "is enough money and provisions to last you. You have to count on a hike of ten hours, all in the valley between the mountains. Naturally not on the roads. We might have to sleep one night on the way, so take blankets, but otherwise very little baggage. You should now set a watch at night to see when the guards knock off."

"One more thing," said Brust. "Tonight we'll get a newspaper. It costs six hundred francs."

7. Baer was a real name for three Saint-Cyprien prisoners. One was Richard Baer, the doctor my father later called by the pseudonym Löwe (see below). The use of the real name here was probably a Freudian slip in a draft in which all other names, except for Judith and Peter, were changed.

"You guys are crazy if you pay that," Ritter said. "But it's no concern of mine."

"What happens once we're over there?" Veilchenfeld asked. "How do we go further?"

"You can hide with my friends, at least for a time, but then you'll need money."

"What happens if they catch us?"

"Then you're probably done for. And money won't help. They'll take that from you anyway."

"And what are Spanish prisons like?" Licht asked.

"You'd look back on Saint-Cyprien," he said, "like it was paradise."

After Ritter left, Ams told them that they were trying to get each of twelve barracks to contribute fifty francs each for the newspaper, which then could be read aloud to the occupants. Brust said that as his commission he wanted to keep the paper.

"Granted," Ams said.

That evening, having raised the money, they got the paper, a French daily from the previous day, which Feuermann read as they stood in a tight circle around him. Suddenly they heard the names of places that were far inside France—Abbeville, Cherbourg, the Somme. In the face of overwhelming enemy forces there had been withdrawals to new strategic positions. They would later learn that what they had been reading was already very old news.

The next morning, June 10, a man came to Licht to tell him that on the previous evening he had talked to one of the men in the other block—Ilot II—whose sister had seen his own wife and Judith together in La Panne on the Belgian coast a few weeks before. They had surely gotten into France. By then the men at Saint-Cyprien were trying every means to learn more about their wives. All postal service was blocked, but Spatz had persuaded the camp commandant to prepare a list of all the internees, together with the names of wives and children, to circulate to other camps in an attempt to learn where any of the women were. They were anxiously waiting for answers.

—⁂—

At about the same time, a growing number of them were hit by a troubling disease with severe diarrhea, cramps, and high fever—at first only a few, but after a week, more than a third had it. The internee doctors needed medications but had none. Gross, who was in charge of the camp clinic, paid no attention to the disease; the French doctors did little more. When one ailing man was brought in, the French doctor asked, "Why the fuss? He's going to die anyway."[8]

Brust came to his friends, who were lying in the sun, and told them he wasn't going to watch it much longer. "Have your hearts hardened so much that it makes no difference to you what's going on here? People are standing in line by the hundreds in front of the so-called infirmary. Occasionally one falls over because he's too weak to stand. I asked them what they were doing there. One answered that they could get constipation pills.

"Then I knocked gently on the door. When nobody came I banged with my fists. Gross's assistant finally showed up and asked if I was deranged. I pushed him aside and got to Gross. 'Are you giving people something or not?' I asked him. 'I don't have anything,' he answered. 'Want to see my medicine cabinet?' and then he showed me a completely empty closet, with the exception of a little package of aspirin. When I asked him if he had a little tea at least, he said no. The best he had was hot water.

"'Then why do you go along with the French?' I asked him. 'Why don't you shove it in their faces?' Gross, the stuffed a shirt that he is, said he was designated head physician and in that post he will remain, even if the whole camp goes to hell. You guys should see the clinic. Or are you afraid?"

"Afraid?" said Ams. "It can't be worse than a field hospital in Russia."

—᠁—

The clinic was a barracks like all the others. On one side of some thirty meters there were three tiny windows.[9] The air was foul and the place swarmed with flies. The patients lay on straw sacks, their bare upper

---

8. The disease was almost certainly dysentery, as later reported by various outside visitors.

9. In a drawing called "Dysentery"—the original is now lost—the painter Karl Schwesig, also a prisoner at Saint-Cyprien and later at Gurs and other camps, rendered it with a sign over the door, presumably left from the time when it housed mostly Spanish patients, that said "Infirmeria."

bodies emaciated, little more than skin and bones. The sweat shone on them like a mirror.

"As far as I can tell, the whole place has one hand towel," Brust said. "They're all terribly thirsty. If they have to go—and for some that means forty or fifty times every twenty-four hours—they have to go outside. There's a latrine across the way from the clinic, but to use it they have to climb a ladder two meters high, even people who can hardly stand. When there's a strong wind or a sandstorm some of them don't make it and lie on the ground until they're found by their comrades who then have to bring them back into the barracks, soiled as they are. The next day somebody takes pity and washes them off under the pump."

There was neither extra food for them nor any kind of treatment. The only thing that was done is that twice a day their temperature was taken.

"What can we do?" Licht asked as they left. Brust said it was all up to Gross.

"We need somebody here who can do something besides standing at attention and saluting. We need somebody who not only knows something but who can stand up to the French. Otherwise the whole camp will go under."

As they left, Licht again looked for Dr. Strohmann, whom he had still not found. He knew that Judith, Peter, and Judith's mother had been seen at the Belgian coast, but that was all. Maybe Strohmann knew more, and Licht asked Spatz if he could somehow get him over into the other Ilot.

"Of course," Spatz said. "Tomorrow morning, you'll go as my assistant." But the next morning, before they could go, they got the first list of women from Gurs, the internment camp near the city of Pau, and the whole place turned into a madhouse.[10] Bauer, the leader of the Pure Germans, stood with the list in hand in the midst of screaming, gesticulating men who at that moment seemed more like children. Those whose wives had been found hugged one another, wept, showed photographs, and assured others that their wives would also be found. There were said to be five thousand women at Gurs. This list had only 250 names. Judith's name was not on it.

10. Among those interned at Gurs was Hannah Arendt. Gurs was a name I first heard from my father, but I don't recall in what context.

Ams shoved his arm under Licht's. "Oh, shit," he said. "Your turn will come."

Coincidentally with the list from Gurs came a new wave of rumors. Paris had fallen, some said; according to others Paris had been by-passed and the Wehrmacht had already penetrated deeper into France. The whole place was a zoo where the animals were restlessly pacing around their cages.

Outside their own barracks, Licht and his friends came on a cluster of people listening to a frightfully emaciated man.

"For some days now," the man said, "a couple of crazies have been walking around here saying you should enlist in the Foreign Legion. They say you should do it in gratitude to France. You have an obligation to help put Hitler down. Yes, maybe we should do it, but only as free and reasonable men who know what chances they have and what risks they're taking. If the Boches capture a Frenchman, he gets interned and that's it. If they get you, they wouldn't shoot you. They'd hang you. We won't do it under pressure. If there's pressure, we stay here patiently and wait."

"He's right," Ams said. "Even so some are enlisting every day."

Not so long after, a pale-faced Veilchenfeld came in and gathered people. "Listen to what I have to say," he said. "The rules for the camp have been tightened. No one will be allowed to go to the latrine at night. In front of each barracks will be a tub, which will have to be emptied every morning. And we have to post a watch at the door from nine in the evening to five in the morning to make sure that no more than one person goes at a time. The French will check.

"Finally, as soon as they can do the installations, the tubs will be placed inside each barracks, and a crossbeam will be set across the door each evening so that no one can go out. Anyone seen outside will be shot."

That same evening soldiers began the work on the installation for the crossbeams, and the first watch was posted.

—⁓—

It wasn't easy. The first night, people wanted constantly to rush to the tub, and Licht, who, with Lofe, drew the watch from one to three, had to struggle to persuade each person to wait inside until the previous one was done. Many had terrible cramps. When Speier, who could hardly stand, came to the door and begged to be allowed out, first whispering, then screaming that he would go in the sand. He couldn't hold it anymore. Licht let him go.

Outside there was a fierce sandstorm, driving sand through all the cracks. The wind came in fierce gusts, and each drove a great cloud of sand against the planks. The man who had been at the tub came in.

"Speier is lying out there," he said. "I tried to help him up, but I couldn't."

Lofe and Licht went out. Speier had apparently been blown down and was now lying with his face in the sand. As they went to pick him up, he said, "Let me die here." Licht and Lofe, making short work of it, dragged him back to his place in the barracks, woke Ams and Veilchenfeld, and went to sleep.

The next morning, Licht almost throttled Spatz. "Tell us exactly," he said in his rage, "where these new rules come from, and don't give us any crap."

"They came out of a blue sky." Ams sidled over. He thought it would be good if someone were there to prevent blows.

"I have a very different notion," Licht said. "Are things going so badly at the front that they're taking it out on us? But that's not what I want to say. What I want to say is that Spatz is not suited for his job."

Spatz blanched. "So what do you think I should be doing?" he asked.

"Scream," said Brust, who had joined them. "Scream and not always swallow."

Licht resumed. "Since you've become the big cheese, have you gone through the barracks and talked to the people there?"

"I get reports from the barracks chiefs and from the doctors."

"Oh," Licht said. "Stand up, little guy, and I'll show you what things really look like."

"Do you know how you're talking to me?"

In the meantime, Brust had also lost his temper. Showing the camp leader the camp, he said in his soft child's voice, was a great idea. A couple of others were now standing with them.

"Okay," Spatz said at last. "I'll come with you."

They began in their own barracks.

"Pay attention," Licht said. "I want to explain things to you. You don't see this man in the dark because they've not allowed us to put in a third window in a barracks of sixty men, but Speier is lying there. Last night the man collapsed on his way to relieve himself in a sandstorm. Other than the charcoal we make ourselves out of animal bones, there are no medications. Other than pea soup and dry bread, there's no nourishment for him.

"Next to him here lies Gallus. The man, as you know, is crippled. He has terrible asthma. At night he's been standing mostly outside the door. Otherwise he would suffocate. Now he won't be able to do it anymore. If he does, he'll be shot.

"Now here's Heimburger; he's sixty-seven.[11] Every morning we have to help him unbend his limbs. He has rheumatism or gout, and lying in damp sand does him no good.

"Now, here are three sick men next to each other. They have the same illness as Speier. Yesterday their temperature was over forty degrees. During my watch last night, each had to go out between five and ten times. It may be that they caught pneumonia from the wind, I don't know.

"Now turn around and look through this room. Have you ever seen anything more miserable? If things continue like this, nobody will come out of this alive."

"Let's spare him the other barracks," Ams said.

"What about the latrines?" someone said.

"Excellent," said Licht. "Come, Spatz, we're going to take a little walk. The fresh air will do you good."

They went through the camp with their eyes nearly shut. In the wind, they could only be understood by screaming.

"Can't you see that you're doing me an injustice?" Spatz shouted.

"Is it an injustice," Ams shouted back, "to show you what's going on here?"

They approached the latrine. From a distance they could already see the pieces of rag and paper flying around the camp. As they came closer,

---

11. There was a fifty-three-year-old inmate named Max Heimbach in my father's barracks. Was my father's use of the name Heimburger a Freudian slip?

Carl Rabus,
Sketches of
Saint-Cyprien
for his graphic
work "Die
Passion."

*© Buchheim-
museum der
Phantasie,
Bernried /
Germany.*

they saw the long line of people waiting. Many had their arms around their bellies. Not many could stand up straight. They kept their eyes shut. Now and then they spit out the sand that had blown in their mouths. None of them spoke. One old man rested his head on the back of the man in front of them. They were like living cadavers.

"What do you think of that?" Ams shouted in Spatz's ear. Then, without another word, they left him standing there.

—⁓—

When Licht finally saw Strohmann in the sick bay in the other block, he hardly recognized the man who had been his own doctor. He'd grown a thick black beard and looked more like an old rabbi than a young physician. He said he was glad to see Licht and apologized for not meeting him sooner, but he'd had little time. And, he said, he didn't know much.

But Licht was angry that Strohmann, knowing how important it was, hadn't made more effort to tell him what he knew about Judith and Peter. "You were certainly the last person in this whole camp of some seven or eight thousand people who saw my family."

"Your family," he said, "is almost certainly somewhere here in southern France. I met your wife, your son, Mrs. Cohn, and your maid, Maria, departing La Panne in the trailer of a car. They were jammed in among thousands of other cars. But however those cars got through, your family would have gotten through as well."

Licht had the gloomy feeling that the doctor wasn't telling all he knew. "You really don't know anything more?"

"I really don't know how it went. One really couldn't worry too much about others."

Wasn't Hirsch, Licht's business partner, with Judith?

No, Hirsch had left for France a few days before.

"How odd," Licht said, "that my partner had left my wife, my son, and the old lady alone."

"As I told you, everybody was looking out for himself. '*Sauve qui peut.*'"

What would he do, Licht asked Ams a little later, if he had a partner and friend to whom he had made a firm promise that in case of urgent need he would look after his friend's family? "Would you go away and leave them behind?"

"Of course I wouldn't," Ams said, "but I'm not the norm."

—ɯɯ—

"The doctors are on strike," Brust said as he sat down with Licht and Ams. "They've announced they won't work with Gross anymore. Two more people died. With that the doctors wanted authority to send the very sick people to the hospital in Perpignan, but Gross wanted to keep them in his own clutches. Guys, I've seen the dead men. They look like they suffocated. Can that just be ordinary diarrhea? It makes me shudder when I think that we might have an epidemic of a dangerous illness."

They went into the barracks to see Löwe, who was one of the striking doctors.[12]

"Tell us," Ams said.

"There's not much to tell," Löwe said. "I don't know anything about Gross's medical skills, but as a human being, he's beyond reach."

"And what did those people die of?"

Löwe shrugged. "You'd have to do blood tests. You'd have to examine stools. It should have done been long ago. But here there's no codeine, no medicine of any kind, and not even towels. We have to work here as if we were without any supplies in the jungle. But I don't want to have any deaths on my conscience. That Gross has to deal with, if that's what he wants. But not me."

"So you're on strike," Ams said.v

"What should we do instead?"

"What does the military doctor say?"

"I imagine that for him, it's just a matter of numbers. What people die of makes no difference to him. The dead get buried, and that's the end of it."

—ɯɯ—

12. As noted earlier, Löwe was my father's pseudonym for Richard Baer. (Lion for Bear: one zoo animal for another). He eventually escaped by way of Switzerland, where he was interned again, and later practiced medicine in New York. "Richard Baer, 68, Physician, Is Dead," *New York Times*, April 12, 1965.

The rumors kept pouring in. They seemed to come almost every half hour, the good alternating with the bad. Only the Pure Germans seemed certain and calm. They strolled along the fence near the shore; they sat in their barracks in the evening and sang old German songs. The great shifts in mood of the others didn't seem to affect them.

There were more lists of women. In their whole circle, it was only Licht, Veilchenfeld, and Brust who had heard nothing. They sat for hours thinking about where their wives could be. But they could do little.

Owing to the chocolate and other things the smugglers brought in, those who had not fallen ill slowly regained some of their strength. But even those who survived the illness were still weak. They lay the whole day in the shady corners of what they called the sun barracks, a roofless shed whose walls sheltered them from the wind. Every so often, as the hot summer sun reached them, they would move to a new spot. But the scraps of soiled paper that flew everywhere like butterflies made sitting almost anywhere in the camp nearly intolerable.

Escape planning again became a common topic. Often they stood by the inland fence in clusters of three or four and looked at the mountains, beyond which lay freedom. But Licht, who thought much about it, also told himself it was probably insane to flee before he knew where Judith was. At the same time he couldn't let himself fall into the hands of the Germans.

Now and then a newspaper would get into the camp. From one they learned of the appointment of the defeatist General Maxime Weygand as commander of the French army, which depressed them all.

They met again with Ritter, who said he'd been in touch with some of his connections and talked about buying or even stealing a little boat in the next town and rowing by night up the Dordogne until they got into the foothills. Once they were in the ravines that led to the pass, not much could happen. "I assume that if the Germans came, we wouldn't be the only ones," he said. "There will be a rush. But we have to avoid the Spanish border controls. For a stretch we could go with the crowd. Then we'd come to the trails I know."

After remaining silent for a while, Spatz asked, "You don't want me on your expedition?"

Prisoners mending clothes outside a barracks at Saint-Cyprien, 1940.
*Varian Fry Papers, Rare Book & Manuscript
Library, Columbia University.*

That wasn't up to him, Ams said, but to whoever led the group. He didn't have anything against Spatz.

"And you, Licht?"

"You know what I think of your efforts here," Licht said. "But that doesn't mean you're no longer my comrade. I'd help you if I could."

"I want to tell you how things stand, without holding anything back," Spatz said. At first he spoke haltingly, then the words poured out. "What's going on is a bottomless obscenity. And I'm part of it. I have to be. Here eight thousand men are imprisoned in a camp that's unhealthy and unbearable in every respect. I don't know whether you know that there are swamps around here. Soldiers who have been stationed here for a while come down with the same sickness that we have here. They get sent to the mountains to recuperate. We can't get to the mountains. We sit here behind barbed wire, waiting for the Germans. And then there's this camp itself. These barracks were thrown up in an emergency. You know about the origins of this hell. One day in December 1938, the French, in a grandiose gesture, opened the border to the refugees waiting on the Spanish side of the border, who then came to this cursed shore.[13] Next they put barbed wire around them. Then they quietly left them in the sand to die. And then they let them build these barracks—fast, fast—and every day so many died, women and children and the wounded—so, quick, the barracks! before the world sees what's happening. Now look around, there they stand: the barracks.

"And then we came. What a jolly thought, locking us into the same camp where the Spaniards had been. Only pity that it was spring. Many more died here in the winter. And now comes Spatz who thinks maybe he can help others a little if he can talk reasonably and politely to the French. What an idiot! Such an idiot. Here he comes and says, gentlemen, just consider. The people you have in this camp aren't your enemies, excepting a few Nazis; they're people whose most passionate hopes and wishes are on your side. 'Extreme suspects,' they answer. Then at least look to the health of these people. Provide at least some medicine and some minimal nutrition. They don't listen. They make notes, which vanish in the files. And if that can't be, at least help sustain people's morale. Tell them the truth, say a few reasonable things. The men here don't die just from hunger and disease but from not knowing. They lie awake at night, they groan, they weep, they curse, Mr. Commandant. I told him, help them with whatever gesture you can. Tell them France is still there and that we enjoy her protection. The man never answered.

"Now back to you. You all look at me questioningly. In every look there's the same not knowing. Everyone who encounters me looks at me with questions. Everyone follows me with questions that I can't answer.

13. After Franco's victory and the collapse of Spanish Republican resistance in Catalonia in 1939, some 400,000 refugees crowded this shore. The French were totally unprepared for the numbers and didn't know what to do with them, so they put barbed wire around them and let them throw up the rickety barracks which became the archipelago of camps in Southwest France—Gurs, Vernet, Saint-Cyprien, Argelès and others—that the refugees from Belgium and France would later be tossed into.

He meets with the commandant, they think. He must know something. Why isn't he helping us? After all, he's one of us. Now you're shutting me out. Licht hates me. Ams suspects me, Brust conspires against me. So what must I do? I'm up against a huge machine, me, a pitiful little emigrant—I'm standing powerless between you and a monster."

He stopped. No one uttered a syllable. Then very quietly he continued.

"The collapse is at hand. Up there, everything is already in a state of dissolution. Not that you can see it from the outside, but I feel it. There's fear in their eyes. They feel hands around their necks, just as we do. They have dark circles around their eyes. They whisper to each other. Great shadows hang over them, just as they loom over us.

"Maybe you hadn't heard, but Italy has entered the war. The vultures are coming. And still I, Spatz, remain at my post, and still I ask for toilet paper and drugs and better food and a little understanding."

They all felt sorry for him. At last Ams said what they all thought. "Spatz, you're a good guy and our comrade, but you're the wrong man in the wrong job."

As they broke up, Spatz was bombarded with still more questions, most reflecting the same fear: What's going to happen to us?

Ams answered for Spatz. "Gentlemen, don't forget that we're not alone on this earth. There are millions of people who have these same dubious pleasures. We're not about to have our heads chopped off, and after all we've been through, we still have had great luck. If the good Lord had wanted us to kick the bucket, the devil would have had us long ago. In all their confusion, the Belgians, having labeled us extreme suspects, had nothing better to do than ship us safely away. Maybe the French will do the same."

—⁕—

The next afternoon, a muggy day, they heard planes, first a formation of three flying south, then more and more, maybe forty or fifty all flying in the same direction, which engrossed and excited them and led to wild guessing. A battle in the Mediterranean, someone suggested. A raid on Rome, somebody else guessed. The Germans had attacked Gibraltar, a third offered, and the French were coming to support the British. But whatever it was, they agreed, it was something big. Only the Pure Germans stood there as if they knew everything and as if it was the most natural thing in the world.

Feuermann collected his friends and told them that the Nazis said it was the French government fleeing to Morocco. Even as he spoke, more flew over.

"The devil only knows," Licht said. "I've counted a hundred thirty so far. They can't all be carrying government officials."

Nobody knew anything in the staff barracks either, but the general lassitude told them something. The sergeants were drinking coffee, their pith helmets on the back of their necks, sweat dripping from their heads.

Ritter came by. "The squad charged with the barracks watch won't be here tonight," he said. "Nobody knows whether there'll be others, but be prepared."

"What do you think about the planes?" Ams asked him.

"Rats. Ordinary rats."

"You mean as in sinking ship?"

"Absolutely. If it had been a raid they would have come back by now. All in the same direction."

Brust had been talking with Mützenmacher, his former schoolmate. "Peace is at the door," Mützenmacher had told him. "At the end of this month I'll be home in Brussels. Shall I say hello to your wife?" Brust told him he didn't know where his wife was.

There had been new lists of interned women, and again Judith's name wasn't on them, but for Licht, as for others, that worry had been overshadowed by worries about their own fate. They just didn't have room enough in their heads for other cares.

At the same time their circumstances were changing. There was no watch at the barracks that evening, so most didn't return to their quarters as the rules required but sat in the dark outside. There was a beautiful moon. Now and then a sick man passed on his way to the latrine. They could hear the frogs in the nearby swamps and occasionally the voices of the guards chatting at the perimeter fence, and then the commands to a squad marching past the fence and out.

"They're gone," Ams said, "and for now we're lying here in the sand without chaperones."

Ritter came by and gestured to Ams to follow him.

"We're not there yet," Ritter said. "In a few hours, they'll have new people. But it's over. France is done for."

"What news have you got?" Ams asked.

"There's talk of an armistice. Yes, their people are getting weak. It's like a sickness, a sort of tuberculosis of character has gotten hold of them."

The new squad, when it arrived, consisted entirely of old men. Ritter pointed out that they had no live ammunition. Some appeared to be drunk.

—៣—

The next evening, after Spatz failed to return to the barracks, Ams and Licht found him sitting at a table in the camp office with one of the new sergeants, a man named Borallo. Between them stood a candle and a half-empty bottle of rum. Borallo, with his glassy eyes, must already have drunk quite a bit, but he seemed to be more angry than drunk.

"Have a drink, gentlemen," he said when Ams and Licht came in. Then he turned back to Spatz. "What was I saying? Oh, yes. I've been in the service twelve years. Not a grand life, but good enough, good food, good drinking, and a wife and child. What else does a man need? I would have been up for promotion next year, but now there won't be a next year. They're negotiating with the Boches in the woods at Compiègne, a lovely French wood. I know it. As they negotiate, the Germans are calmly marching on, always farther into French land, through our fields. . . . Oh, those beautiful vineyards at Bordeaux. Now they'll be eating our grapes. If you're very quiet," he said, lowering his voice, "you can hear them marching. I've been hearing them for days. They're not here yet, but they're awfully fast, these devils, frightfully fast. With one blow they break your heart. With one blow. Now our lives have turned to shit. We've been betrayed, that's for sure. We got told a big lie. Leave Hitler alone, he'll devour the Bolsheviks. Instead he's devoured us."

He stood up. "And, now, gentlemen," he said, "you see before you the new commander of the guard of Saint-Cyprien. You know me. But what am I? An old, dumb wreck. Good night, gentlemen." And then he was gone.

"Now," said Ams, "we know where we stand."

The newspaper they got the next day, confirming that the armistice deal had been signed, listed terms that unsettled them all. As the Line of Demarcation was drawn, Saint-Cyprien would not be in the occupied zone. But the agreement required the French to turn over on demand any individual the Germans wanted. The Germans only had to present lists of those they were after and the French had to deliver them to the German military.[14]

As more details became available there were large assemblages of people trying to parse all the legal niceties. "Are they going to deliver us?" people asked Ams, who had been reading them the terms.

"I'm no lawyer," Ams answered, "but from what it says here, that could happen."

The anxiety increased when new lists, complete with home addresses and religion, were drawn up, which later intensified when the report spread that they were all going to be shipped to Poland. Licht heard it just as he was returning from the little camp post office that had just been set up. He had sent out ten so-called search cards to his family and was near despair that he still knew nothing about where Judith was.

Because he'd hardly slept for several nights, he tried to lie down, but soon he was roused by Ams, who took him to see Löwe, Licht's doctor friend. They found him in a dark corner, together with Brust and Veilchenfeld.

"Can you all keep your mouths shut?" Löwe asked.

"Don't give us any stuff about Poland," Licht interrupted.

"Never mind Poland," Löwe said. "I have something much more unpleasant for you. For some days we've had a new illness that I'm not going to name for now. One died from it today in Ilot II. The symptoms are a high fever, forty degrees at least, sudden weakness, terrible lethargy to the point that the patient has no will to resist it."

"Name it," said Ams.

"Do you know it?" Löwe asked the others.

None of them knew.

14. This was Article XIX, perhaps the most shameful element in France's surrender in June 1940.

Felix Nussbaum, "Draft for a Painting: *St. Cyprien,*" 1940.
The Leo Baeck Institute, New York.

"For a doctor in my position," Löwe said, "it's irresponsible to diagnose before I have confirmation. When I tell you, put three question marks after the name: typhus."

When they asked, Löwe told them that there was only one effective way to control it, and that was through vaccination. "If I could write to Switzerland it could be provided." He had already talked to Gross, he said, and Gross told him he was seeing ghosts. Gross said the dead man had died of a weak heart.

"That's just what we need," said Ams.

—∞—

When it came time to draw the new lists, many barracks resisted. A great crowd gathered outside the administration barracks-cum-office. A message was sent to Spatz asking that the commandant personally come to the camp to explain what the lists were supposed to be for. And soon, indeed, an officer appeared who was quickly convinced that the people before him were determined to resist. After briefly disappearing into the office, he returned.

"I give you my word as an officer," he said, "that the lists are solely for the French authorities and will not be relayed to the Germans."

A breath of relief went through the crowd. It was the first time the camp had been officially addressed by a French officer.

The officer's promise reinforced a bright—and promising—new development. Individuals at Saint-Cyprien who could justify the requests with some good reason—a visit to a physician or a foreign consulate, for example—would be a granted a day's leave to go into Perpignan. It was a radical change from the lockdown of a few weeks before.

Ams and Veilchenfeld were among the first to get a pass. When they returned in the evening, their friends all wanted to know how it had gone. The two were quickly surrounded by people eager to learn about things on the outside.

"Do you want to know what struck us most?" Ams asked.

"Of course," Licht said.

"Well, they have a facility down there called a chair. You can sit on it. There's a thing called a table from which they eat. There are implements like knives, spoons, and plates. There are toilets that I never wanted to get off. And you'll never guess what I did in the afternoon. I took a warm bath in a bathtub, and then I got undressed and got into a clean bed. I tried to sleep but couldn't because it was too soft. So I got dressed, went to a café, heard music while I drank coffee, ate cake, and looked at the girls. And then I said to Veilchenfeld he should poke me in the arm to wake me up.

"So, guys, these things still exist. Nothing is lost. We only think so here in our sand and filth and our fleas and lice. Down there nobody looks for little beasts under his shirt in the middle of the street. And while the faces up here have long made me want to puke, I constantly thought of you. Want to know more?"

They showered him with more questions, which he answered in his usually sardonic way until it was pitch dark and he nearly fell over with fatigue.

—∞—

But just as the new furlough policy brought relief, the fleas became a plague that quickly infested the camp. Nobody knew where they came from—from the straw, from the sand, nobody had any idea. But there they were, millions of little red insects that wouldn't let them rest. Nobody could get much sleep. Several times each night people got up to shake out their shirts. Many slept outside where it was a little better. In the morning, however, it got so damp that they had to retreat to the barracks. Some people were bitten so badly that their legs looked like one large wound. Many became so tense that angry quarrels broke out even between good friends. The smallest annoyances drove calm people over the edge and then to a state of days-long depression.

In some barracks they also had lice. Those who had them were separated from others and were treated almost like lepers. When those who brought their food came to the kitchen, a wide path was formed to let them through.

After the mail blackout ended and the first letters arrived from France and Switzerland, the most interesting reports—many of them from wives telling what they'd been through—were read aloud. But after someone stood up and said, "We are very happy for you who have found your wives and families again. But please be sensitive to those who don't yet know," those who had gotten word sat apart in a corner to read their mail to one another. If one of the unlucky ones who knew nothing wandered by, they hastily began to make small talk.

Each day there was a crowd waiting at the little postal center, though of the few who got mail it was mostly those who'd already heard. The others had to wait twenty-four hours for what was likely to be the next disappointment.

From Ritter, Licht and his friends also learned how the Pure Germans seemed to know so much and strutted around with so much confidence.

"I kept wondering how these swine were so well informed while we never knew anything," Brust said. "The answer is very simple. They have a radio here in the barracks. It almost makes me cry. Long before we were arrested in Brussels, and even before Belgium was attacked, they had organized themselves. They set up a group of twenty or thirty men; each hid a small part of the radio in his suitcase or in his pocket. That's how they got it past all the inspections. Then they reassembled it here. Bauer managed to distract or delay the inspections when it was necessary. One day when the barracks are vacant I'll show you."[15]

"Why do we wonder about the power of these Nazis?" Ams said. "Unbelievable, unbelievable. We have to keep it in mind for the future."

—⁓—

A few hours later they learned from Brust that a commission had arrived that would screen each man. If he met their conditions, he'd be released.

"My boy," said Ams, "get in the habit of thinking logically and speaking clearly. What conditions must one fulfill?" Brust said he didn't know, but the answer would surely be made clear.

And so began the sad story of the so-called Commission de Criblage, the struggle between sick, unlucky, despairing, beaten-down, hunted people and an establishment operating by opaque rules and laws that were incomprehensible to ordinary mortals. Supposedly each case was to be examined on its merits. If the individual met the requirements he would be released. The requirements supposedly had to be disclosed to give each the opportunity to meet them, but of course they never were.

The commission was a great apparatus consisting of a chairman and several former French police commissioners. But it never became clear by what standards the exercise was conducted. The whole camp racked its brains. Did the internees have to satisfy the French or the Germans? That in itself constituted a huge difference, since the vast majority of the interned could have been freed without the remotest danger to French interests while Nazi racism required the dispatch of the Jews into a concentration camp.

The commissioners, working primarily from the lists of the internees, including a secret list prepared by Spatz and the camp administration, met in a barracks near the main gate of the camp. When they came out of their session, Licht could see from their faces that something hadn't

15. One reader of a draft of this story questioned how it would have been possible for the Pure Germans to know that they would all be interned in the same place even before the invasion of Belgium. That might have been a cover story to explain a radio that had been smuggled in by a Nazi sympathizer or, through bribery, by a guard, and to enhance their reputation for cleverness, but I have no reason to doubt that they might have had a radio.

worked. Veilchenfeld, who had already been examined, said they got a phone call, after which the whole thing was broken off.

Once again there were the wildest rumors, until, one day, the truth came out in the form of a directive posted on the wall of he administration building. For the time being no German or Austrian was eligible for release. Now and then somebody was released. When the lucky one was asked, he'd claim to be a Pole or a Romanian or some other special case.

Then it also became known that a German commission would be on its way to examine the internees. And that generated deep worries, bordering on panic.[16]

—៣—

"Two more died today," Löwe said late one evening when he had collected the small group that he had told his fears about typhus, "and there are at least five more suspected cases, who are lying in the barracks among all the others."

"What do you want to do?" Brust asked him.

"That's what I'm asking all of you."

"I'll talk with Gross," Licht said.

"You're not the right person for that," said Ams. He would go.

When he found Gross, he was fast asleep and Ams had to shake him awake.

"Man, I'm dog tired," Gross said. "I've been on my feet for fourteen hours straight today. Can't this wait until morning?"

16. This was the Kundt Commission, a ten-member group, named for its chairman, Ernst Kundt, a mid-level Nazi party official and bureaucrat in Eastern Europe. It included Wehrmacht officers, Gestapo agents, counterespionage agents, and two representatives of the German Red Cross. It had a list of people—anti-Nazi militants, communists, labor leaders, and intellectuals, wanted by the Germans—whom, under the armistice agreement, the French were required to "surrender on demand." Some camp commandants, it was said, allowed those who felt most in danger to leave and hide outside until the commission left. The commission spent a month in July and August visiting all the camps in southern France. It came to Saint-Cyprien on August 12–13. Bervoets, *La liste de Saint-Cyprien* (Brussels: Alice, 2006), 247–248. Pierre Cros, *Saint-Cyprien de 1939 à 1945: Le village, le camp, la guerre* (Canet, France: La Trabucaire, 2001), 122. Anne Grynberg, *Les camps de la honte: Les internés des camps françaises, 1939–1944.* (Paris: La Découverte, 1991), 138.

"Do you think I would have woken you in the middle of the night if it could?"

Groaning, the doctor got on his feet and followed Ams outside. They stood for a moment in an isolated spot. In an ominously low voice that caught Gross's attention, Ams told Gross about the new deaths. "We want to know what they died of."

"As you may imagine, I can't conduct any thorough examination here," Gross said. "But I'm inclined to assume that they died of exhaustion and malnutrition. What else?"

"I told you," Ams said, "that you better pay close attention. If you don't listen more carefully to my next questions, I can assure you that in one of the coming nights a half dozen tough guys will come to ask."

"You're threatening me?"

"I'm glad you're catching on. I have more questions. Five more are sick. I wouldn't like it if they also died of exhaustion."

"What do you want me to do? My hands are tied as much as yours. What do you want?"

"First of all, I want you to speak to the military doctor."

"That's like talking to this fence."

"Then you're not fit for this job. Resign."

For a moment Gross was silent. He had been rattled. Then he said he'd think about it.

"You better have an answer soon. There are impatient people in this camp."

—⁓—

The next day Spatz told them that he and several internees who had been part of the camp administration were being released. "I've long had the release in hand," he said, "but I didn't just want to leave you in the lurch. But now I have to go because my wife will be arriving."

But wasn't she interned in Gurs? they asked.

"Apparently she's also been released."

The thought that women could also be released excited them. It meant that many would soon be coming to Perpignan or the towns nearby. If so, would the men remain imprisoned for long?

Before Spatz left, he made a little speech.

"I leave you with a heavy heart," he said. "Again and again, I deferred my departure, even though I could have left long ago. But I won't be far in Perpignan and will try to be of help to everyone. More I need not tell you."

Only a few understood the real meaning of those words. When Spatz and his colleagues first left the camp, Licht and his friends wondered how it was possible that all those who had been released had been part of the administration. For others, the French commission had been no help. Through friends many had obtained the residence permits for some town or other that they would need if they were ever to get out. But the permits were of little help in getting out.[17]

Licht had heard again from someone else that Judith had been seen in La Panne, abandoned by all, without a car and in total despair. There was no chance that she was in Gurs, and now he didn't know where to turn. Neither the so-called search cards nor the Red Cross had produced any responses. Friends and a relative in Switzerland had written that they had heard nothing.[18] From his brothers in America he'd just had a telegram. "So far no trace of Judith. Connections with Belgium impossible."

He was totally without information. Almost all the others knew something about the whereabouts of their wives. The idea that she was hiding somewhere seemed totally improbable. Some people had been getting news from Belgium, in part through letters that had been smuggled out, in part through various refugee aid groups, but none had a word about Judith. He was beginning to be haunted by the thought that maybe his family was dead.

The first wives of internees from Gurs, all of them released by the German commission, had begun arriving in Perpignan. Among them was Lofe's sister, who told Licht's friends about her flight and said she also saw Judith at La Panne. She was sure that the car in which she saw Judith had driven off and had crossed the border, because the French no

17. In 2013, I learned from the documents in my father's dossier that he had received a residence permit for the town of Gurs, of all places. Whether he was ever aware of that or how he got it I don't know.

18. The relative in Switzerland was almost certainly my mother's cousin, Erwin Schloss, son of her father's sister Marie, who was one of first feminist journalists in Germany. For more about Schloss, see the next chapter.

NOTICE INDIVIDUELLE

Nom : *SCH R A G*   *Israélite.*

Prénoms : *Othon*

Nationalité : *Allemande aurait fait l'objet d'un refus de passeport pour l'Amérique de la part de l'autorité Allemande*

Date et lieu de naissance : *11.10.1902 à Karlsruhe (Alle.)*

Nom et prénoms du père : *Schrag Hugo = Allemande*

Nom et prénoms de la mère : *Sulzberger. Bella = Américaine*

Profession : *Industriel à Bruxelles. 11 avenue de Scarsin.*

Résidences antérieures : *L'Allemagne et la Belgique depuis fin 1938*

Est-il marié ? : _____ *Oui*

Nom du conjoint et nationalité : *Hass Ludik(?). allemande*

Nombre des enfants vivants : _____ *1.*

Date et lieu de l'arrestation : *le Mai 1940 à Bruxelles, et conduit à Le Vigeant*

Situation de fortune : *30000 mille.*

Connaît-il le français ? : *Oui*

Où désire-t-il se rendre ? : *à furs B.P.*

Pièces d'identité : *C. I. belge N°. 2283*

I. passeport National 1J V N17 Y délivré au l'ambassade allemande

RENSEIGNEMENTS DIVERS *du Luxembourg 15 sep 38*

II. voyage assuré (visas et) pour se rendre au Mexique)

Pièces jointes :

IV: certificat d'hébergement
V: attestation de loyalisme envers la France
émanant d'un témoin Caporal Mublstein Eric
engagé volontaire au 23e R.M.E.V.S. 2eme cie
blessé sur le front français

VI requête de son associé concernant
également Jos Fritz

54
41

longer had any controls at the frontier. She also confirmed that Hirsch, Licht's partner, had abandoned her.

As the wives arrived, the commandant at Saint-Cyprien permitted conjugal visits when the wives requested it. Couples could then get together in a so-called *parloir*, a barracks located well away from the other barracks, but still inside the perimeter fence, in which some built little tents out of blankets. Others just lay on the floor. For Licht the idea that one day he would again hear a tender voice in his ears, and not the harsh camp tones, seemed totally improbable.

A few days after he was released, Spatz suddenly appeared again at the camp and took Ams and Licht aside.

"I can get you out," he told them. "I spoke to a lawyer down there. He's a friend of the prefect. I'm not trying to make anything out of this. I'm doing it only out of friendship. But the lawyer charges a thousand francs per man and he's ready to do it for twelve people. Do you understand? Moreover, you have to decide at once. Within three days you could be legally free."[19]

"Listen," Ams whispered. "I don't think much of this. But still we should try. Getting out of here with forged papers isn't for us, but I'd like to disappear before the German commission shows up. The devil only knows what surprises they'll bring with them. So let's risk a thousand."

"But I have to wait here for Judith," Licht said.

"In the first place, you don't have to leave as soon as you have the release. In the second place, it will be easier to search for your wife from Perpignan than it is here. And in the third place, you still haven't gotten the release."

"Judith will have a harder time finding me in Perpignan than she would here."

"Don't be crazy, and do what I tell you," Ams said, and Licht nodded in agreement. When they paid, their names went on Spatz's list.

19. In July 1940, the police arrested a man named Pinar Henrii in Montpellier who passed himself off as a lawyer and charged relatives of internees who were living in towns near the camps fifteen hundred francs on the pretense that he could free their loved ones. Archives of the Département of the Pyrenées-Orientales 109 W 339.

In the meantime, there was more talk about commissions. The French commission resumed its examination of internees at Saint-Cyprien, but only those who were not German or Austrian—Czechs, Poles, Luxemburgers, Belgians—which made crystal clear the reckless haste with which people had been interned. People of all sorts of nationalities who had no business whatever in these camps had been swept up and shipped off with everybody else. And as it became clear who was being released, a lot of people suddenly became Poles. Men no one would ever have suspected were born in Poland suddenly recalled that their cradle stood somewhere near Krotoschin, and the corresponding lists became ever longer.

But the real anxiety came from people who had been to the *parloir* and reported that for three days there would be no visitors, which led to the widespread belief that the German Kundt Commission was on its way. Instructions were issued to clean the place up.

After the report spread, Ams talked to people in the barracks: "That we're all choking in shit here," he said, "that we're being consumed by hunger and bitten by lice and fleas and that we may all die here, I need not tell you. But anyone who believes he can complain about anything to the Germans, as some seem to think, is kidding himself. To them we're a dog who, if he gets up on his hind legs, has to be beaten down."

Later that evening, the French sergeants came into the camp and ordered the preparation of new lists of internees to be completed by ten the next morning, presumably for the Germans. The French sergeants did not deny it.

And of course there were many in the camp whom the Germans were looking for—socialists, labor leaders, journalists, anti-Nazi authors and actors, people who had fled Germany illegally or hadn't paid their emigration taxes—all of whom now feared that they'd be caught. The demand for the lists put the camp administration in a terrible fix. Again and again internees came and pleaded that they not be listed with their real names. Would the French deliver them up to their deadliest enemies? There had to be a way to protect them.

After Ams spoke and the sergeants left, Ritter, who until then had seemed unconcerned, told Ams to get everyone out of the barracks and shut the door. He told them that all the talk was pointless. Now that he was addressing the internee leadership he wanted to make himself clear.

"It's altogether out of the question," he told them, "that we deliver the correct names of endangered people. Whoever is in danger must know that himself. I know it about myself. Why does it concern you at all what people call themselves on the lists? Everybody should register himself as he thinks proper. You can't know the names of thousands of people. You tell the leaders in the barracks that you want the lists, which will presumably go to the Germans for whatever screening they intend to do. Further you tell them that the lists must be completely new and should have no relationship to the earlier lists. If somebody today suddenly recalls his real name, why should the barracks leaders care? They have to enter the name as he gives it."

Things were tense the next morning. When there was a call for the internees to report, many of those who were in the most danger, Ritter among them, had hidden themselves. At about ten a large gray car drove in. When it stopped, a German officer wearing the armband of the Red Cross got out. Accompanying the German were two French officers.

"The man has a mug like Himmler's," said Ams, who was standing next to Licht.

The first thing they wanted to see was the kitchen, where the gigantic Austrians who constituted most of the kitchen help were standing by their kettles wearing nothing but briefs and looking like this was nothing out of the ordinary.

"Who's in charge of the kitchen?" the German wanted to know.

When a man raised his hand, the German wanted to know his name.

"Cohn," the man said, wiping his hands on his smudged apron

"So, Cohn, how much do you have every day to feed people? How much meat do you get? How much bread? How many potatoes? What vegetables?" Cohn tried to list what he thought was sufficient, and the German wrote it all down.

Given those numbers, the German said, things in the camp must have improved considerably, especially since the Pure Germans, who had been released a few days before, were no longer there. And indeed things were better, though not as good as Cohn reported.

The German next wanted to see the latrine.

"Where's the bleach?" he shouted at the French officers when he saw it. It was all in German, which then had to be translated for the French. "This is a revolting pigpen. And all the soiled paper is flying all over the camp."

The French stood there and didn't say a word.

They were then taken to various barracks, where inmates were lying in their compartments. "Stand up," shouted Herbstfeld, the internee who was taking the group around.

Most slowly stood, although the sick people did not.

"What's wrong with them?" the Nazi asked.

"Sick. We have a number that have diarrhea."

"Why the hell don't you take them to the hospital?" the German growled, and again made a note. By the time he left the camp, he had two pages of notes.

"The guy was right," Ams said, "but I'd rather sit in the filth here than let myself be tortured to death in the most modern Nazi facility." There had been few loud complaints. What the German wrote down he'd seen for himself.

That afternoon, the whole camp, thousands of men, was assembled in front of the building where the commission met. Facing them were the hateful Nazi faces they all hoped never to see again: officers in bright white uniforms, their arrogant noses held high and, behind them, the modest-faced but much more dangerous little Gestapo agents. They had the lists in hand and were now going from group to group.

Licht stood together with the others from barracks 25. A young officer was reading off the names, to which the man who was named would have to answer "here." When they got to them, the Nazi asked questions in a tone that was so derisive that Licht would have liked to punch him in the nose.

"Now, Mr. Ams," he said. "You were a communist?"

"No, lieutenant, I was an expert on furs in Berlin."

The German looked at Ams quizzically to see whether he was being made fun of. But Ams put on such a stupid face that the lieutenant said, "I meant politically."

"Politics didn't interest me," Ams said.

"Of course, of course. And your departure from Germany was completely legal?"

"Yes. And I arrived in Brussels with seventy francs and fifty centimes in my pocket."

"And you, sir, what's your name?" he asked Licht, who was standing next to Ams.

"Hans Licht."

"Ah, Licht, yes. You should take in your clothes; you must once have had a nice belly. You saved yourself a trip to Marienbad this year. You had been there earlier."

"No," said Licht. "I've never been to Marienbad."

"Too bad," the Lieutenant said. "Now you'll never again see that lovely place where so many of your friends and relatives had once been. You emigrated legally to Belgium?"

"No, to Luxembourg."

"Ah, that reminds me of the socialist paper that was published there. What was it called?"

"I don't know what you're referring to."

"That's a shame. You missed something there. . . . Yes, and you paid every penny of your emigration taxes. . . . Thank you, thank you. You can spare me the answer."

When he'd finished with them, Feuermann stepped forward.

"Lieutenant," he asked, "is it possible that people like myself, that is non-Aryans, could return to Belgium?"

When Ams heard the question he put on his vulture face. "Poor Feuermann," Licht thought, who knew Ams well enough to know that he now had murder in his heart.

The lieutenant thought a moment and then turned to one of the Gestapo agents.

"Can a Jew return to Belgium?" he asked.

"Impossible," one of them called. "Out of the question."

The lieutenant came back with an astonished child's face. "You heard the answer yourself," he told Feuermann.

After the commission left, they learned from the sergeants that there had been a great to-do between the French commandant and the Germans, who believed that there were some two hundred people in the camp they'd been looking for whom the French were required to deliver to them but who weren't on their lists—or were on the lists under other names. Licht imagined that it must have been quite a scene. They would also get word that there would be no more releases from Saint-Cyprien and that there would be a new commandant.

Nonetheless, Feuermann's question quickly produced a sort of petition to the commandant from those who wanted to return to Belgium. That led to the creation of a roster, which included the statement that "the undersigned agree that they will be given into the custody of the German authorities." When a committee of internees went to the commandant, he explained that anyone who wanted to return to Belgium had three days to register his name. He would then arrange for transport, though he could not guarantee that the people who went would ever get to Belgium. The French role was only to deliver them to the Line of Demarcation. He didn't know what would happen to them after.

That created a terrible dilemma for those longing to go back. It brought the anxiety to a fever pitch. The risk was so great that the question arose whether the poor souls who desperately wanted to go had become so nostalgic for home that they had lost all reason. They huddled in groups. Some lost themselves in hopeless dreams. All sense of reality vanished. It couldn't be worse than it was in this camp, could it? No one would ever get out of here. Here people would die like dogs, with no chance of rescue. Who out there cared? They had written the Red Cross, the Quakers, even an American journalist in Vichy, and gotten no answers—assuming that their cries for help ever reached their destinations. So, out of here at any price.

For Licht, that was unthinkable. He didn't know where Judith was. And even if he had known, he would have come to the same conclusion. Better dead than in the hands of the Nazis.

Shortly before the deadline came for the list, which now included some 1,100 names, a young man named Kassel appeared and said there'd been a miracle.

"My sister has just arrived from Belgium," he said "and brought with her a notebook with the names of the wives in Brussels who, before she left, had not heard from their husbands."

Left and facing.
Karl Schwesig "Stamps."
Schwesig, who was interned
both at Saint-Cyprien and
later at Gurs, drew scores of
ironic "timbres" about the
camps. This is a small sample.

*Collection Gilles Allart /
Jacky Tronel.*

As he read out the list, Licht suddenly heard Judith's name. "Repeat that!" Ams called.

And so the man repeated it, slowly and clearly: Judith Licht, Brussels, Avenue de l'Université.

"Can I see that?" Licht asked. With teary eyes he read the name his wife had written in her own hand.

"Does this change your mind?" Ams asked.

"Are you crazy? My wife has to come here, and I'll write her so immediately." The letters he had written before had apparently never arrived.

—⚉—

At about three one morning, the people hoping to return to Belgium marched off. After the deadline passed, there had still been some shuffling as some who had signed up tried to back out and others wanted to sign up. Because of the strong doubts that Licht and Ams expressed, only

a handful in their barracks joined, but in others half or more decided to attempt this journey into uncertainty. They were prepared to exchange the hell they knew even for an uncertain future. Most hoped to emigrate later with their families. Only a few imagined they could remain in a country ruled by the Nazis. Even after registration for the trip was complete, there were still furious arguments as some tried to persuade brothers or friends to go or stay with them. Each wanted others to verify the rightness of his decision.

"To my mind," Ams said to Licht after all the farewells were said, "the best thing that can happen is that one day we'll see them all back here again."

Among those who marched off was the man who had represented their block of barracks, Ilot I, in the camp administration, and Licht, who succeeded him, now went to the "office" every morning. His main tasks were to try to calm anxious people, to settle quarrels, and in other tiny ways to ease things for hundreds of individuals.

Soon after he took up his new duties, Löwe came to him.

"Now it's become serious," the doctor said. "We have some twenty new cases and five who are on the verge of dying. The sick are suffering terribly. They lie on their straw sacks in the clinic bathed in sweat, too lethargic to wave off the flies. Most have their eyes closed. And of course we have no special diet. What the kitchen sends us is what they have to eat. Mostly it's pea soup, moldy bread, and a tiny bit of beef. If we don't do something in a few weeks, typhus—and I have no doubt that's what it is—will have killed off a large part of this camp."

Licht asked what he wanted.

"I want to do blood tests," he said, "and for that I need your help. I need to get leave immediately to go to an apothecary in Perpignan where I hope the owner, in return for kind words and some money, will let me do the tests myself. I'll be back in the evening with the results."

"Done," Licht said. "I'll put you on tomorrow's furlough roster."

The next morning, after Löwe went off to Perpignan with his blood sample, Ams and Licht went to Gross, still head of the camp clinic, to ask that the sick be sent immediately to the hospital in Perpignan. Gross said he thought it was not typhus but some sort of swamp fever and told them, in effect, to mind their own business.

As he left, Ams said, "You, my friend, already have a couple of deaths on your conscience. As long as the French protect you, I can't do much to you. But my feelings about you are the same as those I have for a flea. If I had my way, I'd take you between my fingernails and squish you."

Löwe did not return in the evening. There could be an inspection, but the night passed without anyone being aware of his absence. The next morning, however, the commandant came to Licht, asking to see Löwe immediately.

"Löwe?" Licht said. "I'll send for him at once."

After a while, Licht reported that Löwe could not be found. "He's probably in the other block," he stuttered.

"I'll wait," the commandant said.

Licht decided he'd find another doctor who could impersonate Löwe. He found one named Moser who was willing to do it. There was of course the danger that the commandant knew Löwe. But when Licht returned to the commandant, the commandant also ordered Löwe to bring his papers with him.

"I have to tell you the truth," Licht confessed. "Löwe isn't here. He's in Perpignan, not for himself, but in the interests of the whole camp. There's a sickness here from which people are dying. We have to determine for everyone's sake what it is. Löwe went to Perpignan yesterday to get some blood tests, which presumably were not completed by yesterday evening. Otherwise he'd be here. If you want to punish anyone, punish me. He did it for me." The others in the room offered to share the punishment.[20]

The commandant began to scold them, but from his amused look, Licht soon concluded that the scolding was pro forma and that nothing would happen. As soon as Löwe returned, the commandant ordered, he should report to him immediately.

Löwe returned at three that afternoon. "Typhus," he said.[21]

"What a damn mess," Ams said. "In the meantime, they learned that you weren't here last night."

"That was the apothecary. He reported me," Löwe said. When they reported to the commandant a little later, he began by saying, "Dr. Löwe, returned from a twenty-hour unauthorized leave."

The commandant looked at him for a moment, and then asked, "And the result?"

After Löwe gave his one-word answer, no one again spoke about the incident.

Löwe made clear that the sickness had so far been irresponsibly neglected, that everyone needed to be vaccinated, that rigorous hygienic measures had to be taken, and that all the sick people had to be taken immediately to Perpignan. Treating people in the camp was impossible.

As the session ended, the commandant shook his hand and told him he was now the head physician and that he would have the vaccine within two days. The day after that they would begin the vaccinations. And he was free to institute whatever regulations he thought appropriate.

---

20. This entire story was independently told many years later by another Saint-Cyprien prisoner, Rabbi Jehuda Leo Ansbacher, in Erhard Roy Wiehn, *Camp de Gurs: Zur Deportation der Juden aus Sudwestdeutschland* (Constance: Hartung-Gorre Verlag, 2010), 429–431.

21. Although his *New York Times* obituary said he crawled under the perimeter fence to get to the city of Pau to have his samples tested, it should have said Perpignan. Pau was much too far.

In the days that followed, the illness claimed more victims, young men particularly. The ambulance from Perpignan came again and again, and the death toll climbed. After his dismissal Gross found no barracks that would take him, and for two nights he was forced to sleep outside until someone took pity on him and found him a corner in the administration barracks. Because he was afflicted by a bad case of eczema he became even more a leper. It was said that he later committed suicide.

As the epidemic raged, no furloughs were allowed. There would be exceptions only in emergencies. At the same time, people became more self-reliant and discipline eroded. Night after night, more slipped away. Most were soon caught and brought back. To travel by train, one needed a safe-conduct pass from the police. How was a poor refugee to acquire such a thing? Forgeries could be bought, but they were usually so clumsy that any inspector could detect them. Those who were caught were confined for two weeks to a special punishment block where they got only half the normal daily food rations and were shackled at night.

None of that frightened them. They had to escape the hell of the typhus. Within a few days, Löwe had vaccinated them all. But he also made clear that it would take twenty-three days before they were immune. More deaths were reported every day from the hospital in Perpignan. Why, in any case, were the internees still being held here? There was an armistice, they were innocent people, many had a valid exit visa. Through his brothers in America, Licht had gotten clearance for a Mexican visa that he couldn't pick up because there were no furloughs.

The escape scenario was always the same. One gave a guard a few francs to look the other way. Then one had to avoid the patrolling gendarmes. Ams and Licht spoke of it constantly. The thing with Spatz, of course, had come to nothing: Spatz and his colleagues had simply started a new racket. They'd found a Vichy senator who wanted to sponsor the release of internees. Some fifty people paid a thousand francs each, but the scheme never led to any success.

A few days later they learned that the 1,100 who had hoped to return to Belgium were coming back. They had gotten as far as Bordeaux, where the Germans detained them, finally giving them the choice of being interned in the occupied zone or returning to Saint-Cyprien, which they all regarded as the lesser of two evils. That produced a furious argument between Licht and the commandant, who wanted to put them all back in their old barracks. It would be disastrous, Licht maintained, to expose them to people who might still be infected with typhus. After consulting with Löwe, the commandant agreed and housed them all in vacant barracks elsewhere in the camp.

But their return ended once and for all the dream of a return to Belgium. Even for the homesick it was now clear that this road was closed. From now on there seemed to be only two possibilities: escape, or stay and die.

The Larousse

In school in the year after our return from Boulogne they gave all the
students large translucent capsules filled with an amber liquid that
were said to be vitamins. We got one every day. I was afraid to swallow mine and surreptitiously threw them away. On some days that
was difficult without being detected; I never could swallow any large
pill without water. Worse, I felt I didn't have a right to my pill and that
some morning, when our teacher, M. Boulanger, handed them out I
would be challenged as a foreigner, a Boche impostor. It was, of course,
not the capsule I would have minded losing; indeed what I minded
most about the capsules, other than the daily need to find an unde-
tected means of disposing of mine, was that through them I would be
exposed as the Belgian I was not. Getting the pill and then palming it
or hiding it in my desk or in a pocket doubled the guilt. Everyone must
have known. In those days, of course, I was always Pierre, not Peter,
however pronounced, but after one year in Brussels no one could have
been taken in by my pretense that I was one of them; yet no one ever
said anything to me. I knew what I was not. What I was, that wasn't so
clear.

The anti-Semitic measures in Belgium would begin gradually in October, four months after our return from Boulogne, when the German military authorities, with varying degrees of cooperation and/ or resistance from Belgian authorities, began to issue anti-Semitic decrees of increasing severity—on the definition and identification of Jews, barring Jews who had fled at the start of the war from returning to Belgium, requiring Jews to wear the yellow Star of David, excluding Jews from teaching, from practicing law and other professions, seizing Jewish assets, "Aryanizing" Jewish businesses and, in December 1941, eight months after we'd escaped, barring Jewish children from the public schools and universities and in other ways segregating Jews from the general population—culminating in the deportations to the death camps in 1942–43. In the summer of 1942, a year after our escape from Brussels, seventeen thousand Jews, nearly all of them foreign, were deported from Belgium to Auschwitz.[1] But I knew little of any of the decrees that had been imposed even before we left.. How much did my mother know? In the year after our return from Boulogne, we probably owed our own relative immunity to the German decrees to the initial reluctance—essentially the foot-dragging and, in Brussels sometimes, to the courageous resistance—of the local Belgian authorities, whose collaboration was necessary in the execution of those decrees, and to the Belgian constitutional ban on distinctions of religion, race, and origin on which it was based.[2] Eventually, of course, the Belgians collaborated, notwithstanding the later pretense of many that they resisted. "The mayors," wrote a Belgian historian, "were anxious to comply without participating."[3]

1. I owe much of this information to the work and generous help of Barbara Dickschen of the Université Libre de Bruxelles. See, e.g., Dickschen, *L'école en sursis: La scolarisation des enfants juifs pendant la guerre* (Brussels, Université Libre de Bruxelles, 2006). Also Maxime Steinberg, *La question juive, 1940–42*, vol. 1, in *L'étoile et le fusil* (Brussels: Editions Vista, 1983).

2. Thierry Delplancq, "*Des paroles et des actes: L'administration bruxelloise et le registre des Juifs, 1940–1941*." *Cahiers d'histoire du temps présent*, no. 12 (2003): 141–179.

3. David Fraser, *The Fragility of Law: Constitutional Patriotism and the Jews of Belgium* (Abingdon, UK: Routledge, 2008), 95. Mayor Van de Meulebroeck appears to have been among the resisters. For an exhaustive discussion, see Rudi Van Doorslaer et al., *La Bel-*

M. Boulanger functioned with determined, one might even say ruthless, impartiality. I don't recall that anyone in the class was ever selected or identified in any way as different, nor was there any talk about the country's condition as an occupied nation. The amber capsule each morning was the only indication in school that things were not normal. The rest of the day, M. Boulanger drove on furiously, filling the blackboards with his schoolmaster's numbers and words and sentences.

The blackboards were on vertical tracks that ran to the high ceiling at the front of the classroom. They could be rolled up and down, two or three behind one another. It was therefore necessary to copy down what he was putting on the board almost as fast as he was writing it. Once he had sent a board full of material on its way to the ceiling, or when one disappeared behind another, it was nearly impossible to retrieve what was on it: multiplication tables, punctuation rules, spelling, maybe a little geography. One hour each day was given to Flemish, which was a new language for most of us in that French-speaking region. The only thing I can remember of those Flemish lessons was that the best grade one could get was a Z, which seemed appropriate since Flemish had so many Zs in it anyway. It was a language of Zs, I thought, the same way German was a language of SCHs and Italian a language of As and Os. I can still see the classroom, particularly those blackboards that M. Boulanger flung toward the ceiling with such energy. But what actually was on them, and exactly what else we did there in the second and third grade at the École du Bois de la Cambre N°8 I've long since forgotten.

In the year after our return to Brussels, the first year of the German occupation, I spent more and more time foraging for food, legal and black market. It became a sort of scavenger hunt; my mother would hear rumors that a certain store had butter or eggs or flour or canned meat, though I have no idea how she knew—maybe there was a grapevine, maybe it was just instinct—and I would be sent on my bicycle

---

gique docile: Les autorités belges et la persécution des Juifs en Belgique pendant la Seconde Guerre mondiale, SOMA-CEGES (2004–2007), accessed July 2014, http://www.senate .be/event/20070213-jews/doc/rapport_final.pdf.

to pursue it. The food was never labeled. Butter, of course, never had been, but often I would bring home cans of something, usually some greasy Spam-like meat, whose origin was unknown, that I thought tasted like soap and which I got from an otherwise apparently vacant meat market up on the Avenue de l'Hippodrome. The cans, which were brought out from the back of the store, would be sold with all the labels removed, one or two to a person. Here, too, there was a rationing system. In my teen-age years, I sometimes tried to imagine that on those foraging bike rides I was carrying messages for the underground, but I'm not sure that at the time I even knew that there was such a thing.

I had no idea where our money came from and probably never thought to ask. My father took some funds from his business before May 10 and left them with my mother, but much of that may have been lost when we lost our former maid, Maria, in La Panne. My uncles and my father's American mother in New York probably transmitted some money. But how it was delivered I never learned—maybe through my mother's cousin in Switzerland, a Moravian Church parson named Erwin Schloss, the half-Jewish son of my mother's father's sister, who seemed to be a common relay point for us. In the spring of 1941, as we were preparing for our escape attempt from Brussels, I even saw American dollars, whose possession was strictly forbidden and which my mother sewed into the lining at the flat bottom of her large beige handbag just before we left. Later my mother told me she'd had a couple of calls from Gestapo agents looking for my father about some sort of currency irregularities. She believed Maria's father in Luxembourg had denounced her—out of what sort of spite I have forgotten, if I ever knew. Had my mother tried to get back the money she had given Maria for safekeeping before we lost her in La Panne many months before? Had she succeeded? But otherwise her financial dealings seemed to have aroused no official concern. Much later, with the help of Belgian archivists, I found copies of some *"délits de devise,"* the official forms based on Nazi allegations, charging my father with currency offenses, which were almost always directed against Jews (in our case, it seemed, principally failure to pay emigration taxes). I also found a copy of a record from the Nazi *Sicherheitspolizei* (Sipo) in Brussels indicating that my mother had registered with the occupation authorities in her maiden name, Judith Anna Haas—the space for religion was left blank, as was the space for the spouse's name. She was certain that use of her married name—and, of course, disclosure of her ethnicity—would have jeopardized her far more with the Nazi occupation authorities than she would have been otherwise.[4]

I recall no close friends in Brussels. I'd had two very good playmates, the brothers Charlie and Josie, who lived down the Rue Orange from us in Luxembourg, and badly missed them, but none in Brussels that I recall. Once I gave one of my Brussels classmates a mechanical toy tank that someone had given me. I told him I had made it myself and had many more, but that preposterous gesture yielded nothing, not even the accusation, which I half expected, that I was a liar. And so I spent a great deal of time that winter studying the Larousse and the various atlases that I found on my father's book shelves, copying or tracing maps, maps of Antarctica and Australia and Africa, and reading about rivers in Russia and mountains in Asia. Most of all I was interested in New Zealand, to which my mother's brother Karl Haas had emigrated in 1933 and where he was now a sheep rancher. I knew almost nothing about America other than what I discovered in the Larousse. (Checking a 1930s edition recently, I learned that it had little about Der Roosevelt, who had no entry of his own, and was mentioned only as the cousin of Teddy, who was colorful enough to have once been a big hero in France). The one exception on America in our apartment was a book just called *Mexique*, which had black and white photos of the great Mexican landmarks and supposedly representative scenes—Aztec pyramids, sixteenth century missions and cathedrals, scenes of peasants in straw sombreros—indicating, as I think about it now, that my parents had been thinking about a migration to Mexico before I ever heard about it.

4. "During the war, in German-occupied Europe, the Nazis also created the *Devisenschutzkommando* (DSK), which had the task of searching for currency, gold, and other valuables in the private possession of Jews and other enemies of the state, which could then be extorted, confiscated or expropriated for the benefit of the German war economy. The persons who were arrested in these contexts, for hidden currency, for example, were accused of '*délits de devises*' [currency offenses]." Sylvie Vander Elst, Services Archives et Documentation, Brussels, e-mail to author, March 29, 2013.

There was also a stamp collection that someone must have given me and which I very carefully maintained and enlarged as the opportunities arose. And so I began to glimpse a world, much of it already history, that was frozen for me as an indefinite present but which, while I hardly understood it all, was if anything more fascinating for it: the profiles of Lenin and Hindenburg; the faces of Victoria and Albert and Charlotte, the grand duchess of Luxemburg; Louis Blériot's plane, the *Spirit of St. Louis,* and the *Graf Zeppelin.* I learned about places many of whose names in the pre-war years have now been all but forgotten; Danzig, Memel, the Anglo-Egyptian Sudan, the French Sudan, Italian Somalia, Siam, Fiume, the Sudetenland, Ceylon, the French Congo, and French Indo-China. A year later, when I was going to elementary school in New York, fervently trying to establish myself, I often tried to display in class the collection of geographical junk I had collected from the Larousse. When a teacher asked for the name of a river in Italy (why, I have no idea), I could wildly wave my hand and say, "Po." I loved that encyclopedic world with its crude (yet, to me, wonderful) pictures and maps, loved the vicarious trips on which the Larousse took me, loved most of all its combination of Euro-centric inquisitiveness and the subtle sense of Victorian assurance and European superiority.

Still there was time for kid things. As I noted earlier, we lived on the edge of a new development—a one-block street called Avenue des Scarabées (Beetle Avenue)—and thus near open spaces, which by then I was old enough to explore on my bicycle. On the other side, across the wide Avenue des Nations, now the Avenue Franklin Roosevelt, was a large park, the Bois de la Cambre, with its lake, its little island that one could reach on a small cable-drawn ferry or by renting a rowboat. There was also a great dark underground storm drain that ran under a grassy hill and emptied into the lake, which I would explore for what seemed like hundreds of meters, though it was probably no more than a dozen. Today the mouth of the sewer is covered by a locked iron gate; we live in a marginally more cautious age. Before the war Maria, the maid, would sometimes take me there, but now I managed to get there alone on my bicycle, despite warnings that I shouldn't cross the Avenue des Nations by myself.

The other way from our house, across the Avenue de l'Hippodrome where the streetcar ran, were the *nouvelles avenues,* acres and acres, it then seemed, of newly concrete-paved streets waiting for houses that weren't likely to be built until the war's end. They were also building a new church there—I always thought of it as "the cathedral," though it was probably something far more modest—but otherwise the area was vacant. A block down the street where the streetcar ran, and to the left, was the school where, for most of two war-interrupted years, I sat in M. Boulanger's class and tried to become a Belgian.

Despite our relative immunity from Nazi attention, and despite the apparent liberality of the first months of German occupation—until the spring of 1941, it was the Wehrmacht (the army), not civilians (i.e., the Gestapo), that really administered Belgium—one never forgot that this was an occupied country. The nightly blackout, the rationing and the chronic shortage of food were reminders enough, and so was the military swaggering on the streets. One learned to identify the uniforms of the young Luftwaffe officers, the Wehrmacht, the Kriegsmarine, the SS. One saw their trucks and armored vehicles on the road, the swastika on government buildings and on official documents. Now and then we had seen the planes in action in France, the Stukas diving over Boulogne, the bombers flying through a sky dotted with the white puffs of antiaircraft fire, the Messerschmitts circling over the beach in La Panne. But now they flew unmolested; it was their sky, and the hope that one of those puffs of smoke would strike home—that there was still a battle—was replaced by angry helplessness before their power.

Like much else about them, their uniforms seemed designed to intimidate, with their high black hobnailed boots, their wide belts, and their leather Gauleiter coats. They made those who wore them seem bigger and stronger than they were (how much height did those boots add to an average man?), and less prone to ordinary human appeal and intervention. Every step those troops took was part of the superman game. In New York later, as the real terror transformed itself into film and radio dramas and into the Chaplinesque routines of slapstick comedians, and as the distance from it grew, we used to make fun of it. "*Kommen Sie mit*"—come with us, generally meaning "You're under arrest"—became a line in a running joke. But when real men in uniform or long leather coats said the words, they provoked a cutting terror and helplessness that one never completely forgot.

—〰—

I never had a clear idea of how we hoped to escape from Brussels. There was an imagined way west, but my fantasy always blurred on the road south from Boulogne, where our first attempt ended in 1940. Around and over me there was endless talk about identity cards, visas, and consulates.

The anxiety about documents was there long before the first Nazi pulled the first Jew off a train, and long before Auschwitz and Treblinka had become camps of extermination, a fear that I had come to know at an early age. It was in the idea of the frontier itself, particularly in the years between the wars. The frontier nourished both romance— new countries, new languages, new flags, new money, hotels, restaurants with their silver serving dishes, and, at the same time, the anxiety. What if one's passport was not in order, a visa not in the proper place? What if, unknowingly, one carried contraband—too much chocolate, too much jewelry, too many cigarettes?

Frontiers were places of danger. For the inter-war generation, as the cultural historian and literary critic Paul Fussell said much later, a frontier was "not just absurd but sinister"; Europe became "frontier obsessed and, like Auden, map-mad."[5] Long before the train stopped, the train that would once have promised both adventure and security— before the uniformed men came through, first those of one country, then those of the other, people would get out their documents—passports and visas, identity cards, tax receipts, exit permits—and prepare their luggage, sometimes rearranging its contents to mitigate suspicion where there should have been no ground for suspicion. Then would come a helpless stillness—in Basel or Strasbourg or Trier or Kehl— broken only by the sound of the opening and closing of train compartment doors and of footsteps as the douaniers and the gendarmes made their way through the train. For much of my life since I have been

5. Paul Fussell, *Abroad: British Literary Traveling Between the Wars* (New York: Oxford University Press, 1980), 33.

reaching for my passport—in anxious replications of those anxious pre-war travelers—miles before reaching frontiers where no one cares anymore whether you have one or not. And of course in some places— at Ben Gurion or at Sheremetyevo or even at JFK sometimes—they still care.

Motion was security. When the train began to move it became a place apart, in which the upholstered compartment and the comforting rhythms of wheels on track coincided also with a temporary freedom both from official interference and the grubby world outside the train window. As long as the train was moving they couldn't detain you, ask you for papers or search your luggage. A moving train, for me, was the only really free country there was.

But mixed with that sense of freedom, there was something else as well. From my earliest moments—and I have it to this day—my presence on a good train, and maybe a room in a good hotel, conferred a sense of privilege, of status that I rarely have in any other situation. Even in those very early years, the need to belong to a place was strongly mixed with the desire to be an outsider. What is the tension between the wish to be part of something and the need to be outside, even above it? Does everyone begin so young to have the desire, even the passion, to be exempt from the things that limit—that ground— everyone else?

My uncles, sons of an American mother, had managed to emigrate to the United States in the mid- and late thirties, but by the time I began to hear the conversations about emigration it had all become far more difficult. At that point New Zealand must have suggested itself as a possibility, as it had been for my mother's brother Karl, though the talk was always about that great abstraction, America. The most important thing that the anxieties about visas and identity cards taught is that one was very little without them, that one became whatever one was in some government office, and proved it with a document officially stamped and signed, sealed and embossed: the prefect of police, the gendarmerie, the consul, the state. That, too, is something one loses only with difficulty, if at all, and that many in succeeding generations will probably never know. In authoritarian states, people are not born equal; they are made equal by ministries and bureaucrats, or, as in Nazi Germany, unequal.

The other thing I learned, as did many other European emigrants, was that freedom and possibilities lay almost uniquely to the west, that wherever the destination would ultimately be it was usually to the west—Mexico, Cuba, Panama, Argentina, the United States, often with the intermediate goal of Lisbon. For a few, maybe Shanghai or South Africa, or maybe Palestine; but in our bourgeois world, the compass mostly pointed west. In that, like generations of others who became Americans, I already had an American orientation. Direction carried with it not only its obvious geographical meaning, but a larger moral and psychological meaning as well. West was right; to the east lay Poland, concentration camps, pogroms, and Stalin. East was wrong.

I don't know when I first learned that it was our status as Jews that marked us for special danger. It must have been among the first social generalizations I learned, although even after the war began I still had no idea what being a Jew was or why it carried the stigma that was so central to our lives. I knew my parents had contempt for Jews who converted to Christianity, but that, I knew, was based on judgments of hypocrisy and cowardice and not on any strong religious loyalty. I had never had any religious instruction and don't recall my parents ever talking about our Jewishness—either then or later—except in terms of persecution and the particular disabilities it engendered. The identity cards were marked with it—across the face of the card in Nazi-occupied countries was a large J or, in France during the war years, the word JUIF—but what it meant, historically, culturally, or in terms of belief, I didn't learn until much later. In the ensuing years I often heard my parents express their distaste for the *Polacken,* the Eastern Jews, whom they regarded as a social embarrassment, but whatever I was to learn about Judaism I would learn from others. In those early years, first in Europe, then in New York, it was Hitler who made me a Jew.

9

"There's a Letter from Papa"

ver since they returned to Brussels—and in the face of all the vicissitudes of their daily lives and the new circumstances of the occupation—Judith had only one desire: to learn where Hans was, to get in touch with him and to go to him. Three times a day she checked the mailbox. And each time she heard that someone else had heard from her husband, Judith's heart sank. From Hans there was nothing. Every search proved fruitless. But she didn't doubt for a moment that Hans was alive. She knew that she would have a very different inner feeling if he weren't. How many weeks was it?

Then, as she came home one afternoon in late July, she saw through the little glass window on the mailbox a white envelope, and before she even got the letter out she recognized the handwriting. She tore the envelope where she stood and tried to read the letter through her tears. When she managed to wipe her eyes she learned at last where he was.

She went upstairs. "Peter, Peter!" she called. "There's a letter from Papa."

"So what does he say?" Peter asked, though he was not nearly as impressed that a letter had finally arrived from his father.

"He says that he's in a camp, Saint-Cyprien, that he's been trying to find me everywhere, and that he's been in despair that he's had no news of us. . . . He's heard nothing from us, nothing." She read the letter again and again. Although she never had any doubts that he was alive, getting the letter was such a great relief that she could hardly describe it. But the letter also brought a new worry. Everyone in Brussels said that Saint-Cyprien was a hellish pit.

That evening she sat down with her mother and told her she intended to go to Hans. "I know he needs me," he said. "Here I'm useless. Peter will be well cared for with you. I have to pull it off—I must get to Saint-Cyprien."

The old woman shook her head. "Of course you know that Jews are strictly forbidden to leave Belgium."

"I'm still going to try. I'll find a way to get around the Nazis."

"Be careful, Judith. You shouldn't play games with the Germans."

All day Judith brooded about her intentions. She asked one person after another, and all gave her versions of the same answer: "Impossible. The only connection between Belgium and the south of France is the transport of Belgian refugees who want to come back to Belgium."

Maybe she could organize such a mission. She put it to a Belgian government official she knew and asked him if he could help. He put her in touch with a man—he identified him as a "travel agent"—named Jacques Pellmans.[1]

"As you know," Pellmans told her when they met a few days later, "most of these trips are run by private humanitarian organizations. But I happen to know people in a Catholic association in the Brussels outskirts. They're prepared to get you the necessary travel documents if you can provide the truck, the fuel, and the driver, all of which you must pay for yourself. They can't incur any expenses that might grow out of this. You also have to commit yourself to underwrite the return trip to Belgium of refugees in the south of France.

"And I travel as what?"

---

1. His real name was Piccard.

"You could probably go as a sort of nurse. Your job will be to look after the old, the sick, and children."

Judith decided at once to try it. She would also see if her friend Anna Taler could accompany her. She knew Taler, whose husband was also at Saint-Cyprien, to be a resolute and courageous woman.

"I think you could easily take another woman," Pellmans said. "In any case, a real nurse would be coming along as well."

When she left Pellmans she contacted Taler, who was immediately on fire with the idea. She was a strong, vigorous woman who should have been a man. From her haircut to the way she expressed herself, everything about her was masculine. She seemed to be afraid of nothing.

The next day Taler went to search garages and storage depots for the necessary gas. Judith herself went to the half-destroyed house outside Brussels where the Catholic group had its little office. The people there were cordial and pleased with Judith's proposal. They'd get the travel permits, said Henri René, who managed the agency. It would not be difficult. He also agreed to find a truck and driver.

René was a tall, sedate man whose quiet modesty immediately evoked trust in those who met him. Judith resolved to ask him to lead the trip. He could deal with the Germans at the borders. He so badly mangled his German that it might make even hardened Gestapo agents laugh.

Not many days later, as her plans firmed up, a man appeared at her door. He said his name was Lisieux, that he owned a truck, and that he would get the gas. And, he whispered slyly, he'd get it from the Germans.

At almost the same time, one of the directors of the Catholic group delivered the travel permits and the travel authorization for Lisieux and his truck.

"Getting yours wasn't as easy as we imagined," he said. "We had to pull some strings. Finally we shoved your Belgian identity card into a stack of other documents and the guy signed them all in one swoop without looking at any of them. And so here is this wonderful little piece of paper decorated with all the Nazi stamps you could ever wish for." It authorized her to travel into unoccupied France and back for the purpose of bringing back Belgian refugees. It was, the document said, all in furtherance of German interests.

But Lisieux's crazy idea that he'd get the gas from the Germans almost wrecked the whole project. He'd gone with his travel permit to the German fuel depot and asked for a hundred liters of gasoline. The man at the window took the paper and vanished with it into an adjoining room.

"Out of the question," he said when he returned. Worse, somebody had written "invalid" in large letters across the face of the permit.

"I'll stick the permit on the windshield," Lisieux told Judith. "It's usually so dirty that nobody will be able to see it."

Taler then reported that she could get gas from a black marketer in Antwerp for fifteen Belgian francs a liter. It was an insane price, but what could Judith do? Their travel permits had a time limit. Waiting longer would jeopardize the whole trip, so Judith decided to buy the gas.

Peter followed Judith's plan with the greatest interest. He really couldn't understand his mother. She was so terribly afraid of so many things, moths especially. How could she undertake a thing as large and dangerous as this? Every time he sat down at dinner he'd growl in a snarling Nazi voice, "Frau Licht, you're under arrest."

As Judith's émigré friends learned of her plans, many came with requests: one woman wanted a package delivered to her husband; another wanted to send money; another had letters. Almost all wanted her to persuade their husbands to return to Brussels. She should try to ease their fear of the German occupation and to use her own trip to convince them that one could cross the Line of Demarcation illegally if one wanted to. They were glad to know someone who would bring their husbands news first hand. But they shied from any similar venture, which they regarded as unimaginably dangerous. Almost none thought it would succeed.

—❧—

Even as Lisieux's truck was waiting outside the door of their apartment building, Judith went one last time—perhaps pro forma—to consult her mother.

"You have to do what you think right," her mother said.

When she came out, Peter was standing there, looking over the large gray vehicle that was waiting for her.

"What should I tell your Papa?" she asked as she reached for his hand.

Placard with the order from the German military authorities in Belgium requiring all Jews to register as Jews.

Creative Commons.

"I don't know," he said. "You'll know."

She could hardly separate herself from him. How long would it be before she saw him again? Maybe she never would.

On the way out of Brussels they picked up Taler, who brought her bicycle and, as she climbed in, told Judith she'd stuffed dollars into the frame. "Look it over," she said, "and see if anyone will notice. Surely these guys won't have x-ray machines or begin taking things apart with screwdrivers." She hoped to stay in the south of France with her husband, and send for her children later, while Judith was determined to return to Brussels to get Peter and her mother. But those plans for the future were unimportant next to what faced them now.

They came next to the office of the sponsoring Catholic organization where they picked up René and the real nurse. They were given green armbands, the only identification they had to show that they were nurses. The real nurse showed no sign of awareness that Judith was not one, though she seemed to know. In their first hours on the road, she gave Judith and Taler a little course in counseling and first aid.

At the first control point, only the truck was checked. Nobody was interested in the occupants. At the border between Belgium and France, René got off and, in his quiet, commonsense way began to talk to the German officers. Judith and Taler crept into the farthest corner of the truck. Through the sides they could hear René's broken German and the terse answers of the Germans. Suddenly a soldier appeared in the truck.

"Are any of you carrying any money or foreign currency?" he asked.

"No," they said, as they thought of the dollars in the bicycle.

"It's not so impossible," the soldier said. "Yesterday we caught a guy with a hundred thousand francs." He gave them all a quizzical look. Then, apparently satisfied, he left.

They were now in occupied France, riding through ravaged towns between ripening fields. Trees in the little orchards and gardens were heavy with fruit. New life had begun to leave the carnage of the past behind.

They spent the night in a pension in a little village. As they got out of their truck German soldiers gathered around them, wanting to know all sorts of things. For the Jewish emigrants, it was not easy to be surrounded by men wearing the swastika. Later, when they were alone, Judith and

Anna Taler parsed everything that the Germans said or asked. Even as they lay in bed they racked their brains about what one or another of the Germans' words signified. They'd given René all their papers. Maybe no one would find them with a passport bearing the *Judenstempel*.

During a sleepless night, they heard boots outside their window. "They're watching us," Taler said. But neither dared look out. They'd rather not know. Only toward morning, with the echoes of the boots gone, did they get any sleep.

—m—

Now came the next worry: the Line of Demarcation. Brussels had been full of stories about the partition of France with this cruel and senseless barrier. There were reports of the arrests of people trying to cross illegally, of shootings, of transports to concentration camps in the East, some true, some imagined.

Shortly before they got to it, they stopped briefly to work up their courage. They were all wrought up, though they tried not to show it. They played a sort of cops and robbers game, with one side playing Nazis interrogating the others, all of it a sort of drill for what they thought might lie ahead.

René told Judith she should try to look as German as possible. "If you can, do your face and hair to the Nazi taste."

Judith took her mirror, braided her hair and wrapped the braid around her head for the Gretchen look. She wiped off her lipstick and the rouge from her cheeks, giving her a somewhat pale and undernourished appearance.

René laughed when he saw her. "But don't forget," he said, "that after the German checkpoint come the French. When we have the Boches behind us, you have to again become Madame Licht as fast as possible."

As they were again on their way, the skies let loose with a fearful cloudburst. The truck slushed slowly through the pouring rain, which crackled against its roof and sides, ending all conversation.

Suddenly they stopped. René, who had been sitting with the driver, got out. Two German soldiers had been standing in the drenching rain before a shed at the side of the road. As René approached them, they decided they were getting too wet and went inside. This presumably was the line.

Nobody on the truck dared say a word. Judith thought the others must hear the pounding of her heart. She was holding her head between her hands. Her eyes were closed. She didn't want to see what was coming. She was reminded of the moment in Boulogne when the Germans came into the cellar. Even now, she expected to hear the order, "Everybody out!"

They continued to wait. It was taking longer and longer as the rain continued to clatter against the truck. She didn't know what she'd answer if they asked if she was a Jew.

Suddenly they were moving again—it was as if nothing had happened—and they all jumped up to get a last look at what was said to be this most terrible of all European borders. In the heavy rain they couldn't see much: a road as straight as an arrow, full of puddles, a gate with its black, white, and red stripes, and a swastika flag of a size that no one had ever seen before. Its sheer size was intimidating. But that was all. There were no machine guns, no barbed wire, no troops.

Now came the Vichy French. After driving a good distance—was this all no-man's-land?—they stopped again. Carefully they looked out. Before the truck stood a black soldier in a French uniform with red pants, a fez on his head, and in his hand a huge red umbrella. It was still pouring.

"When do we get to the French border control?" René asked him through the window.

"You've already passed it," the soldier said.

In the rain they must have driven right through it, assuming there was one at all. They had arrived in unoccupied France, greeted by a black colonial soldier with a red umbrella. When the rain let up, they imagined themselves to be a little like the Israelites who had crossed the Red Sea with Moses thousands of years before and had arrived on the other side with dry feet.

When they briefly stopped in the next town, René came back to tell them how smoothly it had gone with the Germans. But they couldn't help feeling they owed much to the fact that, even for the Nazis, it had been raining too hard.

And then they got the bad news. Lisieux had left his bag with Judith's and Taler's passports in the place where they stayed the previous night.

At first Judith refused to believe it. She thought René was joking when he told her. Now, as he gave her his word of honor that it was true, she didn't know what to say. She knew that her passport with its *Judenstempel* could fall into the Nazis' hands, and then the whole scheme would blow up in her face. The Gestapo in Brussels would be notified, making her return impossible. For Taler it wasn't so bad, since she planned to stay in the south of France anyway. But Judith, who had briefly believed that her biggest worries were behind her, now stood under a cloud of uncertainty that would hang over her as long as she was in the south of France.

René tried to reassure her. "Look at the bright side, Madame Licht," he said. "There's a solution for everything." And, he reminded her, she still had her Belgian identity card.

They spent the night at a little inn a little farther along. But before she went to bed Judith asked Lisieux if he knew a place where she and Hans could hide. She told him that she was going to urge Hans to escape from the camp.

"I can arrange that for you, Madame," Lisieux said.

Judith knew that he was capable of promising more than he could deliver.

"How do you propose to do that?" she asked.

"That's my secret."

"When will I know?"

"Probably tomorrow."

The next day, without any further incidents, they stopped in Toulouse, where they left the nurse to begin collecting the lost sheep for the return trip. Then, instead of taking the direct route to Perpignan, Lisieux turned off into the mountains. The whole way he had a secretive look on his face. Nobody could explain it. Only Judith had an idea what it was about. Finally they stopped in a tiny village. Just outside was a sign marked "Les Martys."

Even the word village was an exaggeration. Along the main street there were maybe ten or a dozen houses. The other inhabitants were scattered around and about, some hidden in the surrounding hills, some behind overgrown gardens.

As soon as Lisieux stopped and got out of the truck a man came in an oxcart and greeted him like an old friend. For a time they stood in quiet conversation.

Finally Lisieux returned to Judith. "It will work," he said. "The man I was talking to is the mayor of this town. He's ready to take you and your husband in, and if necessary, Mrs. Taler and her husband as well. He's a good old friend. I told him you were decent, quiet people. That your husbands will have fled from Saint-Cyprien, of course, he will not know."

"Can the mayor decide everything?" Judith asked.

"In this place he has police power. He is, if I may say so, his own prefect."

"What's this town like?" Taler asked.

""Wonderful," Lisieux replied. He took on the manner of a tourist guide and announced, "Les Martys has three hundred inhabitants. It is twenty-three kilometers from the nearest large city. Its prime source of income comes from dairy farming. It once produced a good deal of wine, but since France began choking on its grape harvest they've given up the vineyards above eight hundred meters. There are many vacant houses in Les Martys, and I'm sure you'll find a place in one of them."

They drove slowly down the hill to the city of Carcassonne, which really was twenty-three kilometers away, as Lisieux had said. The sun was setting behind them as they passed along the Canal du Midi. When they got to the hotel in Perpignan, it was pitch dark.[2]

—∽—

For Licht, August 17 was a trying day. In the morning there was a row after the French camp authorities complained that internees were walking around the region without leave. In the afternoon a sergeant came into the camp with another advisory that anyone caught wandering around outside the camp enclosure should be shot.

For dinner there was the usual swill—hard peas and moldy bread—which didn't improve the mood of the inmates. Through much of the

2. It now takes a little over an hour from Carcassonne to Perpignan by the fastest route. In 1940, it must have taken some three hours.

camp, angry men gathered in little clusters—the familiar eruption of camp rage.

Licht stood in one of the half-demolished barracks among a group of surly barracks leaders when Lofe suddenly burst in and dragged him outside.

"Guess who's in Perpignan," he said.

Licht had no idea. "I beg of you," he said, "don't tread on my nerves unnecessarily. Tell me already."

Lofe momentarily took delight in Licht's curiosity and then quietly said, as if it was the most ordinary thing, "Your wife."

"Don't talk nonsense," Licht said.

"I don't kid about such things," Lofe answered. "Mrs. Judith Licht arrived by truck from Belgium last night. So did Taler's wife. "

For Licht, the troubles at the camp suddenly became a secondary issue. The quarrels of internees, the camp rage, the finagling of the French, even the typhus—how important were they now? Judith Licht was here, his Judith Licht, who for months had been lost to him.

For a moment he was almost speechless. The only word he could utter was "Man!" He sat down in the sand, then said "Man! Man!" a few more times.

He hardly slept that night. He tried to imagine how she would look. Had she changed? What had she gone through, and what could she tell him about Peter, about Brussels, about the business? For a moment he thought that maybe Judith would really know a way he could get out of the camp. But then he gave that up. So many wives had been sitting around for weeks trying every possibility to rescue their husbands and getting nowhere.

Early the next morning, Licht, Anna's husband, Erwin Taler, Ams, Brust, and Veilchenfeld walked the eight kilometers to Elne, where they would catch the bus to Perpignan.[3] Licht had risen at daybreak, shaved and washed in the icy water of the fountain. He had put on the clothes

---

3. This seems puzzling. Had they arranged for day furloughs? What travel permits did they possess? Or had they simply taken advantage of the confusion and demoralization in the early months of the Vichy regime and the accompanying rash of desertions and inattention among the camp guards?

he'd been arrested in, which now were much too baggy. He had cursed as he tried to tie his tie over his loose shirt collar, which wrinkled and folded in on itself.

It was the first time that Licht had seen the area outside the camp. They walked through fields and meadows until they reached the main road leading to Elne. They didn't talk much; they were too preoccupied with their own thoughts.

—⁊⁊—

Judith, despite her nearsightedness, recognized him from his gait and his brown jacket and gray trousers. She couldn't make out his face until he was standing in front of her.

To Licht, when he first saw her, Judith looked unchanged. He increased his pace, but he decided that it would have looked too dumb to run. Then she was in his arms, both of them speaking at the same time, neither answering the other. They just wanted to hear the other's voice. What was said in that moment was unimportant. Things became relatively normal only after Licht had taken Judith's hand and they settled into the hotel dining room.

Then Licht remembered that he hadn't introduced his friends. "This is Richard Ams," he said. "And this is Louis Veilchenfeld, and Lofe you know."

Judith shook their hands, though for the moment she paid them little attention. She had eyes only for Licht. "You've gotten thinner," she said, "but it does you no harm. And you have a few more gray hairs, where you still have any."

"You're totally unchanged. But tell me about Peter."

"He's okay. But if I start to tell you more, I'll get into my own story and then I won't stop until tomorrow morning."

"And I have to be back at seven this evening," Licht said.

"You're not going back. In that paradise of yours there's an epidemic of typhus, and you can't really believe that I'm going to let you return there for one moment."

"That's impossible. I can't leave illegally. Here they check all the time. One can't hide. In any case, I couldn't stand life in hiding."

At that moment Anna Taler and her husband joined them.

"My Heinrich, of course, isn't going back," Taler said. "A few are dying every day over there and I wouldn't like to become a widow here."

"We were just discussing that," Judith said. "Hans wants to go back, but maybe he'll think it over. What do you think, Mr. Ams?"

"He has to be very careful. The punishment barracks at Saint-Cyprien isn't pleasant."

That afternoon Judith arranged a sort of general assembly. She'd seen that Hans wasn't able to reach a decision by himself. She wanted them to make clear to him as quickly as possible what would happen in the camp without him.

They took a cleared table in the empty hotel dining room—Ams, Lofe, Brust, Veilchenfeld, the Talers, a friend of the Talers named Kreuzberg, and the Lichts. "We can talk a long time about the past," Judith began. "But the important thing is the future. I don't want Hans to go back to the camp, not now and never again, period."

"That's impossible," Licht said. "An escape like that has to be carefully prepared. One has to know where one will go. Staying here in Perpignan is out of the question, and traveling is possible only with a *sauf-conduit*. Otherwise one will be arrested at the next stop."

"So what if I had something prepared?" Judith asked.

"I have to know what it is."

"A little village, for example, that I won't name now so that if people are questioned they can say they don't know."

"And what about the prefect?"

"There's no prefect there. The mayor decides."

"That's impossible. There is no such place."

"I assure you. I found the place. You and I and Lofe, the Talers and Kreuzberg can all find housing there. You only have to say yes."

"And Ams? "

"Ams of course also, if he wants. But if I heard him right, he doesn't want to leave the camp, at least not illegally."

"And Veilchenfeld?"

"I have my own plans," Veilchenfeld said. "Brust and I have decided to return to Brussels."

Licht looked at Ams, who nodded. "My dear Licht," Ams said. "You're looking at this old Richard Ams as if he were to blame that there are

people on this earth as crazy as Veilchenfeld and Brust. For that I have
no more responsibility than you. I certainly can't endorse their plans.
To be honest, I'm just too burned out to take on any responsibility. In
the past it might have been different. Now I say let these two idiots go, if
that's what they want to do."

"It's not an easy decision for me," Veilchenfeld said. "I'm terribly afraid
of the trip back. But Brust and I have our wives in Brussels and at the
moment we have no chance to emigrate. We also understand from Judith
that the Boches won't eat us up. We belong with our better halves."

"We're a funny group," Kreuzberg said. "We're behaving as if it were
up to us to make choices. But others are deciding for us. In any case, I'm
ready to give that little village a try."

"So are we," the Talers said.

Lofe waited to see what Licht would say. A battle was raging in Licht's
head. Everything in Licht bristled at the idea of living illegally somewhere. He longed for quiet, for rest, for freedom. Against all that there
was the fear of illegality.

"I can't come to a clear decision," he said at last. "You all know I want
to get out of that filth. But to be honest, I don't believe in that wonder-
town where the mayor alone makes all the decisions."

"Shouldn't we try?" Lofe asked. "Maybe there is such an exception
in France."

"I also think you should try," Ams said. "In any case you shouldn't
worry about me. I badly want out of the camp, but I want to fight for my
freedom. I have a right to be released. I have a document in hand showing
that I've been denaturalized."

"But you advise me to go?" Licht asked.

"The only thing for you is to get out of here. Things will work out in
the camp. You'll simply disappear from the list."[4]

"You're a remarkable group," Judith Licht said. "At this table we have a
gathering of every possibility: the man who only wants to get out legally;
the man who wants to get out illegally; the man who wants out but can't

---

4. Omission from the list didn't happen. "Othon" Schrag's camp dossier had several
official entries showing that he'd escaped.

get himself to go; and those who want the easiest way out—to return to Brussels."

"Is that the easiest way?" Veilchenfeld asked hopefully.

"At the moment, certainly," Judith said, thinking of Lisieux's truck and the nurse in Toulouse. "You'll almost certainly get over the Line of Demarcation, maybe with a few heart palpitations. And in Brussels, if you've done nothing to get under the Germans' skin, at this moment probably nobody will bother you."

"I'll never go back to Brussels," said Licht. "A hundred times better to stay here."

In the long pause that followed, Judith looked at the men's faces. On everyone there were residues of the life in the camp. The lines between nostrils and chin were deeper; the furrows on their foreheads remained even when they were not frowning. But it showed most of all in the haunted look in their eyes. Even Ams and Kreuzberg, who were still full of energy, were unable to erase the past from their faces.

"I'm returning to the camp," Ams said.

"I'm going to Brussels": Veilchenfeld.

"I'm going to the little village": Kreuzberg.

For the Talers it had long been a done deal.

Licht took a deep breath. "What are your plans?" he asked Judith.

"I'm staying as long as you need me. When you're again able to stand on your own feet, I'm going back to Brussels to get Peter."

"All right, for God's sake," Licht said.

"Of course, I'll try it too," Lofe said.

—⚹—

They set their departure for Les Martys for the day after the next. The inmate who ran the canteen would bring the few things that Licht still had in the camp to Perpignan. They would all meet in Perpignan the evening before.

Licht and Judith spent most of their last day in the park, where Licht, who thought he saw a pursuing gendarme around every street corner, felt safest. For all those on the run from Saint-Cyprien, the park was a sort of sanctuary where, under some unwritten law, the police didn't set foot. Even when there were sweeps on the streets and raids in the hotels, the police seemed to obey the rule.

Licht would probably have gotten sick if he'd had to remain in the city much longer. He felt he was on the edge of some form of madness. There were heavy weights on him. He looked like a hunted animal.

Judith tried her best to calm him. She was aware that there was constant danger, but she also knew that Licht was drifting into a sort of paranoia, a psychosis of fear not based on anything real. She was struck by how much stronger were her own nerves than those of these men, who had been so shaken by what they'd been through. She seemed much more firmly anchored to the realities of life, despite all she'd experienced.

Late into their last night in Perpignan, they all sat for hours in Judith and Hans's room debating, once again, the question of the return of Belgium. But only one thing was clear: they all had to run risks—Ams in the camp, the others on the outside. Anyone who left an island had to decide what was the least risk. There was no clear answer for any of them.

The next morning, like people taking the air, they walked casually to the garage from where Lisieux's truck would take them to Les Martys and then take Brust and Veilchenfeld on to Brussels. It would be the last time they would all be together in this little city that had played such a large and largely unpleasant role in their lives. The office of the prefect was here; this is where the German Commission sometimes met. Some of their friends had been caught in the raids here.

Licht thought that of them all maybe Ams was facing the most difficult prospects. In a way, the others were betraying him. All those who had been closest to him every day were leaving. He alone remained in his job in the barracks. When you came down to it, Licht thought, what swine we all are.

They boarded the truck and shook hands one last time with Ams, who was standing tall and rigid, with an ironic smile on his face. "Write now and then," he said, "and if you're longing to see me, come visit. I'll always have a bed ready for you."

The doors and the rear gate of the truck were shut. Under the canvas covering the bed of the truck, it was a little as it had been in the cattle cars. But Judith was sitting next to Licht, and next to Taler was his wife. They heard Ams call "Au revoir!" and then they were off.

Once they had left Perpignan, Lisieux opened the back of the truck so they could see the sunny, peaceful summer countryside. They rode past vineyards, orchards, and farmhouses, through low hills. Along the way, people watched with some mixture of curiosity and compassion. Children waved at the "returning refugees."

The men recalled their last trip on a truck, from the Elne railway station into Saint-Cyprien, now with the hope that that was forever behind them. Any gendarme who wished could still flag them down and send them back to the camp, to the fleas, to the typhus, and to despair.

On the road out of Carcassonne, they stopped in a little town so René and Lisieux could get something to eat. The other men didn't trust themselves to leave the truck. Why endanger the happy illusion that they were merely on a Sunday outing?

Lisieux parked the truck at a hotel. Judith and Anna Taler, protected by their green armbands, went out to shop, and then they all had bread and sausage and sat and waited for Lisieux and René, all the time fearing they'd be discovered. Licht wondered what he'd say if someone asked what they were doing there—his first answer, he thought, would be that they were Belgian refugees on their way home—but no one bothered about them. Only the two long-awaited men came and said they'd had a wonderful meal and good wine.

How important, Licht wondered, is food and drink next to freedom? What would I give to shake the feeling that I was being hunted, if I could again look without fear directly into a gendarme's face?

The truck now turned into the mountains, steadily climbing until they stopped at a small shuttered guesthouse where Lisieux got off and announced they were in Les Martys.

Not many minutes later Lisieux introduced Licht to M. Didier, the mayor, who immediately invited them to a little tavern for coffee.[5] He had a strong, compact build, the face of a farmer, and remarkably bright blue eyes. Licht had the feeling that it would be hard to fool Didier; he'd

---

5. Didier's real name, as indicated earlier, was Paul Ilhe, which my father acknowledged in an author's note in his novel *Sons of the Morning* (New York: Doubleday, 1945). "Monsieur and Madame Ilhe," he wrote, "sheltered the author, his wife and friends in a small French village when they were hiding from the Gestapo." The identity and the other details of the place were confirmed for me in 2013 by the mayor's office and by Patrick Claret, the grandson of Rene Ilhe, the brother of Paul Ilhe. Patrick and his mother still live there.

see through everything. He picked up things at once, and despite a small speech defect, his replies came like bullets from a rifle.

Lisieux opened the conversation. "Here are my tourists," he said.

"Tell me your situation," Didier said, turning to Licht, "and what I can do for you."

Licht said they were all Belgian refugees who had been living in France, though they had never been registered anywhere, always in flight.

"What nationality?" the mayor asked.

Licht had feared the question before it was asked. Their papers still identified them as German even though the Nazis had denaturalized them. What should he say?

"Show me your papers."

Licht showed him his identity card.

"You're German?"

"I was German, but I've long been denaturalized."

"You're Jewish?"

"Of course, here's the stamp."

At this point the mayor's demeanor changed.

"I'll be glad to take you into my community. But I can only shelter you for two or three weeks, at most, without reporting your presence. Any longer won't work. For some time now, the gendarmes have been coming here almost every week."

Licht got a terrible shock. The dream is already over, he thought. Lisieux had misunderstood or maybe misreported the situation.

"What do we have to do," Licht asked, "if we wanted to stay indefinitely?"

"You have to get a residence permit from the prefecture in Carcassonne."[6]

That's impossible, Licht thought. The prefect will ask all sorts of questions; there'll be an investigation. And it was even possible that despite whatever their friends could do, their escape might have been reported.

Lisieux cut in. "You know the prefect well, don't you?"

---

6. My father identified the town only as "M." presumably, again, to shelter those who helped them.

"Yes, he's a great friend."

"Now, listen," Lisieux said. "You don't have to know everything, even though you're the mayor. These people can't submit any official application, but I can vouch for their decency and propriety."

"All well and good, but it's impossible without the permit from the prefecture."

"Fine, but could you simply ask the prefect for a permit for six people, without asking whom it concerns?"

"I'll try it, but I'll have to go personally."

"I'll drive you tomorrow to Carcassonne. Mr. Licht and maybe one other will come with us. They'll bring their papers. You'll see the prefect alone, and only when he says yes will the documents be presented. And then everything will be settled."[7]

"Agreed." The mayor expressed his sympathy for the Belgian refugees—he'd had a few in his village some weeks before. "But please don't believe that we French are any better off. Almost all our able-bodied men are in German prison camps. Most of their families have had no news. People ask me every day how such a terrible collapse could ever have come about."

Licht responded evasively to Lisieux's plan. He had to tell the others and allow them to think whether the plan made any sense. At last the mayor stood, paid for their coffee, and they returned to the truck. He greeted the others and cracked a couple of jokes with the women, whom he seemed to like. After he left, Licht sat down with the others at the side of the road and told them what had taken place.

He was quite without hope, and so was his version of the discussion with the mayor. The prefect would never grant the permits without seeing their papers. Thousands had tried, lawyers and politicians had intervened on people's behalf, women had fallen on their knees—and still they denied the permits. They were not allowed to issue them to Germans, especially Jews, even if they wanted to.

"Of course," said Licht, "our good mayor doesn't know that, but I know it and you know it and we should start thinking right now what we'll do if the permit is refused."

---

7. I've always wondered how much all this help from Lisieux cost my mother.

Judith, who sensed the mood her husband was in, wanted to try to steer him away from his worries. "Right now we have to find a place to stay for the night," she said, "and to get something to eat. Beyond that things will sort themselves out."

"Once we have something in our stomachs," Anna Taler said, "everything will look better."

Lisieux had gotten the key to an abandoned little inn, an ancient, dilapidated building whose rooms smelled of mold and dust. When they opened the shutters, they discovered that most of the floors were covered with sacks of straw where, it appeared, earlier refugees had slept.

They bought bread and cheese, lit a small fire in the wood stove, and brewed coffee, but no one had much of an appetite. All were occupied with their thoughts. Only the two women behaved as if everything were in the greatest order. To a stranger, it might have looked like a boring tea party where, for some reason, no one spoke.

Licht couldn't control his anxiety. "What will happen?" he asked. "Let's assume the permits are denied—there's a ninety percent chance that's what will happen. To my mind that will leave only two possibilities: back into the camp, or back to Belgium."

—⁊⁊⁊—

The next morning, Lisieux drove Licht, Judith, Lofe, and Didier to the prefecture in Carcassonne. Licht's fingers twisted anxiously together. He felt like a man on his way to the guillotine. He had no hope. It would take a miracle—did such miracles ever happen?

Didier was joking with Judith. He didn't say a word about what they were going for. He was talking mainly about where he would have lunch. To Licht, listening to the conversation around him was like listening to Martians who had come to earth for a picnic.

"Why are you making such a gruesome face, Monsieur Hans?" Didier said. "Isn't it wonderful to ride through the sunny mountains of France, to look forward to a good lunch and a good glass of wine and at the same time to have such a pretty wife? What else would you want?"

"I'm worrying about what's coming," Licht replied.

"What's coming?"

"Yes, about the authorization."

Didier laughed. "That will take care of itself. Accustom yourself to think no further than about what's right here." He put his arm around Judith's shoulders. "Am I not right, Madame?"

"Of course. Hans worries too much."

They were now driving through the narrow crooked streets of Carcassonne, stopping finally at a square planted with large trees. Judith and Lofe waited on a bench in the square while Didier and Licht went into a café.

"Let's drink a Kirsch," Didier said. "It will cheer us up."

With their glasses standing before them, he had Licht tell him again what he wanted. Then he stood, reached in his pocket for the beret that he apparently brought for the occasion, stuck his cigarette into the corner of his mouth, and said, "Wait here for me. I'm sure I'll be back soon."

Licht sank into his troubled thoughts. He drank two glasses of cognac, which seemed to do him good. After that everything looked a little brighter.

Twenty minutes later, he saw the mayor coming back, even though he was still a good distance away. Before he got to the open door of the café, he called: "We won! But come fast, come fast. This can all still be arranged this morning."

The short-legged Didier walked so fast that Licht had no chance to ask questions. He hardly knew what was happening before he stood in a large wood-paneled room. There, sitting at a table, was a man of fragile appearance who looked mostly over the glasses sitting on the tip of his nose. His eyes did all manner of contortions to avoid looking through them.

"You have all your papers?" he asked.

"Yes, sir." Licht laid a stack of documents on the table, passports for those who had them, identity cards for those, like Judith, who didn't.

"Take them to my secretary over there and spell your names."

Licht swept them up and took them to an elderly woman sitting at a typewriter.

She not did deign to look at him. With her, it seemed, everything was about numbers and documents; the creature that stuck them in front of her was of no consequence.

She rolled the blank forms into her typewriter and said, without looking up, "Tell me the names, or better, spell them." Licht did as asked.

When she was done, she yanked the forms from her machine and took them and the carbon to her boss.

The mayor stood in a dark corner of the room, watching with pride what he had achieved.

The prefect slowly and thoughtfully dipped his pen in the ink, signed the forms, carefully folded the papers and handed them to the mayor.

"So then, next Sunday," Didier said to the prefect. They shook hands. In the hall outside, Didier handed Licht the documents.

He didn't know what to say. He felt like he'd just gotten an eleventh hour pardon. He stuttered a few words of thanks until Didier interrupted. "But it was nothing, Monsieur Hans. Let's go have a little something."

"Let's first go and tell the others," Licht replied. "They've been worried about how all this would end, and then we can go drink as much as you like."

Even from far off, Lofe saw Licht's happy face. "It went well," he told Judith who, because of her shortsightedness, couldn't see anything. They stood to meet Licht and the mayor. Licht had to show the papers again and again. It was so wonderful, unbelievable, that one could again walk around like a free man.

—☽—

They spent one more night in the old inn in Les Martys. The only sad and fearful people among them that evening were Brust and Veilchenfeld. The thought of the Line of Demarcation and what followed weighed heavily on them. Ever since their fears that they'd have trouble getting residence permits in the little village proved wrong, and that they could have stayed there like the others, they were even more worried than before. And now the option of remaining was closed. And so at their last meal together they were depressed. The cheer of the others made it almost seem as if they were in an alien environment.

Licht could easily imagine himself in their position. "You could always stay," he said. "I'm convinced that in the end the mayor could also get you the residence permit."

"We've been telling ourselves the same thing," Veilchenfeld replied. "But we're staying with our plan. Nothing's really changed for us. The reasons we want to return to Brussels haven't changed."

"I don't want to deter you in any way," Licht said. "Maybe you'll turn out to be right. But if you do it, you have to be totally committed—otherwise you'll never make it."

"That's right," Judith said. "If you're going into it halfheartedly, then you're better off staying here. When I came, I only thought: 'I have to get across no matter what happens.' Even if they had held me back I would have tried a second time and a third. I would have kept trying again and again."

"Judith is right," Brust said. "I'm firmly committed to do it. No doubt I'm scared. That I don't know what to say at the Line of Demarcation is troubling, but something will occur to me."

René shrugged. "Maybe it will rain," he said. "Maybe on the way, I'll scare up a document for you from some Belgian committee."

"So you all believe that we can risk it without too much worry?" Veilchenfeld asked. "Give us for once an unambiguous answer."

"I think I'm the only one who can judge that," Judith said. "I think you run a great risk, but not so great that men shouldn't try it. Is that unambiguous enough?"

"Thanks very much," Veilchenfeld replied. "And now to all, good night."

Soon they lay down to sleep. All became quiet. Sometimes Licht's straw bed rustled. Now and then he heard the clucking of a chicken. But something is missing, he thought before he fell asleep. And then it came to him. What was missing was the pressure he had felt around his heart ever since his arrest. For the first time since that day, it was gone.

—∿∿—

The next morning, the mayor rented Licht and his friends a vacant farmhouse that obviously hadn't been occupied for years.[8] It was full of spiderwebs, and a thick layer of dust lay on all the furniture. Lisieux drove his truck to the door to unload their baggage, and now all who were staying stood by as the others prepared to leave.

---

8. According to Patrick Claret, the mayor's grandnephew, who sent me a photo, his family owned and still owns the house. Now restored, it's a sturdy stone farmhouse. It's hard to imagine it as the ramshackle place my father stayed in.

"No big scenes," Veilchenfeld called. "We'll make it."

"And if not," said Licht, "come back here."

"Say hello to Brussels," said Judith. "And don't forget to call Peter and my mother. And tell them that whatever happens, I'm coming back to get them."

"And what shall we tell the Nazis?" Brust asked.

No one answered. They all felt the suppressed fear that the question raised.

René came around in his customary calm, down-to-earth manner. "We'll see to your passport, Madame Licht," he said. "And somehow we'll slip it over the line."

He was the last to climb in. He put on his sunglasses and Lisieux started the engine.

"Don't forget to get in good with the post office people and the tobacconist," Lisieux called to Licht. Slowly the truck started down the dirt track that led to the main road a few kilometers away. Brust waved for a long time with his handkerchief.

"Don't any of you have a handkerchief?" Anna Taler asked. When no one answered she wiped her eyes with her sleeve.

Then they all turned toward their new home. If they were to live here, they'd have to clean everything from the bottom up.

10

Les Martys

The house had been vacant for years. It had once been inhabited by farmers, until they could no longer extract enough from the rocky soil to feed themselves. The terrain was hilly, the road to the distant market difficult. In the early years of the twentieth century, as it became too hard to glean a livelihood from the soil, like many local farmers they moved to the cities to work in the factories. The house and the land became useless and remained abandoned until a very different kind of inhabitant brought a different kind of life.

There was a large living room on the ground floor, with a fireplace on one side and a table and a couple of chairs. The adjoining kitchen had a wood stove and a water pump that rarely worked; the alternative was to haul water from the well with a bucket. There were three bedrooms on the second floor, each with a large bed and one chair. Many window-panes were broken, the holes covered with cardboard. Everything was damp. The rains had left stains where the water came through the roof and the holes in the windows.

Nonetheless, to the escapees from the camp the little house seemed like paradise. After many months they had a home in which life could move in some sort of order, a kitchen in which to cook, a table where they could eat, and real beds in which to sleep.

There were six of them: Judith and Hans, the Talers, Lofe, and the Talers' friend, Kreuzberg. As soon as they arrived, they planned for the management of this new household. They drew up a budget for their weekly expenses. The wives would take care of the kitchen on a rotating basis; the men had to chop fire wood, bring in water, and clean the rooms.

The mayor's house was not far. On the first morning his wife came by, bringing vegetables from her garden, a gift for the new household. She offered help. If there was anything they needed, they should let her know. For them all, it was an unaccustomed feeling that suddenly strangers, people they didn't know, seemed to care about them. They were no longer hunted exiles, but were treated with consideration and respect. The postman who came in the morning stayed to chat about the weather. He was pleased when Licht told him how much he liked Les Martys, how lucky they all felt that they could be here. The postmistress inquired as often as she could about how they liked every little thing. It didn't take long for them to feel that they'd been accepted.

But there remained a shadow of fear that this idyll could end in a rude awakening. One fine morning there might be officers at the door to take them back to Perpignan, back to Saint-Cyprien, back to the camp. In the middle of a guessing game, at play, or during their work, the specter of re-internment would run through the house. They heard little from the camp. No one there knew where they were. To reach them, it was necessary to write Lofe's sister, now in Marseille, who relayed the news.[1]

---

1. "Lofe's" sister, who was divorced, had been interned with her fifteen-year-old daughter at the huge French camp at Gurs, had been released with her daughter or maybe bought her way out, and, like many other *Gursiennes,* had made her way to Marseille and Perpignan. I first heard the name Gurs as a boy from my father, who probably heard it from her. Her real name was Gertrud (Lefo) Kayser. Her part of my father's story is pretty well corroborated in Gertrud's daughter Liane's memoir in Robert B. Kahn, ed., *Reflections by Jewish Survivors from Mannheim* (Mannheim Reunion Committee, 1990), 97–98. Mannheim Jewish Survivors Reflections June 1990, accessed July 2014, www.jewishgen.org/yizkor /Mannheim/images/Mannheim Survivors Reflections June1990.pdf. Unfortunately Liane died before I had a chance to speak with her.

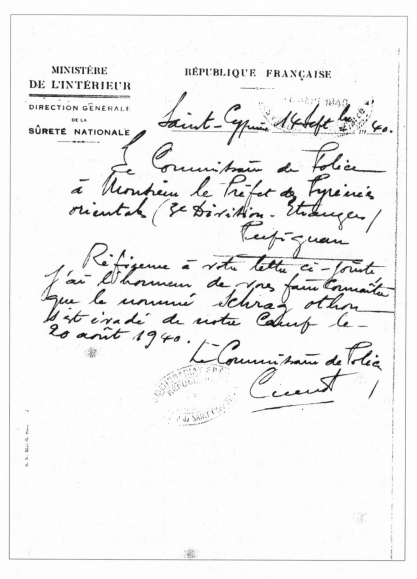

Memo from a police official at Saint-Cyprien notifying the prefecture that "Othon" Schrag escaped on August 20, 1940, one of many documents in Otto's camp file.

Archives of the Department des Pyrenées-Atlantiques, Pau.

Soon after their arrival they were invited to the confirmation of the mayor's son, for which they accompanied their neighbors to the little village church. Those sitting around them were mostly women, drawn and exhausted people, many in tears. Some of their husbands, brothers and sons had been wounded or killed in the war; some were in German prison camps. Now they sat and thought about better times before the war.

Life had been hard for them even before, as they struggled against the difficult conditions that nature imposed on them to put bread on the table. Now it was nearly impossible. Now the whole load was on their shoulders. Their loved ones were confined behind German barbed wire. Most had had no news. They looked at the little group of emigrants not as strangers but as if, in their own misfortune, they somehow belonged.

As the young boys and girls slowly walked to the altar to receive the sacraments from an old priest with white hair, Licht thought he was dreaming. Unbelievable, he thought, that I'm sitting here with Judith in this little French church, that I'm a free man, that my life may again have a small hope for the future.

In those first days of freedom, they all allowed themselves to enjoy an unburdened present. Nobody wanted to talk about the past or the future. What they liked best was to lie in the sun in silence, and at night they played charades and other games of the sort that Licht hadn't thought about since he was a child. They all knew it couldn't last and all feared the end that had to come.

It was Judith who first lifted the veil. "Our life here is wonderful," she said one evening. "I can believe that we might want to stay here for the rest of the war, maybe even for the rest of our lives. But you know that I must return to Peter. The boy is alone in Brussels with my mother. He is well cared for. But we must one day be reunited, and the future, about which no one has spoken, has to come. I have to try, by whatever means, to return to Belgium and, you my dear Hans, have to help me."

There were daily debates without resolution. As the same things were said again and again, it became ever more clear to Licht that Judith could not be persuaded to stay.

They'd subscribed to a Toulouse newspaper, which came daily by mail and which was their only contact with the outside world. From time to time it carried announcements from one or another transportation company about return trips from France for Belgian refugees. Although Judith followed those announcements closely, she kept putting off a decision. For the moment she had to stay with Hans, who, she felt, badly needed her.

Over time, food shortages in the village became ever more severe. There were no potatoes, bread was rationed, butter was not to be had. The weather turned cool and rainy. Every day they set a large fire in the fireplace, which wasn't sufficient to really warm the room. The bedrooms were damp and cold, and when there was a heavy rain, they had to close the shutters to prevent at least some water from coming through the broken panes. The laundry was always damp. Nonetheless, life was bearable. If it had been up to him, Licht wouldn't have changed anything. The one worry was that Peter wasn't there. So Judith's intended return became a looming concern.

Toward the end of September they learned from the paper that the Germans had issued an order forbidding the return of any Jews to Belgium. The border would be closed to them. When Judith read the news, it ended her calm and restraint. From then on, she feverishly sought a way to return to Peter as soon as possible.

Her inquiries at the transportation companies always yielded the same answer: Jews without a German travel permit would not be taken. That made it clear to all that the return would be particularly difficult. She began to fear that it would never be possible.

At the same time a new shadow arose. As Judith thought about her next step, it forced the others think about their own future. Lofe put it to them in the clearest manner. "It's obvious," he said, "that we have to emigrate. The temporary situation in which we find ourselves has to end sooner or later. It's possible that the French will simply forget us and let us stay in Les Martys for the rest of our lives. But that can't work. We have to return to our lives. We have to confront the new difficulties. We can't hide from them for all eternity."

"Two things are necessary," Lofe continued. "We have to get a permit to leave France. To get that, you need a visa to enter some country overseas. So getting that visa has to be the first step."

Licht despaired that for them, who had escaped the camp, it would never be possible to get an exit permit from France.

"Then we have to go illegally," said Lofe.

They were badly divided. Kreuzberg and the Taler family were in no hurry to leave. They hoped, if at all possible, to spend the rest of the war in Les Martys, to farm the land, send to Brussels for their children, and enroll them in school in that little place. They dreamed about making this little French nest their ultimate goal.

For Licht and Lofe, the ground underfoot was on fire. For them, this town was a transition point. The faster they moved on the better. They believed that all overseas entry visas could become still more difficult to get, that many countries could close their borders entirely, and that sooner or later, the Germans would appear here and smash all plans, all futures, and all hopes.

One day Judith Licht found a notice in the Toulouse paper in which a man named Martens offered to take Belgian refugees by car back to Brussels. Licht wrote him to ask whether he could even take a Jewish woman. "Come to Toulouse so we can discuss it," came the reply. That made it necessary to obtain an internal travel permit, a *sauf-conduit,* from the local gendarmerie, and its availability probably depended as much on the mood of the gendarmes as on anything else.

But a couple of days later, the *sauf-conduit* indeed arrived, a lovely red piece of paper with the stamp of the gendarmerie and the signature of the commandant authorizing Judith and Hans, in furtherance of their emigration, to travel to Toulouse. Everyone in the group looked at this wonderful document from all sides, passing it from hand to hand as if it opened the door to the whole world.

The next morning, on the bus to Carcassonne, where they would get the train to Toulouse, Judith was totally preoccupied with one terrible question: If she was asked at the Line of Demarcation whether she was a Jew, what should she answer? Licht, as if sensing the cause of her uneasiness, suddenly realized that in a few days she might be gone, and he would again face the uncertainty of not knowing, waiting for smuggled letters and reports from people who had themselves been smuggled across the borders. He recalled the months at Saint-Cyprien when he had no news, and it made him shudder that he might be thrown into that uncertainty again. About all the more terrible things that might occur he tried not to think at all. The German edicts had become so strict and were so mercilessly enforced that even for Judith, failure could lead to arrest and the concentration camp. That would be the end of everything: Judith in a concentration camp, Licht in Les Martys, Peter and Judith's mother in Brussels.

In Carcassonne, they had an hour to stroll before they had to catch their train. The city was still crowded with Belgian refugees; many stood on the streets or sat in the squares in their dark shopworn clothes. Everywhere one had to possess ration stamps to get something to eat; the wonderful French pastries of old, the sausages, the hams, the cakes, were gone from the shop windows. Now and then they encountered a car of German soldiers and officers. The French didn't look at them, but anyone could read from the expressions on the Germans' faces how proud they were, how grand was their self-regard, and how low and contemptible they thought anyone who didn't wear their uniform. Even in Vichy France, supposedly unoccupied, they were an occupying force. It made Licht's heart pound each time he heard their loud, rattling voices, as if they owned the world.

—∞—

In Toulouse, they checked into the city's best hotel: the better the hotel, they were told by an acquaintance from Brussels, a man named Heber who was himself living in Toulouse without a permit, the less the danger of being stopped and detained. That evening they met Martens, who told them that he regularly made the trip to Brussels and that from time to time he took people illegally. And while that was especially dangerous, he said, he believed he could manage it.

"Of course your name can't be Judith," he said. "That sounds too Jewish. Also you can't have a Belgian identity card, because I can't doctor those. Do you have any other papers?" Judith happened to be carrying her old Luxembourg identity card, which delighted Martens. They should come to his office the next morning and he would change the name Judith to Edith, a name with which the Boches can't find fault. When he quoted his fee for the whole affair, which was quite reasonable,

Judith told him that in all likelihood she would travel with him, but first she wanted to determine from the German Commission in Toulouse if there was any chance of getting a permit.

To Licht, the man seemed solid. He did not look like a professional swindler, but rather like a sort of small businessman trying, in the face of the hard economic conditions, to make a little in the human smuggling business. He was himself accompanying his clients, which seemed to reduce the risk.

The next morning, when they came to his office, Martens told Judith she must make a clear decision now on whether she would make the trip with him. He couldn't dally any longer. Even more stringent travel restrictions could be imposed at any moment. If Judith would give him her Luxembourg identity card, he would show her his wonderful method of changing her name.

When Judith handed him her card, he brought out two vials, one with a white fluid, the other with a red fluid. With one he dabbed out the letters "Ju" leaving only the "dith." He could now, if Judith agreed, put in a lovely "E" and then she would be Edith Licht.

Judith couldn't decide whether she was willing to go along with the forgery. Inherently she was reluctant to travel under a false name. She was willing to take responsibility for all sorts of dangers, but even so she wanted, as a general principle, to avoid any overt act, like document forgery, that was subject to criminal punishment. Again and again she said, "Yes, it's possible that I'll have fewer difficulties if I travel with that document. But if I'm stopped and I'm traveling with legal documents, probably the most they can do is to send me back. If I travel with forged documents, they'll lock me up."

At last, after a long interval of indecision, Judith told the man that she was ninety percent certain she would travel with him, but for a definitive answer he should come back to their hotel that evening.

Licht sensed that his wife needed more time to think—that she wasn't as firm in her resolve as she had been in Les Martys. She would now walk around all day trying to decide.

"What would you do?" she asked him.

"You know that I would never make that trip, that I regard it as sheer insanity to return to the Nazis. We have no news from Brussels. We don't know what's happened in the meantime. Your passport that was lost in the occupied zone could have been found; maybe the Nazis are making follow-up inquiries about you. You could get into the worst possible mess. I think the whole thing is a crazy adventure."

"But you know that I have to get Peter."

"We'll get someone from the Red Cross to bring Peter out. That's the simplest thing in the world. Nothing bad will happen."

"And what about the furniture, the household, and my mother?"

Licht didn't have the courage to say that given the circumstances, it was hard to take an old lady into consideration, that first consideration has to go to the young who still have their lives before them. Judith could not allow everything to go to smithereens to help an old woman for whom any illegal travel was out of the question in any case.

When Martens returned that evening Licht told him that Judith couldn't decide to make the trip with him, that she probably wouldn't go at all, but that when he returned from Belgium, he should get in touch.

"I don't believe," Martens said, "that I'll do it again. These things have become so difficult and so dangerous that this will be my last trip." The next morning, Hans and Judith returned to Les Martys. They were happy to leave Toulouse and to have that stress behind them. Licht was especially relieved that Judith was not going away. He hoped that maybe she would be of a different mind and stay indefinitely. When the bus brought them back to their village solitude, the woods already had their fall colors; everywhere there were leaves on the roads; the air was fresh, giving both the feeling that they were coming home.

—⁂—

Talk in the house now turned to the emigration of Licht and Lofe. Licht had heard from his brothers in America that steps had already been taken to get him a Mexican visa. But to get it he had to travel to Marseille, and he was reluctant to undertake that trip because he'd heard how dangerous it was there for people who'd escaped from the camps. The newspaper also reported on the frequent raids and roundups, the *rafles,* on the streets, in the cafés, and in other public places, leading Licht to defer his trip to the consulate from one day to the next.

And beyond that loomed the question of how to get out of France. Lofe's sister told about a priest in Perpignan who smuggled people over the Spanish border. He knew the officials on both sides and went once or twice a week, and so far he had lucked out. She told of others who had hiked across the Pyrenees through the fog in long overnight treks. But for both Licht and Lofe it was first necessary to obtain a Spanish visa, for which one required a Portuguese visa, which in turn required an American visa. And that, for the time being was entirely out of reach. Thus they had to think about some other destination, maybe in Cuba or South America. What were the possibilities there? They asked Lofe's sister to make inquiries.

Judith concluded from the Toulouse newspaper that there were ever fewer opportunities for transportation back to Brussels. The Line of Demarcation could be crossed only two days a week, and all who crossed needed a permit from the Germans. As she saw the possibilities for a return begin to fade she became ever more anxious, an anxiety that spread and infected the whole house. There were squabbles over trivial matters. Letters from Brussels, usually written in code, were misunderstood, and the quiet and comity of the early days became a memory. Conversations became sterile: each knew what the others were thinking.

Then, like a gift from heaven, one day there appeared Dr. Max Geierle, a Swiss who had lived for many years in America and was affiliated with the New York law firm with which Licht's brother was also associated. He'd flown in on a Pan-Am Clipper to Lisbon three days before and had found them through Lofe's sister in Marseille. For them all it was almost unbelievable that here sat a man who not long before had been in the distant, longed-for freedom of America and had landed here amid their semi-imprisonment. Even greater than the astonishment, however, was the uplift that followed his declaration that he was here to help, that he brought letters from America, and that he was prepared to go to the consulate in Marseille to pick up Licht and Judith's Mexican visas and try to get one for Lofe.

Judith asked him what he, as a lawyer, thought of her plans, and what could happen to her under the worst circumstances, to which he responded that she knew more about the Nazis than he did. But under no circumstances should she return to Brussels until she had the Mexican visa in hand—not only hers, but also those for her mother and the boy. When she asked about the lost passport, he assured her that for people in those circumstances the Mexicans would issue *Titres de Voyage*. Because it was reported that the French would never grant an exit visa to any male under forty—presumably to prevent avoidance of military service—that also resolved a problem for the thirty-eight-year-old Licht, who could now "lose" his passport and claim to be forty-one.

After Geierle left, they marveled that some people could still cross borders freely. "On the sixth of October I'll be in Zurich, on the twentieth in Paris, on the seventh of November I have a seat on the Clipper to New York, and if I can't make that I'll take the next or the one after that," Geierle had said. This man seemed like a creature from another world, no sign of uncertainty or fear, no haunted expression. He was calm, confident, and down to earth; he seemed to them like an image of their own personalities in a time long gone. So, presumably, had they all once been. But they'd forgotten all that. Today they were only shadows of what people of their culture and social status once had been.

Not long after Geierle's departure there was a notice in the newspaper from a M. Delfosse stating that he was arranging his last voyage to Belgium. Judith, who was again certain that she had to go back, could no longer be deterred, and Licht, who was unwilling to be responsible for holding her back, accompanied her once more to Toulouse. Two days before, they had received their Mexican documents stating that they were stateless and that Licht was forty-one—frail documents that nonetheless made Licht, the escapee from Saint-Cyprien, feel a bit more secure. If he was stopped, he could at least show his intention to emigrate.

By the time they arrived in Toulouse most of the Belgian refugees had left, only to be replaced by forlorn new faces in the same old clothes and coats, people from the border provinces of Alsace and Lorraine whom the Germans had evicted from their homes, and whom France tried to take into its small southern cities and share with them what little it had.

—⁂—

I recall almost nothing from the many weeks my mother was gone—or exactly how long it was. The clearest memory was of the picture postcards my parents sent from Carcassonne with black and white night photographs of the floodlit walls of the castle. I loved that castle, the Cité, and very much wanted to go there.[2] I remember the melody I often whistled—mostly, I think, as I rode my bike—and that I only later learned came from Tchaikovsky's *Capriccio Italien*. I must have heard it on the radio. I remember a somewhat older girl I occasionally talked with on the street near our apartment but about whom I re-member almost nothing, except that she was from Guatemala and that I found the pattern of the veins on her bare legs strangely attractive. I must have continued to run errands for the household—searching for meat, eggs, and butter, the cans without labels—but who the house-hold consisted of I haven't the slightest recollection. Was there a maid? Who did the cooking? Who made sure Peter took his bath?

From my earliest encounters with my grandmother, I always found her a little austere and reproachful, with her dark ankle-length dresses. Did we ever play games together? Did we talk at dinner? Did she ask about my day at school or what I learned? Did we talk about the Ger-man occupation or anything about politics? Did she ever try to tell me about her late husband, my grandfather, Ludwig Haas, who died the year before I was born? She must have had no end of stories. The ques-tions remain unanswered. Now, many years after the fact, my sense is that most adults of her generation and social class—and maybe my parents' as well—tended to stereotype and patronize children. My mother would later tell—how charming she thought it was!—that one night when I was five or six we came home very late from a train trip somewhere. I was asked by my grandmother (as was the patronizing fashion) whether the other passengers didn't think it strange that a young boy like myself was traveling so late, and I was said to have re-plied, "I'm sure they didn't notice I was a child." It was probably an ac-curate description of my own state of mind, and of theirs.

2. I finally got there in the spring of 2013, during my trip to do research on this story. The view of the walls of the Cité from outside hadn't changed from those postcards, but on the inside it was jammed door-to-door with postcard and souvenir shops, crêperies, and an array of other vendors for the tourists.

11

Cavallo's Bus

There was no light in the war-darkened streets of Toulouse. One could hardly see a hand before one's eyes. Judith groped her way along the walls. Each time she stepped off the sidewalk she was afraid of falling. Now and again she heard steps and occasionally a voice. She shivered in the cold. I can still turn back, she told herself. I haven't yet taken the last step. Suddenly she wished she would get a severe pain, maybe appendicitis, something that would allow her to turn back without losing face. Was that a stitch in her chest? No; it was nothing. It was all part of this life. In undertaking these adventures, she'd better get used to it. Maybe I'll miss my ride, she thought, half in hope, half in fear; maybe my watch is wrong, maybe the Italian driver and the vehicle will be gone.

But the bus was standing in the appointed place. The door was open and a couple of her fellow passengers were already sitting there; the driver was asleep between the seats on the floor. Judith coughed; the man shook himself, yawned loudly, and sat up.

"I'm Madame Licht," she said as the driver got on his feet. "I've arranged with M. Delfosse to travel with you."

"My name is Cavallo," he said. "What's your nationality? Show me your papers."

"M. Delfosse is completely in the picture."

"Delfosse here, Delfosse there," Cavallo replied. "I'm the owner of this bus, and I decide who rides with me and who doesn't. Show me your documents."

Judith gave him her Belgian identity card.

"You're German." He said. "Taking you is out of the question."

"I arranged it with Delfosse. I've paid for the trip."

"What did you pay?"

"Fifteen hundred francs."

"That really thrills me. For fifteen hundred I should take you illegally over the border? Others pay five thousand francs."

Judith became angry. "I arranged that with Delfosse. He understands the circumstances in which I travel exactly. Fifteen hundred is the fare he charged. I assume that you will honor that agreement."

Cavallo thought about it for a moment, then he growled that Judith should for God's sake get on. This is an unpleasant fellow, she said to herself after she took a seat. Maybe she should ask how he proposed to take them over the border. But then she thought better of it, lest he become still more bullheaded and hostile and refuse to take her altogether. As dawn broke and she looked around, she noticed that there appeared to be Jewish faces behind her. For the first time she didn't feel so bereft.

As they drove out of Toulouse, Cavallo began to sing Italian folksongs in a loud voice and with great passion, so much so that it began to get on the passengers' nerves. A heavyset older man, a Belgian, seated next to Judith began to whisper. "If that guy would only stop."

"What can one do?" Judith asked.

"Naturally nothing. I believe he sings to keep himself from falling asleep." The Belgian was obviously glad to have someone he could connect with. He now tried to keep the conversation going. She should regard him as her friend.

Judith had an oppressive feeling when she thought about what the next hours might bring. Although there wasn't much conversation among the other passengers, she heard enough to sense that even those who were making the trip legally didn't know what awaited them—were traveling into the unknown. Nobody could properly imagine what things in the occupied zone or in Belgium looked like. Some had no news whatever from their families; many had no idea what might have happened to their homes.

There was something almost surreal about this transport in which forty people were sitting together, none of whom was sure exactly where the trip would end. None knew what awaited them when they crossed the Line of Demarcation. Beyond lay a mysterious realm that they only knew from rumors, a place that they saw only as a shadow. Behind it were the rules and laws of another world. What did they know about the monstrous machine that ground humans into dust, that rendered what had once been a person into nothing but a shell? She recalled Hans, in his uncertainty, once reading to her Hamlet's lines about how

> The dread of something after death,
> The undiscovered country from whose bourn
> No traveler returns, puzzles the will
> And makes us rather bear those ills we have
> Than fly to others that we know not of . . .

They stopped. Hidden behind some trees there must have been a house into which Cavallo now disappeared. After several minutes, he returned with three men lugging heavy crates marked "Caution. Fragile," which they carefully stowed on the luggage rack of the bus. After they boarded, Cavallo turned to the passengers.

"I have the honor to introduce," he said, "the members of the Italian Commerce Commission. They will accompany us." That's not bad for me, thought Judith. If these guys really belong to a commission, then inspections of the bus won't be so intense.

Toward midday they reached the vicinity of Agen. The others went for lunch in a large hotel, while Judith, who wanted to be alone, went on her own into a small café where the owner told her that they had almost nothing to serve. "We used to serve trout and chicken and what you will, but since the start of this lousy war that's all over."

Judith didn't want to talk. She was sad and alone, and she thought about how long a road there already was between her and Hans. All the quiet little villages they'd passed through, the vineyards, the streams and bridges they'd crossed—all that already separated her from him. How will it be at the end when the distance is fifty or a hundred times as great?

German guard post at the Line of Demarcation between German-occupied France and Vichy France. The sign, facing unoccupied France, posted in the early days of the occupation, forbids Jews from entering the occupied zone and defines who is considered a Jew. Travel for Jews and many others in the other direction would soon also be severely restricted.

Bundesarchiv, Bild 1011-017-1065-44A and 45A / Photo: Becker.

As they drove into a pitch-black night it began to storm, and she had the feeling that the bus moved only slowly and with difficulty. And as the border came closer, Judith felt herself growing weaker and more anxious. Others seemed beset with the same anxiety and conversations became sillier. The old Belgian, perhaps thinking that this was the moment for more intimacy, tried to take Judith's hand. She made herself as small as possible and wished she had a magic helmet, like Siegfried's Tarnhelm, that would make her invisible through the coming hours. What would she do if they hauled her off the bus?

Cavallo stopped the bus and asked that the bulbs in the interior lights at the rear be unscrewed. "If the Germans ask," he said. "Tell them the light isn't working." In addition, he told all the people traveling without legal documents to seat themselves in the rearmost rows of the bus, where Judith was already sitting. So here we're again together, Judith thought. How clear and simple the separation. In Europe a Jew is illegal. The others are legal. They can sit in the front rows. The Germans can look at their faces. Where we are, the light must be darkened.

The Belgian, who now sat in front of Judith, turned. "I have a broad back, Madame," he said. "Hide yourself behind me. I am your shield. And when we're through, we'll celebrate."

The bus went slower and slower until it stopped and the door opened. Outside, holding powerful flashlights, stood the Germans in their leather coats.

"You're late," one of them said to Cavallo.

"We had a couple of breakdowns. French gas these days isn't worth a damn."

"Show me the list," said another of the Germans, as he stepped into the bus.

The three Italians greeted him with raised arms. Smiling, he thanked them.

"Ah! I see the gentlemen are again making a trip," he said. "Now who else do we have here?" He glanced at the list while his colleague shone his light around the bus. "I'm going to read each name. When your name is called, come forward."

That does it for me, Judith thought, and probably for the others in the back rows. But Cavallo, who knew how it all worked, had listed those with documents at the top of the list. The first six really had to step forward. After that the whole thing became too boring for the German.

"I still have a long way to go," he said to Cavallo. "If everybody has to climb out of his seat and come forward it will take too long. Turn on the lights in the back."

"They don't work," came the cries from the bus.

"Then I'll read the names. When your name is called identify yourself."

Each time someone said "here," he shone his flashlight at the person.

"Judith Licht," he called.

"Here," Judith answered.

The Belgian made himself as big as he could. Judith shrank behind him. The beam of the light found the Belgian, swung to the left and the right, and rested for a moment on the face of a French woman in the same row. Then, satisfied, the German called the name of the next person on the manifest. As the German passed all the others without objections, even those with names that might have aroused suspicions, it became clear to all that there was a special arrangement between the Italian and these officials. Otherwise would they have allowed passengers with names like Kohn and Rosenbaum to pass?

With a "Good trip" and the Hitler salute for the Italians, the Germans left. Cavallo started the bus, and within minutes they had left the Line of Demarcation behind.

"So that wasn't so dangerous," the Belgian said, turning to Judith. "Even with the Boches, it's possible to arrange things."

"Did you see their faces?" asked the Pole who was sitting next to Judith. "Do they all look like that?"

"I saw nothing at all," said a small woman who had been sitting with her arms curled around her knees. "I kept my eyes shut, as we did as children. We thought that that way no one could find us."

"I looked right into that guy's face," the Belgian said. "Now, the first chance we get, we'll celebrate. You don't cross the Line of Demarcation every day."

—⚏—

They spent most of the next day dawdling in Bordeaux. Cavallo had evidently decided to drive mostly at night. He seemed to feel that he was freshest at night. Or maybe he also thought that by that means he could avoid official checks. During the day he slept somewhere. Judith, like some others, spent part of the day in the little café where they had stopped at dawn and part of the day walking the streets of Bordeaux. Judith sent Hans a postcard. The cards that were permitted carried a printed form in which the sender could enter words in the allotted spaces. But at least Hans would learn that she had arrived safely in Bordeaux.

Late that evening they stopped at an inn crowded with German soldiers, where the host had prepared a special dinner, and where the three Italians were welcomed as if this were home. They offloaded the crates—which, it turned out were crates of champagne—and there began a great feast. They shared the room with German soldiers and officers. To Judith, the more relaxed and joyful the event became the eerier it seemed. The old Belgian, who had drunk a lot, became ever more attentive. He tried to take her in his arms, and the more Judith resisted, the more insistent he became. Finally she left, and sat in the bus.

After some time, two of her fellow travelers came to tell her that Cavallo wanted to speak to her.

"If Cavallo wants something from me," she replied, "he can come here himself."

They left, and a few minutes later they returned to tell her it wasn't only Cavallo who wanted to see her. It was a German officer.

That made her heart race. Had one of the others on the bus denounced her? What would happen now? She was so frightened she could barely stand, but she managed to accompany the two inside.

The German was very polite. "I understand," he said, "that you speak German."

"Yes," Judith replied. "A little."

"Then please help me, and be my interpreter. I have some bills to settle with these gentlemen," he said, indicating the Italians. "They speak only Italian and a little French and we can't understand one another."

Much relieved, Judith replied that she'd be glad to do so, and translated as they negotiated the champagne deal until they finally came to agreement.

"Where are you from?" the German asked.

Judith quickly invented a story. She was born in Belgium near the Luxembourg border and had spoken a lot of German at home, and was now going back, glad that her flight was over.

"I wish you all the best," the German said.

The Belgian again approached Judith, but since he was so unsteady on his feet, she managed to avoid him.

—ൕ—

In the early dawn the next morning, as they drove through the avenues of Paris, it struck Judith that even streets can change their looks. What once had been the city of light was so dimly lit that people sometimes had to grope along the sidewalks. She recalled the bright young face Paris had shown when she walked the Champs Elysées with Hans at the time of the World Exposition in 1937. Now it looked old and wrinkled. The buildings seemed to bend under the weight of the French misfortune. Policemen stood forlorn on the dark corners; only when one came very close could one even see them. There were no lights in the windows. Here and there one met German military people, soldiers who paced up and down with their rifles before some of the city's government buildings: the Quai d'Orsay, the Chamber of Deputies, the War Ministry. Everywhere she saw the same gray figures, all part of the great German war machine. Workers with their hands in their pockets, their coats buttoned to the neck against the cold, scurried along the walls of the buildings.

The most notable transformation, however, was the empty streets. Gone were the wild Paris taxi drivers who in a prior war had helped save the city. Gone were the luxurious private cars that one would have seen in other times even at this hour of the day. The very air smelled different. There had always been something special about the atmosphere in Paris. Now it reeked of rot, smoke, and dirt.

A winter sun came out later in the morning and the fog lifted, but Paris did not lose its sad look. The streets swarmed with uniforms. Where were the iridescent colors of those old pictures? Gray, brown, and black were the colors now moving through this city. Even the French, Judith saw, had been darkened by those colors. Knowingly or unknowingly, the French too were now gray.

There were long lines outside bakeries, meat markets, and groceries, where no loud word was spoken. People had learned not to speak carelessly. One never knew whether there was an informer nearby who would report careless words. Judith recalled something she was told on that earlier visit. "Could you ever imagine a French breakfast without butter, croissants and rolls ? If it happened it would lead to bloodshed."

Cavallo, who usually could be moved only with effort, was unexpectedly punctual in preparing to depart that afternoon. It was only after some effort that he was persuaded to wait for one woman who had been delayed. He would have left her in Paris.

Again they rode in darkness, and toward midnight they crossed into Belgium. There was no real inspection at the border, and customs was a pure formality; no one bothered about the people in the bus, and in the early hours of the morning Cavallo dropped Judith a few blocks from her home on the Avenue de l'Université. That was close enough for her to walk, he decided. As he handed her her bag, he told her that if she ever wanted to travel with him again she'd have to have a permit from the Germans. "If you don't have those papers, I won't take you."

—m—

After Judith left, Licht could hardly sleep. Should he have forced her to stay? Was he a weakling? Every trip to government offices frightened him. Every interrogation before an official condemned him to near panic. Maybe he really should have taken the responsibility and said no to her intended return. Maybe he should have fought it out. He allowed a woman with little experience to undertake an adventure that he himself would never have dared. Wasn't that something for which he bore a heavy responsibility?

When the bus brought him back to Les Martys, there was a letter at the post office for Judith from her mother. He tore it open.

"Peter and I are well," she wrote, "although we very much miss you and Hans. The other day we had a very unpleasant visit and I'm glad you hadn't come back. Stay with Hans and don't come here. The damp winter climate here is bad for your rheumatism and southern France is surely better."

Licht had to sit down. He wanted to scream. What should under no circumstances have occurred did occur. The Nazis had come calling on Mrs. Cohn and questioned her. Whether that stemmed from Judith's lost passport or something else, he didn't know. There was no way to learn anything except the bare facts from the veiled language that letter writers in Nazi-occupied countries had accustomed themselves to. "Visit" had become an international code word for "Gestapo." "Climate" and "weather" described the circumstances of those concerned. The warning not to come back could not be clearer. And yet Judith was under way. He saw her sitting on a bus that brought her ever closer to the danger. He imagined how relieved she'd be when she safely crossed the Demarcation Line, and how shocked she'd be when she got home and her mother told her, in her calm, factual way, what had happened.

But what in God's name had really happened? Licht gave the letter to Kreuzberg, who read it with compressed lips. "What a mess," he said. "If your wife is smart, she'll try to come back at the next possible moment."

In the succeeding days, the quiet of the village again lulled Licht into an even greater torpor than it had before. He knew that he had to make things happen, to prepare for his own future. If he did nothing, he might sit here forever. To have any chance of success it was necessary to have many irons in the fire. But he couldn't bestir himself: the place was so lovely. Up here one could smell the earth; here a brisk wind blew; here there were trees and grass, dogs and cows; here was life as it should be lived.

It was Lofe who shook him out of his lethargy. "Something finally has to happen," he declared one morning. "I have no intention of burying myself in this nest for the rest of the war. There are countless possibilities for getting out of France. Some of our friends have already succeeded. We sit here while Mr. Hans Licht simply can't bring himself to do anything. If you want peace and quiet at any price, this is not the place you're likely to get it forever. Things will not remain unchanged here. One day the Nazis will be at our door and then the dream will be at an end. I intend to start doing things, and if you wish, I'll do them for you, too."

"What can one do?" Licht asked.

Since legal routes were closed for them, Lofe said, they had to choose an illegal way. He'd heard from his sister that in Marseille the Belgian consulate issued identity papers for those who had during their flight from the Germans lost their own, or had, for one or another reason, fled without documents. All one needed was two forms of proof showing that one was who one claimed to be, and it would be easy to get them. By that means one would finally be rid of the accursed German passport and could then travel to Lisbon on the Belgian documents. In Lisbon one could once again allow oneself the luxury of living on a legal basis. "I'm going to go to Marseille to see what I can do for both of us. Is that all right with you?"[1]

Licht agreed. He was happy to have someone else take things in hand. Lofe would handle things well.

"There's of course yet another possibility," Lofe said. "From Perpignan you can walk across the border any day. My sister knows people who do that, but naturally I'd rather have documents in hand. The chance to walk across the Pyrenees is never lost."

In reality, that route was already closed. Although none of them thought of it, it had begun to snow even at the lower levels in the Pyrenees, making the mountain paths impassible until spring.

Ten days after Judith left, it also started to snow in Les Martys, though at first it mostly rained and blew, leaving the bedrooms damp and uncomfortable. At midday, Licht was called to the post office for a phone call that was to come through a bit later from Toulouse.

"Who was it?" he asked the postal clerk.

"A woman, but she didn't give her name."

---

1. The Belgian government, now in exile in London, severed diplomatic relations with Vichy on September 5, 1940, so her information, if it was ever correct, was probably long out of date. "In the apocalyptic atmosphere of 1940 Marseille," Lisa Fittko later wrote, "there were new stories every day about absurd escape attempts; plans involving fantasy boats and fictitious captains, visas for countries not found on any map, and passports issued by nations that no longer existed." Fittko, *Escape through the Pyrenees* (Evanston, IL: Northwestern University Press, 1991), 105. Fittko and her husband Hans were probably the most active of those, referred to by Lofe below, who walked refugees through the mountains.

"Are you Hans Licht?" came a woman's voice, when he picked up the receiver.

"Yes."

"My name has no bearing on this. I traveled with your wife from Toulouse to Brussels and I'm now back. Your wife arrived safely. At first, for whatever reasons, she wanted to come back here immediately."

"And now?"

"Now she's going to stay a little while."

"Is there no danger?"

"That I don't know, but your wife said you shouldn't worry. In four weeks she'll be coming."

"Do you know anything else?"

"No, that's all."

12

Brussels Encore

Because she didn't want to disturb her mother, Judith spent the early hours after Cavallo dropped her sleeping in the building concierge's flat. At seven, after she awoke, she walked anxiously to her own door, where a young woman, apparently a maid she had never seen before, met her.

"Who are you looking for?" she asked in French.

Judith noticed from her accent that she must be German. "I am Madame Licht, and I've just returned from France."

"You're Madame Licht. That's unbelievable, and you're arriving just now. Just now you have to come?"

Judith was frightened. "What does that mean?"

"I don't know if I should be talking about that," the young woman answered. "Mrs. Cohn is still asleep. But maybe it would be better if you knew before you saw her."

"So speak already. Is it Peter?"

"No, no, he's fine. Everything is okay. Only the Gestapo was here about three weeks ago and asked for you. For you and Mr. Licht."

They had gone into the kitchen. Judith had to sit down. Her thoughts were a carousel. They had to leave quickly; there was not a minute to lose. They mustn't catch her. It was Peter who brought her back to reality.

As always, he had long been awake, looking repeatedly at the alarm clock. When would it be time to get up? But he heard sounds and then voices. That could only be his mother, that surely was his mother, even though it seemed impossible. He got up, put on his bathrobe and his red slippers and went into the kitchen and there, really, was his mother. The first thing he told her was that he had new friends who were living with them.[1]

"You didn't know that?" the maid asked. "You didn't get our letters?"

"I know nothing," Judith replied. "How did you get those friends?" She looked at her son from all angles. He looked well, taller, though certainly not heavier. It would be dreadful, she thought, if I now had to leave him again. If I only knew exactly what's wrong.

"Yes," said Peter. "Hans and Eberhard Taler are with us, also Ferdinand Kreuzberg."

Judith had to laugh. Here was the mirror of Les Martys: the parents there, the children here. The maid explained that she had the three children in her care, that one morning the Gestapo had come to the Kreuzberg apartment to confiscate everything and seal the place off. There was an arrest warrant out for Kreuzberg.

Mrs. Kreuzberg had developed severe ailments since her husband had been interned at Saint-Cyprien, and was so impaired that she couldn't move without help. As the Nazis rummaged through her house, she took a lethal dose of something that had already been prepared and killed herself. The maid, who had been too busy with a hundred other tasks in the emergency to look after the woman, had already begun to pack the most important things she and the children would need wherever they went after their eviction. When after some time she returned to Mrs. Kreuzberg's room, she was dead. In her desperate need, the maid turned to Mrs. Cohn, who immediately took them in.

Peter, of course, was thrilled to have the new friends. What he most wanted to do at that moment was to show his mother the lot next to the

---

1. Of these friends I recall nothing, but I left it in, even though I think it may have been fiction, because it is so integral to my father's story. And, of course, it could be true.

apartment where they had their fort. It was almost an afterthought when he told her the Nazis had been there.

"Why?" she asked.

"I don't know," Peter replied. "But they took Oma's money."

—∿∿—

When she walked into her mother's room, she found her mother still in bed.

"There you are," her mother said. "I'm so happy you're here. But it's terrible at the same time." Judith didn't kiss her mother; she never did. Her mother hated shows of superficial tenderness. Like two men, they shook hands. Judith knew it wasn't necessary to do more.

"You have to leave again immediately," said Mrs. Cohn. "Not much can happen to me." She recounted for her daughter how a few weeks earlier agents from a special section of the Gestapo appeared to ask for Licht.[2] "My son-in-law," she told them, "was a German and was interned by the Belgians and taken to southern France."

"And what about your daughter?" they wanted to know.

"She's also in the south of France," she'd replied.[3]

"A tax lien has been issued against your son-in-law," one said. "When we find him he's subject to immediate arrest. While we can't arrest him now, we have to confiscate his money. What does he have here in the house?"

Mrs. Cohn was a very precise and conscientious individual. As she did every day, she had done all her accounts the previous evening. She knew the balance exactly.

2. It was the SiPo, the police arm of the *Sicherheitsdienst* (SD), not the Gestapo, searching for money and valuables that Jews emigrating from Germany took with them, without paying the taxes they supposedly owed. I recently received documentation from the Service Archives et Documentation, the Belgian archives in Brussels, indicating that such a charge had indeed been leveled by the Nazis against my father.

3. My mother would subsequently register for a new identity card in Brussels under her maiden name, Judith Anna Haas, without any indication that she was married or any declaration of religion (see below). In 1943, those cards would be used as an "administrative tool in the organization of the deportation" of Jews to Auschwitz (Gert De Prins, FOD Sociale Zekerheid, DG Oorlogsslachtoffers, Brussels, e-mail message to author, May 28, 2013.

"Nine hundred sixty-one marks, fifty pfennig," she had answered.[4]

"Give it to us," he said. "Otherwise there's nothing?"

"Not a pfennig."

"No dollars or other foreign currency?"

"Nothing."

One of the agents had examined the bookcase. Licht had a library of some two thousand volumes. The agent pulled out a fat book and found sheets of paper that had been slipped into it. "Here's a letter," he said.

And truly, even when they still lived in Germany, Licht sometimes stuck letters that he particularly wanted to save into certain books. "Yes," the agent said. "That's the usual Jew hiding place." But he did nothing further. Then they gave Mrs. Cohn a receipt for the money they'd taken, and left. But now, of course it was very troubling that Judith was there again, first because the Germans knew she had traveled illegally to southern France and, second, because of that alleged tax lien.

Judith first thought that the best thing she could do was to return to Hans immediately. She went for advice to every possible friend. Veilchenfeld, who had made it back safely in Lisieux's truck from southern France, strongly urged her to stay. He had in the meantime become the director of the Jewish Committee in Brussels and through that association perhaps had information that others didn't have.

—∿—

After she'd been back some ten days and nothing had happened, she began to feel a little more secure. Yet while she had begun to pursue many possibilities, she'd made little progress. The matter of the tax lien continued to loom. In Licht's briefcase she found German certificates that were only issued when all emigration taxes had been fully paid. Through an attorney she submitted those documents to the German authorities in Brussels, who had in turn forwarded them to officials in Bruchsal, the town in southern Germany where the Lichts had lived before they emigrated. Now they were waiting for a response. She had also got a new Belgian identity card despite the fact that she had trav-

---

4. I assume that there were other funds. I'm also puzzled by "accounts" in German money.

eled illegally: the passport that Lisieux left behind on their trip south had apparently never been found. Like all others, she also got her food-rationing cards.

The transformation of life in Brussels was nonetheless shocking, Like all the other countries they had conquered, the Germans had infested Belgium like a plague of locusts.[5] The granaries and food warehouses had been stripped; the shelves in the shops were nearly bare. Ration stamps were required for everything, yet each month more stamps were left over for goods that were unavailable. People who wanted to nourish themselves adequately had to buy the necessities on the black market. But who could afford that for the duration? Who could pay 65 to 70 francs for a pound of butter, 140 francs for a liter of oil, 70 francs for a dozen eggs, between 70 and 140 francs for a pound for meat, depending on quality? The assets of Licht's business were frozen; not a centime was available. The Belgian bureaucrat who handled the matter, Judith soon learned, was a narrow-minded little man who had the fear of the Germans deep in his bones.

The streets, like those in Paris, were dominated by the German military. Behind the city's windows, the hatred grew daily. Even before Judith had left for France, it had been there like a little bud. But that was before people began to go hungry. Now they saw their children grow paler and frailer by the day. As Judith stood in line waiting to get into a butcher shop, she looked with curiosity at the faces. She would have liked to read the thoughts behind those pinched and frowning foreheads, where misery always left its first marks. No one spoke. They looked anxiously at the little packages those ahead of them carried out of the shops. They counted those ahead of them and tried to calculate whether they, who stood twentieth or twenty-fifth in line, would still get something. They burrowed themselves into their wool shawls and every couple of minutes took the small step that brought them closer to the entrance.

---

5. In 1943, two years after he wrote this, my father's novel *The Locusts* would be published in New York. In interviews and publisher's handouts, he'd be quoted that his story, about locust plagues in Kansas in the nineteenth century, was in part prompted by the Nazis' sweep through Europe.

After a wait of about an hour at one shop, Judith got her little package of meat. This was her ration for the week. Even if she still had stamps, it was unlikely that she would get any meat for them.

As she turned a corner, a man approached her. "Do you need meat?" he asked.

"Naturally I need meat. How much?"

"Dogs sixty francs a pound, cats according to size."

Judith shuddered. The man followed her for a few steps. "I once sold beef," he said. "But since those guys over there have been here (indicating a couple of German soldiers across the street), this is how I try to make my living."

"I'm not buying this," Judith said.

"Not yet," the man replied.

—w—

In some respects, Judith faced the same problem as Licht. He couldn't apply for a French exit permit without the risk of being identified as an escapee from Saint-Cyprien. Similarly, she couldn't seek legal passage out of Brussels without the authorities now discovering that she had returned to Brussels illegally. Even after consulting lawyers and knowledgeable friends she could come to no conclusion. As the weeks passed and she lay awake at night worrying, she thought how much simpler it would be to give up on getting the necessary papers and travel illegally. But then there resurfaced the difficulties that Peter and her mother represented. How could she assume the risk and strains of travel for the old woman and the young boy? Everybody had advice and suggestions. There was this firm; there was that group. Each time she drew back before she took some crucial step.

Over and over Judith had to wonder about the situation in which Jews found themselves in Belgium. Although the Germans occupied the country, they hadn't yet intruded very much into its internal administration. The early anti-Jewish measures still appeared to her to be narrowly framed and indifferently administered by the local Belgian officials.[6] The

---

6. As indicated above, neither my mother nor I then seemed to know much about the anti-Semitic decrees—the forced registration of Jews, the impending expulsion of Jews

pressure to emigrate was thus not so great as in Luxemburg or Holland, where there were Nazi civilian administrations, meaning that in every respect it was Nazi law that applied.

At the same time, emigration had become more difficult since there were virtually no foreign consulates left. Aside from the American consulates in Antwerp and Brussels, and of course the German, few countries had consular representation. Before her trip south to get Hans out of Saint-Cyprien, when Judith had applied for an American transit visa she was told she first had to get the Mexican consulate in Brussels to certify that she had a visa to immigrate there. But as the American officials well knew, Mexico no longer had any representation in Brussels. Now, thanks to Geierle, at least she had the Mexican visa.

Some weeks after Judith's return to Brussels, the Taler and Kreuzberg children got travel permits, giving them the right to travel as far as Paris, where they would have to ask the prefecture and the German authorities for permits to travel into unoccupied France. A few days later she had learned that Jacques Pellmans was in Brussels.

After she phoned him, the smuggler came to the apartment and quickly agreed to take the children. He would go in a few days. He would also get the documents the children needed to travel on from Paris. "But you, Madame," he said, "are making a terrible mistake. You're sitting here in Brussels and deferring your departure from month to month. Make a decision. Leave everything as is and travel with me. I'll certainly take you across the Demarcation Line. Today and tomorrow that still works. When you're ready to go, it may be too late."

Judith replied that she wasn't ready. "Nothing is finished. I haven't yet so lost my head that I'm going to throw it all in and go away."

"But what are you then giving up?" Pellmans asked.

---

from public schools and universities—that the German military authorities had already begun to issue in Belgium. The German commandant in Belgium, General Alexander von Falkenhausen, who would take part in the failed anti-Hitler plot of July 1944, would later be tried by the Belgians for his role in deporting Jews to the death camps. Despite testimony that he tried to save Jews, he was convicted and sentenced to twelve years at hard labor, of which he served four.

"Can't you see that I have to fight to save part of my husband's assets, to take my mother along, and therefore to travel legally and to bring my affairs to some state of security and order?"

"You're not for this age. Your ideas and thoughts still echo the gray past, when people and places were stable. We've become nomads, and we have to take on the attributes and instincts of nomads."

"I can't change it," Judith said as the conversation ended. "Take the children. Take them safely to their parents. I myself have to stay here until I sense that I have fulfilled my obligations." As Pellmans left, still shaking his head, Judith called Peter. "The children are going to leave," she told him. "But we'll follow soon."[7]

—⁓—

The next news from Licht arrived a few days later. Things in southern France were so unsettled, he wrote, and the consulates threw up so many difficulties, that getting the chance to travel on from there might take months. Judith should therefore try to find a way to go directly to Lisbon without passing through the south of France. It would be especially difficult if Mrs. Cohn, who would have no residence permit, were to come to Les Martys, where she would be illegal. Judith under all circumstances should try to go to Portugal directly.

After lengthy conversations with her acquaintances Judith finally decided to apply for German travel permits under her maiden name, thereby separating her from the name Licht and the arrest warrant that the Germans had issued for her husband.[8] Veilchenfeld, as the head of the Jewish Committee, had told her that while the Germans were thorough, "even here, sometimes the one doesn't know what the other does," so much so that some agencies work against others. "The military are in ongoing battles with the Gestapo. If you apply for a travel permit today, they will check with the German mission, but it's hardly certain that they've ever heard the name Licht. And the financial division of the SD

7. It seemed to have occurred to no one at the time that Pellmans (Piccard) could have taken me to my father, as he would do with the Taler children. But maybe fathers of our class in those days weren't expected or prepared to take care of children.

8. She did indeed use her maiden name, according to documents I received in 2013 from the Belgian archivists.

is far removed from the passport office. And since the occupation, the German mission in any case leads only a shadow existence."

Nonetheless, Judith opted to use her maiden name when she applied for the travel permit through Veilchenfeld's Jewish aid group. That application was in fact soon granted—for her, for Peter, and for her mother. That left her free to travel to Paris. But again there came letters from Licht trying to dissuade her from going to southern France.

She also needed the Spanish and Portuguese transit visas to travel legally to Lisbon. And here, as in southern France, the Portuguese required evidence of an American immigration visa or a similar document from some other country. In addition, she needed evidence that she had booked a berth on a ship and had paid for it. There was no direct connection from Portugal to Mexico, which was why the American visa was necessary. And her experience with the bureaucrats at the US consulate had left things looking nearly hopeless.

All that, plus the difficulty of crossing the Line of Demarcation again, left Judith with the feeling that all her efforts were leading nowhere. She became uneasier by the day. She sought advice from every possible person, many of whom listened with only half an ear. They had too many problems of their own. Those who listened urged patience. "You must wait." When she told people that she might try making the trip without the necessary documents they told her she was crazy.

"Illegal?" they asked. "What a thought. You must be sick. You've run off the tracks. Do you know what that really means, illegal?"

When Judith shook her head, they told her it would lead her to prison or to a concentration camp. Was she thinking of her son? Maybe it was all the same to her what happened to her, but had she forgotten Peter and Hans?

"I'm terribly afraid myself," she would answer. "I'm not brave. But somebody has to have some courage. At the moment when it's necessary to act, one finds it. It's only before that one has heart palpitations."

Gradually she reached a firm decision that she would travel illegally. What had been a frightening specter had become part of her. It was now in her blood.

13

The Paper Chase in Marseille

Other than what he'd gleaned from Mrs. Cohn's ominous letter, Licht knew little about any of this. It was only later that he learned any details. All his endeavors were directed to the goal of leaving France as soon as possible and meeting Judith in Lisbon. He had no doubt that one day those efforts would be successful, at least insofar as they concerned Judith. She had let him know that she would come in about four weeks, and he knew that when she put her mind to something, she usually succeeded. It was of course possible, maybe even likely, that it would take much longer and that when she arrived he'd no longer be there. But he believed that she'd come.

Lofe had returned from Marseille, where he and his sister had made some connections, bringing a whole collection of forged documents. If he wished, he could be a Pole or a Russian. All the documents had his photo and an official-looking stamp of one sort of another and were signed and sworn to by two witnesses.

"I advise you," said Kreuzberg after he looked at the documents, "to go to Marseille and determine from the consulates how to get out. I would never believe that you'd succeed with these papers. You can use them to fool a gendarme who stops you on the street, but not the Gestapo agents who may examine you at the Spanish border."[1]

Licht and Lofe, who understood, obtained *sauf-conduits* and a few days later left on their information-gathering trip. From Lofe's sister they had learned that there was a strict inspection at the Marseille train station. Licht had written a friend to determine whether their *sauf-conduits* would suffice and was told they would not. The friend would meet them at the train.

"Follow me into the station restaurant," he told them on the platform as they arrived. "There's a way from here through the station to the hotel, where they don't check your identity card."

"But I have one," said Licht.

"But I don't," said the man, whose name was Lucien Fischer. "I'm living here illegally."

He led them through the restaurant restroom, which also served the hotel, into the hotel lobby, and then onto the street. That wasn't just Fischer's private route. All Marseille must have known about it. Almost certainly it was known to the police, but they for some strange reason tolerated it. One of their men, a grim-faced officer, stood at the station gate no more than five meters from the restaurant, and woe to anyone who had no identity card.

"I want to go immediately to the American consulate," Licht said. "Since I have my Mexican visa, it should be easy to get my American transit visa."

"Next, dear Mr. Licht," Fischer said, "we're going to a café, where you'll meet many knowledgeable people. You'll still have time for the consulate."

---

1. It's almost eerie how Anna Seghers's great novel, *Transit*, written in exile in Mexico at nearly the same time as this story but not published until 1944, reflects the gray light and resonates with the overtones of the consulates, the cafés, even the smells of the Marseille of this time and the people who, like the ones in this story, chased documents through the maze of its streets. Her story could be the story of thousands, and no doubt was in part so intended. Seghers's grim running joke was almost perfect: to get a permit to stay, you had to prove that you intended to leave.

On the way they stopped at a hotel where they managed to book a room. They were lucky; the city was overcrowded. Two large hotels had been commandeered and occupied entirely by French or German officials. The city was also packed with refugees unable to return to the occupied regions of Europe. Marseille had become a great catch-basin of refugees with nowhere to go.

The little café where Fischer took them was itself crowded with all manner of people, men and women speaking a dozen languages but French almost not at all. He seemed to be well known there. When their coffees came, Fischer told them a lump of sugar had already been put in their coffee. Others got saccharin.

"Now please pay attention," Fischer said. "You can probably get your Portuguese visa quickly if you have your American visa. And that depends on how well the American consul slept the night before. What you can't get is the Spanish transit visa and the French exit permit. The Germans have simply prohibited them, and therefore nobody gets out of here legally."

"Despite that," Lofe asked, "couldn't we apply?"

"If you tried to apply they'd give you a questionnaire that would make your eyes pop out. Not even a person with documents could answer all those questions, much less a person like you, who escaped from a camp. And that's not everything. A few days later, the gendarmerie will call to make a so-called *enquète*. What was left out of the questionnaire, these snoops will now want to know."

"It's unbelievable." Licht said. "On the one hand they want to get rid of us and torment us so long in the camps that we're ready to flee into the jungle; and then they won't let us go."

"My dear Licht," said Fischer, "I see that you've come from a remote mountain retreat. The mechanism here is something that could have been invented by Hitler personally, and maybe was. The French really want to get rid of us. They rightly ask themselves how they can feed us. The Germans answer that it's not so simple. First, there are still a few guys among you that we want to get our hands on, and second, we can't be sure how many of these refugees will run to help the British. Better this way. And if a few thousand Jews get ground down, better yet."

"So there remains only the illegal route?" Licht asked.

"What is the meaning of illegal?" Fischer asked. "Did they arrest and haul you off to France legally? Was Belgium occupied legally? In God's name, forget your old bourgeois ideas. Every day, dozens of others travel through Spain to Portugal, slipping through every conceivable hole, but for people like you, who still lug around the heavy pelt of legality, the holes are too tight."

Licht knew all that. He had been in the same situation when he escaped from Saint-Cyprien. In Les Martys in the meantime, he'd again become accustomed to a clandestine sort of bourgeois life. Now he would have to leave that nest.

"I might be able to get a Spanish visa," he said.

"Impossible," Fischer said. "Whoever told you that is a swindler."

"But if I got it, could I then get out of France?"

"You're in the wrong place for that. For that you have to go to the Café Excelsior in Perpignan. But don't convince yourself that the Spanish will let you through." The whole thing gave Licht the creeps.

After they left the café, Licht and Lofe strolled slowly down the great avenue called La Canebière toward the old harbor. There were few cars, but the street was busy and swarmed with police. People trying to get the day's Swiss newspapers, which had just arrived and quickly sold out, surrounded the newsstands. It was these as yet uncensored papers that carried the real news of the world. The coffeehouses were crowded. Many went there just to keep warm and sat for hours in front of a cup of coffee.

As they were about to enter a small restaurant, they saw their friend Ruckert from Saint-Cyprien, hurrying to get off the street.

Licht called to him.

Surprised, he stood still for a moment, then whispered. "Don't go in there, it's full of informers. Come with me to my room, there we can talk."

He was maybe forty, a man of few words with the worn, lined face of an older man. Ruckert seemed to have become acquainted with every concentration camp in Germany. For whatever reasons, even in 1933 he'd been ground in the gears of the Gestapo machine, and for five years he had been unable to rescue himself. He never told how he finally got away, but everyone who came near him had an uncomfortable feeling.

He led them away from the main streets into a small alley in the inner city, then across a courtyard, through another house, and to a sort of shed filled with every conceivable piece of junk. Using a large key, he opened a door that the others hadn't noticed and led them into a room. "Sit wherever you can," he said.

There was really nothing to sit on. Licht pulled two flimsy crates from the corners. Ruckert sat on a couple of sacks on the floor. "This is my bed," he said. A narrow ray of light came through a tiny window, making the whole place even sadder and drearier.

"I have to warn you," he began, "Marseille is a hot and dangerous place. You walk around as if you were on secure ground. But everything here is shaky. You don't see it from the outside, but people like me know it."

"How so?" asked Licht, who had the feeling that he was sitting with someone who didn't have control of all his faculties.

Ruckert began to whisper. "Naturally, I can't tell you everything. But I'll try to make clear what concerns you. There are at least a thousand informers here. Among them are former internees from Saint-Cyprien who, of course, know us. Just as you went to enter that restaurant, I saw two inside. They sell the names of us illegals. The police hate them like the plague but they have to deal with it when they point someone out. Otherwise they go to the German Commission and complain about the French police. But those are not the only dangers. Beware of the passport forgers. Don't buy any forged papers. Right now, they're peddling Czech passports. Pathetic phony crap. Don't get involved with these guys. It could endanger your life."

"So what should one do?" Lofe asked.

"Wait. There's all kind of things going on underground. I can't tell you details. It will still take some time until all is ready. But it will ripen here. There are already cracks in the ground on which the Boches stand. The unrest grows daily. The police do their work halfheartedly. One of these days Nazis will hang from the streetlights on the Canebière. I have a rope here. One of these days Schneidebreck will hang from it."

"Is that the one from the camp?" Licht asked.

"Yes. He has at least a hundred on his conscience. Whole raids have been started on his say-so. He wanted to catch me, too. Thank God that

I have good friends. They live all around here. They're French, mostly—former communists and socialists. They're young men who were led into battle and were suddenly alone, without officers, when the Nazis attacked. Here beats the heart of France. From it will come our future. And that's why I say wait. Or don't you want to be here for the great cleansing?"

Licht stood up. He had a headache and had to get away. "I've had enough of Europe," he said. "I want to have a life again that makes sense."

The next morning Licht went to the visa section of the American consulate, a large gray building near the prefecture. Having heard so much about how they did things, he had his heart in his mouth after he finally got into the building and mounted the wide stairway to the second floor.

The place was jammed with people, overflowing to the street, most of them women crowding around a fat man who, in his blue suit, looked like an important person. He had barricaded himself behind two tables. For Licht the depressing atmosphere was almost tangible. When he got to the front of the line and asked the man whether, having obtained a Mexican visa, he could now get an American transit visa, the automatic answer was "No."

"I'd like to speak to the consul personally," Licht insisted.

"That's me," the man said.

"I have to have the visa. Otherwise I can't get to Mexico. There's no direct connection by ship from Portugal to Mexico."

"There is," was the response.

Licht knew that wasn't true. "Can I get it if I prove to you that there's no connection?"

"No," the man said. "But you can try." Then he moved the line along.[2]

2. No one then knew about memos like the one circulated in June 1940 by Breckenridge Long, who headed US State Department's visa division, to the effect that "We can delay and effectively stop for a temporary period of indefinite length the number of immigrants into the United States. We could do this by simply advising our consuls to put every obstacle in the way and to require additional evidence and to resort to various administrative devices, which would postpone and postpone and postpone the granting of the visas."

The crowd of refugees waiting outside the US consulate in Marseille hoping to obtain an American visa. On some days Otto (Hans) was part of it.

United States Holocaust Memorial Museum.

On his way out, Licht recalled that when he was in Saint-Cyprien, friends in Switzerland had put him in touch with an organization in Marseille that helped emigrants.[3] After much searching he found the office, where he was taken to see a Miss Patrick, an older Englishwoman in a bright little room overlooking the harbor.

"I remember your name," she said, although she probably had no idea who he was. "I'm glad you're no longer in the camp. Tell me your story and I'll see if I can help."

It was refreshing that someone would talk to him like that. Licht told her everything that had happened, including the story of his visit to the American consulate. Often his narrative would be interrupted by the

3. This almost certainly refers again to my mother's cousin Erwin Schloss, the Moravian cleric in Berne who was involved with refugee relief organizations.

telephone. Each time, when she was done, she said, "Please excuse me. And please tell me more. It all interests me very much."

When he was done, she promised to intervene at the American consulate so that he could speak to a real consul. "Whether you'll get a visa I don't know, but I'll give you a recommendation that you can take to Mr. Stanwick and maybe he'll grant your wish. Keep me in touch and do nothing rash. I may also be able to help you with Spain."[4]

—ᴍ—

Licht went to get a cup of coffee in the same café where he'd been with Fischer the previous day. And there was Fischer again, in a corner, reading a newspaper.

"So what have you accomplished?" Fischer asked. "Have you spoken to the American consul?"

"No. You know exactly how difficult that is."

"Difficult? One only has to know the right route."

"Which route? Is there anything one can do?"

"The fat guy behind that table does the same thing with everyone. He says 'no' to everybody. By saying he's the consul, he tells people there's no one higher to speak to. Of course that's a lie, but a lot of simple people, women especially, buy it. But there's a way past him. You act as if you work there. When the guy turns his back, you shove your way through and get in the line of those who, on the basis of some secret document or other, are allowed to see the consul's secretary. And there on the right sits an amiable blond youngster. He'll give you a slip with a firm date and time when you can see Mr. Stanwick personally."

4. The vice consul in Marseille at the time was a man named Myles Standish, who, with Hiram "Harry" Bingham, the other visa officer at the Marseille consulate, collaborated with Varian Fry and the American Emergency Rescue Committee. They took considerable risks to help artists and intellectuals running from Hitler, not all of them Jewish, get American visas. Standish was the man who spirited the popular novelist Lion Feuchtwanger out of the loosely guarded San Nicola internment camp. In October 1940, when Feuchtwanger arrived in New York, thanks to Fry and Standish, he jeopardized Fry's whole clandestine operation by blurting out many of the details to the *New York Times*. "Flight Described by Feuchtwanger," *NYT*, October 6, 1940.

Licht found all that very useful. He had the introduction from Miss Patrick in his pocket, but in case that didn't work, he could try the other way.

The next day he went to American Export Lines saying he wanted to book passage from Lisbon to Veracruz.[5]

"There is no such service," said the clerk.

"Would you give me a statement in writing to that effect?" said Licht as he pressed fifty francs into her hand.

"With the greatest pleasure."

With her letter in hand he went back to the consulate. As before, people stood in long lines and waited. Many of those who had been there before nine were still there at eleven. People spent whole days in consulates. A young woman who worked there told how the incoming mail was tossed into laundry baskets and never read. People who couldn't come personally—those who couldn't get travel permits from the police—were out of luck.

When Licht stood again before the fat man at the table, the man took the letter from the shipping line, read it—what it said Licht of course knew—and told Licht to wait in the next line. Mr. Lawrence would call him in. Of all those who waited in those long lines, he was one of six or eight who had gotten this far. The others, who had been standing there since morning, were looking with envious faces at the few in the little group waiting at the inner door.

After a half hour Licht was called in. He showed his papers—including the recommendation from Miss Patrick. Lawrence said almost nothing. After he looked at all the documents he began to fill out a slip and make an entry in a ledger.

"This is your appointment," he said. "Be punctual."

—⁂—

When Licht got into Stanwick's office a few days later, the man didn't look up and didn't say a word. For him, Licht didn't seem to exist. By then

5. Under the terms of the Neutrality Act, ships of American Export Lines, probably the biggest US steamship company in transatlantic service before the war, had by then already been ordered to call no longer at Marseille.

Licht, who, despite the order to "be punctual," had been kept waiting most of the day, was so furious that he'd resolved to create a scene that this lackey would remember for the rest of his life.

Although no one invited him to sit, Licht sat down on a chair and, again without being asked, began to talk about the run-around he'd gotten. Now Stanwick looked up. Maybe it was Licht's voice; maybe it was because he spoke the fluent English that he had learned from his American mother.

"I've been here waiting since this morning at nine," he said. "I have a Mexican visa and need an American transit visa."

Stanwick leaned back in the swivel chair at his desk, put his feet up and began to rock. "Others have been waiting much longer," he said in a weary voice. "We have an enormous workload. Nobody asked you to come here and wait. You didn't have to wait."

Licht held his tongue. Better now to remain quiet until he saw what Stanwick would do. If he didn't issue the visa Licht could still say all the things that were on his mind.

Stanwick looked at the papers that had been laid before him. Then he went to the sink in the corner of the office and began to wash his hands. As he was occupied with the soap and water, and without turning, he said, "I'll give you the visa."

Licht didn't know whether he'd heard right. The man had spoken to the wall. But as he turned, drying his hands, and began to fill out an appointment slip, Licht knew that he'd won the battle. He was to return in three days to pick up the visa.

—⟁—

When Licht and Lofe, who in the meantime had also managed to get clearance for his visa, returned to the consulate, they were led into a room and seated in front of a young woman, who rolled a long blank into a typewriter, laid Licht's passport next to it and began to type. When Licht, in answer to her question, said his destination was Mexico, something terrible happened.

The woman tore the blank out of the typewriter, balled it up and threw it in the wastebasket, "There are no transit visas for Mexico," she said. "The order came through yesterday."

Licht's eyes were spinning. For a moment he couldn't see the woman clearly. She looked to him like a caricature out of a funhouse mirror. Lofe quickly seized the moment. "My friend made a mistake," he said. "First we're going to Panama, then later maybe to Mexico. But that doesn't interest you."

"Why didn't you say so?" she answered, and ran a new blank into the typewriter. Licht began to breathe again. The Panamanian visa he'd bought as insurance a few days before was really worth the seven thousand francs he paid for it. What insanity was this? They let us go to Panama, in the Canal Zone, an American possession. But to Mexico, where we can do them no damage, even if we wanted to, they won't let us go?

There were no further problems. The visas were issued, Stanwick signed them, and with their vest pockets stuffed with American documents they left the consulate.[6] That same evening they traveled back to Les Martys. On their return they learned that the Talers had received a telegram from Switzerland telling them that their children were on their way. But there was no word from Judith.

—❦—

In late January, soon after their return from Marseille, the rain and light dustings of snow they'd had so far were followed by a heavy snowstorm. The power went off, candles had to be lit, and the blasts became so powerful that the house shook. Although the shutters were closed and there was a blaze in the fireplace, it was bone-chilling in the room. The snow came down the chimney; the flakes hissed as they hit the fire. They all put on coats and pushed so close to the hearth that their feet were almost on the burning wood, yet they were still freezing. As the candles burned down, they all went to bed.

There was snow in Licht's bedroom. The flakes came in heavy swirls through the broken windowpanes. On the floor was a puddle, and next to it a little snowdrift. There was even snow on the bed that Licht carefully brushed off when he climbed in. It was hard to keep his candle lit. Again

6. According to US immigration records, my father's visa was dated December 27, 1940, Lofe's (Lefo's) January 14, 1941, some two weeks later, and his sister's and her daughter Liane's on January 10. But they were all issued in Marseille, and were all transit visas.

and again, gusts of wind blew it out. Although there was no moon, a pale light in the sky illuminated the landscape. The flakes fell in waves like rolling fog banks. With every blast of wind there came a sound like the hiss of water. The next morning, when Taler went to open the door to get more wood, he found that the wind had driven a great drift in front of the house. It was impossible to go out.

The storm continued without interruption. They had almost no provisions. There had been no way to store much and, in any case, there was little to buy. If they couldn't walk into the village to shop, they'd have nothing to eat. Worse, they couldn't get any more wood.

And of course, they couldn't cook breakfast. They got blankets and cushions from their beds, and from the damp wood that remained in the fireplace they coaxed a meager fire. It was hard to get even those little sticks to burn. It was only with the help of a lot of paper and the little brushwood that was still lying around that they got a weak flame. And that didn't last long. The snow coming down the chimney soon doused even that weak source of warmth.

The room went dark. The little stumps of candles remaining from the previous evening they saved for the next night. They couldn't open the shutters—the snow outside was too high. And in any case they were completely iced over.

They tried to climb out the upstairs windows, but couldn't. They also tried to shout, but the wind snatched the words away and no one heard them. There was not a soul in sight. Nor, as the wind threw clouds of snow across the landscape, could they see much else. The sky looked as if the storm would never end.

Licht recalled their days in the cattle cars. This, too, was a form of confinement. But to be stuck in a French farmhouse in a snowstorm was altogether different from being shipped from Belgium in locked cattle cars. Calmly he stretched out on his mattress.

"Remind yourselves of those cars," he said. "Then you'll consider yourselves to be princes here."

—∙∙∙—

It was still snowing the next morning, and although the storm had abated it seemed likely that, even if the sun were soon to come out, it would take days before they had any contact with the outside world. But that afternoon, the mayor and two other elderly men from the village came and shoveled a path to the house and cleared the huge drift that blocked the door.

"Maybe," said Lofe to Licht, "there's some news about our Spanish visas. Maybe your wife is on her way. We're sitting here like we're on a remote island. Tomorrow we need to try to get into the village. If the sun shines we should be able to do it."

And the next day, indeed, they succeeded. Although completely exhausted, they got to the post office, but found it closed. The postmistress, who lived upstairs, looked out a window when she heard their voices and told them that neither the telephone nor the telegraph was working, and of course there was no bus service and no mail. There was no telling when it would be resumed.

With great effort Lofe got a little bread from the baker, who himself had hardly anything. But because he had taken the refugees to heart he gave them a little of what he had. They even got a liter of milk as a gift from a farmer, a woman.

Licht was glad that the snowstorms made it impossible for him to leave. He hated the thought of Marseille. The faces of Fischer and his friends depressed him. He had his American visa, but that was hardly the end of it, and the thought of having to walk again from consulate to consulate sickened him. Of course he had to get out of France. He also knew that Judith would try everything to get to Lisbon. Sometimes he thought she might already be on the way, while he was still buried here in the snow. But there was little he could do.

Lofe didn't let himself be discouraged. Once he had the camp behind him, he regained his balance and his confidence. The unceasing efforts and the endless walking about didn't trouble him. Selling was his trade; it's what he'd done all his life. He was at home in waiting rooms. Nonetheless he could never separate himself from Licht. He had to have someone next to him to whom he could unburden himself. He had accustomed himself to Licht's erratic manner. He started in on him again.

"Consider that it will get harder from day to day to get out of France. Don't forget that you have a future, and don't risk everything because you're afraid to make things hard for yourself."

Licht knew that Lofe was right. "I'll go with you to Marseille again," he said. "I have to do something. Otherwise I'll never see Judith and Peter."

—⁂—

The first mail that reached Les Martys after the storm underlined the urgency. A letter from Judith saying that she would travel in the coming few weeks had been carried over the Line of Demarcation. There were in addition three other letters, two from people in the concentration camp at Gurs and one from Judith's cousin in Switzerland. All three advised Licht in coded language to leave as soon as possible. The Germans were looking for him. The cousin in Switzerland wrote in an especially urgent manner. He had always advised that he should wait until Judith could meet him. Now the tone had changed. "You have to get to Lisbon as fast as possible," he wrote. "You can't wait for Judith anymore. For you, everything is now at risk." He promised to explain later.

Licht and Lofe left the next day. The mayor's eyes were tearing as they said goodbye. "You'll have it good when you get to America. You can begin a new life. I'll remain here as mayor and all the old things will get uglier from one day to the next."

The road to Carcassonne, where they would take the train, was still covered with a heavy layer of snow, and the bus moved slowly on the steep hills down from the village. Everything looked different from the time when they first arrived. Was this trip, Licht wondered, the end of a chapter in their lives?

—⁂—

In Marseille, the great harbor lay nearly idle, the huge cranes rusting; only now and then did a ship bring grain and other urgently needed goods from Africa. And most were not for French consumption. The German supervisory commission determined which part—usually less than a fourth—went to the hungry French, and which part went to the Germans. A lot of men were walking around in tattered uniforms, some because they hadn't yet been demobilized, some because they had nothing else to wear. Buying anything required ration stamps. The mayor's office determined case by case who needed a coat or a suit and who didn't.

Licht and Lofe, who had arrived the evening before, walked through those sad streets to the little café where they were to meet Fischer. It seemed to be his hangout. Maybe he spent his nights there: he certainly didn't look so rosy. Apparently a number of his acquaintances had been picked up in a surprise raid and shipped to a camp. He hadn't been caught, but he didn't seem all that secure. He too was trying to decide how he could turn his back on France.

"So you're here again!" he called to Licht and Lofe. "You could by now have been far across all the mountains. But now before you undertake anything new, you have to tell me very clearly that you are firmly committed to take any path—*any* path—that will lead to your goal."

"Listen," Lofe answered. "If that weren't the case, I would certainly not have come back to you. To arrange a legal emigration, there are other places to which one can go."

"Of course. But even with illegality there are nuances. I can give you a whole range of options, from sneaking over the border to a trip with a forged diplomatic passport."

"The whole range is fine by me," Licht said. He wanted, if possible, to be pushed into the works without too much thinking. He wanted someone else to handle it and do the planning. He knew that it was only that way that he could reach his objective. The price was seven hundred American dollars.

"Is that too much for you?" Fischer asked.

Lofe wanted to know if that was for one of them or both.

"No, that's for each of you, of course."

Licht whistled through his teeth. "At today's exchange rate that's nearly a hundred thousand francs. For that, one should get something really first rate."

"For that you get, to begin, the satisfying sense that you've helped England and de Gaulle."

"You can get that at a cheaper price."

"And the seven hundred dollars isn't everything that's required. In addition, you have to perform certain services."

"That sounds very secretive," Licht said. "But maybe we've become a little slow on the uptake in the mountains and don't understand things that others grasp at once."

"So what about the seven hundred dollars?" Fischer asked.

"In principle," Licht countered, "if I can get an exit permit I'm prepared to spend that amount. Obviously I'd be willing to perform any services for England and de Gaulle that I could."

Fischer went to make a phone call and soon came rushing back. "We're going at once to see Frederic DeFerre at his house. Come quickly, the man doesn't have much time." Lofe said he'd met DeFerre in the café before. He said he was a little Frenchman with a tiny mustache and a pointy face.

At DeFerre's door they were met by a young woman holding a child by the hand. Without speaking, she led them into a sitting room where they found DeFerre, wearing a housecoat and slippers, studying a stack of Swiss newspapers. For a French residence of that time, the place was unusually warm. It was crowded with furniture. Two potted palm trees made it impossible to pass without lowering one's head.

DeFerre stood, shook everyone's hand—DeFerre's was a woman's hand, Licht thought; but the grip was very masculine. In that little man there was a lot of strength.

"You want to leave France?" he asked.

"Yes," Licht replied, "and as fast as possible."

"What nationality are you?"

"Stateless, originally German."

"May I see your papers?"

Licht and Lofe both gave him their passports.

"Are you Jews?"

"Yes."

"So listen," DeFerre said. "You know what the Deuxième Bureau is?"[7] When Licht nodded, he continued. "Okay. Pursuant to the goddamn armistice it's become a pauper. The government may no longer fund it. All the former intelligence agents are sitting around, and we're trying to seize every opportunity to get the means to further the interests of the old France; all our information goes to de Gaulle and the British. If I'm to be of any service to you—for example getting you a permit to leave

---

7. The pre-war French military intelligence service.

France—then you have to do something for us. That means you must support us financially and fulfill certain assignments."[8]

"I'm ready to do whatever you wish," Licht said.

"Don't go too far with your promises. I'm not sure you'd be inclined to, for example, join a team of saboteurs."

Licht hesitated. "For that, I would probably be ill-suited. But I would do whatever you'd find appropriate."

"For the moment, nothing will be asked of you, except for the payment. Nor can I promise you anything definite now. It all depends on what the general decides. Leave your money here in a sealed envelope. If I get you the permit it comes due. If, contrary to expectations, it doesn't, you'll get every penny back." When Licht asked how long it would take to get a decision, DeFerre made a phone call to someone he addressed as "major" and "*mon commandant*" and, after a short conversation, told them to return with the money that afternoon.

—⁜—

They spent the intervening time in Fischer's café, where Licht told Fischer that he deserved to get something out of the deal, and offered him a hundred dollars if it went through, which Fischer readily accepted. "Above all," Fischer said, "you have to keep your mouths shut about everything you've seen and heard. What goes on behind the scenes here you wouldn't believe. You've only gotten a glimpse of it today. Everything is just in a state of preparation. If the British were only willing to better support things here and not leave people in financial straits, a lot more could be accomplished. So naturally they try to raise money by every possible means. I'm sure they'll put your seven hundred dollars to good use."

"Is the former French army still involved in these things?" Licht asked.

"Of course," Fischer answered. "It's the army. The army is doing the whole thing."

8. DeFerre sounded not unlike the real Captain Henri Frenay, a French career officer who was posted to the Marseille garrison after the Armistice in 1940, where he began organizing a formal military resistance organization.

A small, portly man passed their table. "He's one of our best people," Fischer whispered. "He organized the recent explosions here."

"He doesn't look like a spy," said Licht. "And not at all like a terrorist."

"You're wrong," Fischer whispered, leaning across the table. "Here anyone could be a terrorist. One day every woman, every child will do what she's been told to do if it strikes the Boches. This is not an isolated group of conspirators. It's a large network. It can't be suppressed. To do that, one would have to post an armed German soldier next to every Frenchman."

—⁂—

The same woman opened the door when Licht returned to DeFerre's house, again holding the child's hand. DeFerre was sitting on the sofa with a military type, presumably the "major," who wore the rosette of the Legion of Honor in his lapel. On a little table before them stood a bottle of cognac and two large glasses. Before each sip, they inhaled the aroma, then closed their eyes as if they were dreaming.

"If I understand correctly, Mr. Licht," said the stranger, whose name Licht didn't catch, "you want to help our organization with a generous monetary contribution and, eventually, if they're requested, to perform some services."

"Yes, sir."

"Mr. Frederic vouches for you and for your friend. I was satisfied with that, but you'll understand that the general wanted other references."

"My best reference," said Licht, "is that the Germans are looking for me."

"For what?"

"I don't know. There's a charge that there's some tax proceeding against me, but I don't know if that could be sufficient cause for them to be after me in France." Licht also showed the man a friendly letter he'd had since before the war from a member of the French parliament. "That's at least something," the man said. Then he paused and began to pace the room.

"We have a terrible need for money," the major resumed. "We're tired of hanging on with our teeth. We're not getting help from anyone. So for the most part we have to pay for everything we do ourselves. If the British can't be persuaded soon that our work here is vitally important for them, then we have to give it all up."

He stopped in front of Licht. "Promise me, something, Mr. Licht," he said. "If you get your permit through us, then before you leave, come to Mr. DeFerre, who will give you an assignment to carry out in Lisbon. Do you speak English?"

"Yes," Licht said.

"Good. So you'll promise that you won't leave for Lisbon without taking your assignment."

"I promise."

"And now deposit your seven hundred dollars with Mr. DeFerre. It won't be touched if you don't get your permit. Give me all your papers, even the Mexican visa."

Licht did as he was told without saying a word.

"I promise you nothing," the major said, as he shook Licht's hand, "but please be assured that I have enormous interest in getting your fourteen hundred dollars for France."[9]

—⟶⟵—

The next day, Licht went looking for Ruckert. He decided that he must have changed his hiding place because there was not a trace of him in the shed where he'd been before. The people who lived nearby said they didn't know him, or pretended they didn't. It was as if the earth had swallowed him. Licht would have been eager to learn more about the underground's activities in France.

That evening, a man named Medingiers, whom he'd first met in Fischer's café, told Licht that he'd failed to obtain the Spanish visa that he had promised to get him. He'd asked for a tidy sum.

"What's with you and the Germans?" Medingiers asked when they'd settled in Licht and Lofe's room in the poorly heated hotel where they were staying.

Licht again replied that he didn't know. Maybe it was that tax matter. Why did Medingiers want to know?

9. Fourteen hundred dollars was then just a little less than the average annual income in America.

"I really shouldn't say, but I have to do it so you don't stumble into a situation that might cost you your head and neck."

Licht's heart began to pound. "Please tell me what you know. For some time I've been warned from all possible sides that they were looking for me in Brussels, presumably for failure to pay German emigration taxes."

"Lofe can easily get his Spanish transit visa. I got a provisional denial for you. And yes, I met my Spanish friend and asked for an explanation. The thing is this: for a transit visa, the Spanish need to get clearance from the German mission in Madrid. In your case the clearance was refused. No reason was given. But my friend also said that despite all that, he believes that with the right connections he can bring it all off. But I wonder whether, given these circumstances, you want to travel through Spain. "

"I don't know. But in any case, get me the visa. Whether or not I use it depends on what other possibilities I have. How long would it take?"

"My friend and I arranged a code, and I'll call him tomorrow evening. He says it will take a couple of days. And he must pay others what he himself would have earned. But he promised he'd do me the favor."

"It makes me want to puke," said Licht. "What should I do?"

"It's a difficult situation," Lofe said. "Some people get to Lisbon by way of Morocco, but for Morocco you need the special approval of General Noguès, and a one-time German may never get that. In addition, there are very few connections between Casablanca and Lisbon."[10]

Licht called DeFerre and arranged to meet him in Fischer's café, where he got a table in the rear, from which he could see who came in.

"I'll try to reach the major," DeFerre said after Licht had told him his difficulties. "Of course I can't promise anything, but I can imagine that you can also get to Morocco."

"What would you do if you were in my shoes?"

10. Charles Hippolyte Noguès was the French resident-general in Morocco. In the early months of 1941, Varian Fry also managed to send refugees by ship from Marseille to the French Caribbean island of Martinique, and from there to New York. Among them was the French publisher Jacques Schiffrin, whose son André, then five years old, would become my publisher at Pantheon and the New Press in New York many years later. Fry, *Surrender on Demand* (New York: Random House, 1945), 187–188.

"I would travel through Spain if I got the visa. Nobody will ask about it. But since my whole life has consisted of dangers, I'm no judge. You've heard the name Pellmans?"

"Of course I've heard the name. I know him personally. He wanted to take my wife illegally from Toulouse to Brussels. Before getting to the Line of Demarcation he was stopped and questioned by the French and with that my wife lost her willingness to risk the trip with him. Is he here?"

"He arrived today and said he knows you. He also took some kids to Les Martys."

"What!" shouted Licht and Lofe at the same moment. "He took the children?"

"Do you know what that's about?"

"Naturally," Licht said, and then told DeFerre the whole story. "And where is he now? He must have some letters from my wife."

"Calm yourself," DeFerre said. "He has them. He asked about you. How come you didn't give us his name as a reference?"

Licht was astounded. "You mean he's one of you?"

"Eureka! He's been working with us for a long time. Through him we've gathered a lot of intelligence about Belgium. He'll soon be here."

For Licht, everything concerning himself now became secondary. At last he would get direct word from Judith. Maybe now all the plans would have to be changed.

At last, a small figure came through the door. After looking about for a moment, he saw them. "Bonjour, M. Licht," he called. "I bring you a thousand greetings from Mme. Licht. Yes, she's doing very well. What resolve! She's going to try every possibility to get to you." He came to the table and greeted the others.

"And how are things up there?" DeFerre asked.

"Not at all well," Pellmans said. "We're hungry; we feed ourselves on dogs and cats. Every now and then we cause a little mess, but so far we've been mostly lying low. Things aren't bad enough yet. In Paris they're much further along."

"What about the air raids?"

"Weak. A little on the coast, otherwise nothing. Our nice little railway junctions don't interest the British. And sometimes Brussels has gone for many weeks without a single air raid alarm." Then he pulled some letters from his pocket.

"Naturally these aren't the latest news. These things are at least four weeks old. My trip with the children was one of the longest I ever made."

Notwithstanding the age of the letters, Licht was happy to get three from Judith and one that Peter had written himself. Judith wrote that she was unshakable in her determination to come either to southern France or to Lisbon. Licht had written her again a few days before that if possible she should go from occupied France directly to Spain and Portugal without touching the unoccupied zone. He couldn't imagine that she and the boy could manage the enormous difficulties in getting through this place. Even if the trip took longer she should try to bypass it.

"And how does my son look?" he asked.

"He's skinny," Pellmans answered. "But these days all children in Belgium are skinny. What should make them fat? Only the Boches get fat."

When Licht asked when he was going back, Pellmans looked questioningly at DeFerre.

"Mr. Pellmans is leaving tomorrow evening," DeFerre said. "And if you want to give him something to take to your wife, meet him here at three tomorrow afternoon." Then he stood and said, "He and I are now going to see the major. We have some things to arrange."

—∞—

For Licht, the next days seemed to be a constant seesaw between hope and despair. Each call to DeFerre brought the same response. "Still no answer." When Licht asked what the major said, he was told that the major had hopes. It was enough to make him crazy. He and Lofe sat for hours each day in Fischer's little café and stared at the door. They imagined that DeFerre would appear at any moment and say, "It's all set." But he didn't come. One day even Fischer didn't show up. People were saying that maybe he'd been arrested.

"You have to get away from Marseille for a couple of days," DeFerre said the next time they called. "Some diplomatic thing is going on, but nobody knows what. The police are beginning to lock people up, even people with valid documents. Better you disappear."

"Easy to say," answered Licht. "But where should we go?"

"I'll talk to my wife. Maybe you can stay with us."

That evening, as they were about to turn from a side street into the Canebière, they saw gendarmes taking a group of people toward the port. Among them were some Jews, but others as well.

"There's Ruckert," Lofe whispered. "Have they finally caught him?"

"Do you trust yourself to return to the hotel?" Licht asked. "Since my conversation with DeFerre I have the awful feeling that they may be waiting for us."

They decided to go directly to DeFerre's place, where they found the family at dinner.

"What a surprise," DeFerre said. "Join us. There's plenty."

Licht knew he couldn't eat until he had some idea of what was going to happen to him. He told DeFerre about the people who'd been arrested that they'd seen on the street. He told him about his feeling that the police might be waiting for him and Lofe in the hotel.

"I don't believe that," DeFerre said. "But if you're worried, you can sleep here. The rooms upstairs are occupied, but here in the living room there's lots of space." If he could, Licht would have hugged the man.

It turned into a pleasant evening. The whole family sat convivially around a floor lamp. DeFerre talked about earlier times, but not as if they were ended, only interrupted through temporary misfortune. The spirit of France, he said, was invincible. The nation would rise again in all its greatness, as it had many times before.

If that really was France, Licht wondered, how could its recent collapse be explained?

Licht and Lofe spent a restful night in easy chairs in the DeFerre living room. DeFerre went to their hotel and learned from the manager that Licht had worried unnecessarily—no one had been looking for them. But DeFerre checked them out, paid their bill, and brought their luggage back to his own place.

"You better stay here through the next day," he told them. "Yesterday they arrested about three hundred people and interned them on a ship in the harbor, and the arrests are continuing today. Nobody knows why. There's something pending, but even the major doesn't know."

It embarrassed Licht and Lofe to accept the man's hospitality. "We can't repay you," Licht said, but they were glad they found this hiding place. And that afternoon brought the answer to the mystery of the arrests. The Spanish dictator, Francisco Franco, was passing through on his way to see Philippe Pétain, once a French World War I hero, now the prime minister of Vichy France, and the Italian dictator Benito Mussolini, so they tried to sweep anything suspected of being anti-fascist out of the way. That was the reason for the arrests.

"You wouldn't have believed what you would have seen today," DeFerre said. "All the streets were blocked off by military people and gendarmes. They were stationed at every crossing, every square in southern France. In the motorcade to the right and left of this guy they'd put six heavily armed guards on motorcycles. Cars with cops in front, cars behind, all moving at the same speed, something that even the best assassin couldn't have taken on. For this they arrested people not only here, but in Perpignan, in Montpellier, in Nice, and they'll keep them in custody until Mr. Franco returns safely to Spain."[11]

The next morning DeFerre told them that he'd heard from the major that the exit permits had been approved. It might take a few days, but they had his word of honor that they would get them.

—◦◦—

When, after three days of nervous waiting in another hotel, Licht and Lofe finally got their passports with the exit visas, they could hardly believe it. "And everything is okay?" Licht asked when DeFerre delivered them.

"Better than you could have expected. At the same time they gave you an entry visa for Morocco. But I'm to tell you not to waste another day. Leave as quickly as you can. Take the path through Morocco and don't wait for the Spanish visa."

"How should we thank you?" Licht asked.

11. The Franco-Mussolini meeting took place in February 1941. The *New York Times* reported that Franco's trip was attended by "extraordinary police measures," including a prohibition of conversations in all foreign languages and "numerous preventive arrests." Lansing Warren, "Franco and Petain Meet This Week," *NYT*, February 11, 1941.

"I'm not to thank, but to France you still have an obligation. Before you leave, let me know when you're going. Then you'll hear more."

"You were right," Licht said. "I have to admit that sometimes you're right."

"Now what are we going to do?" Lofe asked.

"The devil only knows. For the moment I'm so happy about this visa that for a couple of hours I won't think about anything else."

"At least come with me to the shipping lines."

"The shipping lines?"

"If we're going to go to Morocco we have to reserve places on a ship."

"But I'm not sure I'm going to go by way of Morocco."

"How else do you want to get out of France?"

"Maybe we'll still get Spain."

"So suddenly you're the optimist."

Licht knew that Lofe was right. But it annoyed him that he couldn't at least enjoy the knowledge that he'd achieved one goal, and that he'd now have to walk around to the shipping companies to get a berth.

"Go alone this time," he said. "We don't always have to go around like Siamese twins."

"Should I reserve space for you, if I find one?"

"Do as you wish. You have my blessing for whatever."

Fifteen minutes later Lofe was back.

"We have to get back to the Commissaire du Port as fast as possible. Everybody who leaves has to have permission from the French authorities."

"But we already have that."

"It's not enough. The port authorities have to certify that you can board."

"Then is that all?"

"Okay, listen, I don't want to keep anything secret. Before you decide, you have to know that before the ship leaves people from the German Commission will be on board to check the passengers."

"What a disgusting mess," Licht said. "Do you know what they're checking for?"

"Nobody knows. But before the last sailing they hauled three people off the ship."

"So what should I do?"

"My guess is that you should risk it."

Licht knew that somehow it was the Nazis who were controlling his nerves, and knew it was not something he could long stand. He saw before him the men with those ugly faces, some in uniform, some in civilian dress, with long lists of names, searching for the name Licht. He heard them say: "Licht, Hans Licht, from Brussels?" That's not something he could risk.

"For me," he said to Lofe, "it's out of the question."

"What does it get you? One of these days, they'll catch you here, too."

"That's right. But they don't have me yet."

"Go with me in any case. It won't hurt to have the Commissaire's stamp in your passport. You can still decide what you'll do."

—⁓—

There was a long line of people outside the Commissaire's dockside office, few of them French. Through the door, Licht could see the Commissaire, an elderly man, going through a list of names as he dealt with each person. Licht wondered whether that wasn't the Germans' wanted list. Maybe the Nazis had arranged it so that all their hopes would now be smashed. With a shaky hand he gave the man his passport showing the page with the exit visa, so he might get a quick decision. He didn't dare look at the man. He saw only how his dimpled heavy hand took the passport, and began to go through it from front to back. When he got to the last page, he started paging from the beginning again. Then the hand left the passport and brought out a list. With a pencil, he went through the names. Now and then he stopped. Then the hand vanished and returned with a stamp, and began again to leaf through the passport. Suddenly, it seemed, the page with the exit visa had vanished. The hand couldn't find it. At last it came to it, pressed the stamp on the page, snapped the passport shut, and returned it.

Outside afterward, Licht had to wait a fearfully long time for Lofe, who emerged at last, pale as a ghost.

"It was a near thing," he said. "There was a Lofe on the list and it took the guy forever to get it through his head that the other Lofe was born in Warsaw and that his first name was Schmul. At last he gave me the stamp."

They went in search of a ship that might take them from Marseille to Oran. Few took civilian passengers. Most had been taken over for military transport. Finally they found one that would take them.

"How does it work?" Licht asked the clerk at the window. "Are there any document checks before boarding?"

"Of course," the clerk said. "First there's the control for currency."

"And then?"

"Now and then people from the German or the Italian commission come on board."

Because he didn't want to arouse suspicion, Licht didn't dare ask what kind of check the commissions carried out. But they made provisional arrangements for a crossing to Oran a few weeks later that would take about three days. From there they would have to travel by train to Casablanca. But Licht also intended to go to Perpignan to make one more try for the Spanish visa.

"The ship possibility won't go away," he said. "That route will always remain open."

"Fine," Lofe said. "But let's set ourselves a deadline and not walk around forever in Perpignan."

"No need for that. We already have a time limit, since our exit visas expire on the twenty-third of March. We've got barely a month."

"I'm not going to wait that long," Lofe said. "If I don't get the Spanish visa soon, I'm going by ship."

"You're free to do that. But you may have to travel alone. And be careful that you don't get lost in the desert."

"I don't want to travel alone. I don't want to leave you if it's not absolutely necessary. We've seen everything through together and we should stay together to the end."

"You're a good guy. But you have to think about what's at stake for you. You have your sister here, and what you decide will affect her as well."[12]

---

12. From the documents I've since discovered, Lofe (Lefo), as I indicated above, had not only his sister there, but their mother, Marie Süsser Lefo, and his sister's teenage daughter,

"My sister is independent and self-reliant enough. If necessary, she'll manage alone. But I want to stay with you."

The next day, they took the train together to Perpignan. Before they left, Licht and Lofe, as they'd promised, went to DeFerre's house to get instructions directly from the major.

"I was glad to be of help to you," he said. "What we want in return is completely safe and will, I hope, not sit on your conscience."

"Whatever you want we will do," Licht said, "if it will serve our common purpose."

"Whether it will do much good, I don't know. You're just one of many who are delivering the same news, but until now all our efforts have had no success with our friends across the Channel. Here in Marseille and its environs there sit about eight hundred French pilots who are prepared to help England. Despite all the German checkpoints, we think we could get them to North Africa. But there has to be a plan on how they get farther on. It's therefore vitally important for the British to send somebody here to help organize this thing. You should therefore go to the British consul in Lisbon and tell him what I just told you. Tell him also that we can't wait much longer. We're losing our people. You'd think they'd be happy over there to get our help."

As they left, the major said, "We'll meet again one of these days. You'll then find that France, despite everything, has remained as it has always been, a great nation."

—⁂—

When they met Medingiers in their hotel in Perpignan the next morning, he told them they'd come at the right time. "My friend phoned me yesterday to tell me that a Spanish transit visa has been approved, even for Mr. Licht. How they did that over there, I don't know. Tomorrow or the day after at the latest you can go to the Spanish consulate here and pick them up."

"Now I really have a choice," Licht said after Medingiers left. "What to do? I've heard nothing from Judith. At the ship the Germans may be

---

Liane. It was not unlike my father to omit all mention of dependents—and maybe not unlike a lot of men of his class and time.

waiting for me; the same could happen at the Spanish border at Port-Bou. Which do you think is riskier?"[13]

"That's hard to answer," Lofe said. "I'm going to toss a coin—no, I'm serious!—heads is Spain, tails is the ship to Morocco." He took a five-franc piece from his pocket, tossed and caught it, and laid it on the back of his other hand.

"Spain," he said. "Let that settle all debates. If things go wrong, it's nobody's fault. Nobody made the decision."

"You'll see," Lofe's sister said when she met them that afternoon. "It will go well. Right now we're having a good streak. It's been that way my whole life. Streaks of good luck or bad luck. Like in roulette, where red and black rarely follow each other. Right now we're on red. We can safely play it again."

13. Port-Bou, the Spanish border town, now commonly Portbou, is also the place where in September 1940 the great German-Jewish philosopher Walter Benjamin had committed suicide. He'd been smuggled over the Pyrenees into Spain by the legendary Lisa Fittko, had been arrested by Spanish police, and was on the verge of being sent back to France. The manuscript he was carrying and refused to part with, perhaps his magnum opus, was never found. Fittko, a Jewish émigré from Vienna, had escaped from the camp at Gurs and then, with her husband Hans, led countless treks of refugees through the Pyrenees into Spain. See, e.g., Fittko, *Escape through the Pyrenees* (Evanston, IL: Northwestern University Press, 1991). Working with the Fittkos was one of the ways Fry used to help his clients out of France.

14

Across the Bloodied Spanish Earth

The train made its leisurely way along the shore. They passed the little station at Elne, where they and their fellow internees had been unloaded less than a year before. The station, which had seen so much misfortune and misery, now seemed to be hardly used. Tens of thousands of unhappy men had come through its gates: Spaniards, Germans, Austrians, Poles, Jews, Christians, row upon row, column after column, the old, the young, the crippled, the hungry, passed through this place. Now this homely brick building was sunk in sleep. A cat played on the platform; the station attendant sat on a bench smoking a pipe. When would this Elne ever come back to life? Maybe there'd be new uniforms standing here, German or French or who knew who, and the old horrors would wake to a new life. But maybe in a few years, as Ams had predicted with characteristic irony, there'd be tourist guides here from Cook's and American Express, come to show the warm hospitality with which the French had sheltered its refugees.

In Cerbère they all had to get off to clear French customs and border control, and again there was endless waiting. The agent checking exit visas must have taken a liking to Licht. When he saw Licht's passport he looked at it with astonishment, saluted and wished him bon voyage.

But it was not to be the last French gesture. Licht and the others were now led into a large customs shed, where they underwent a thorough inspection. Each passenger had to undergo a body search. The agents seemed to take pleasure in harassing people one more time. Who, Licht thought, were people like him and his fellow refugees other than a rabble that one wanted to be rid of? And yet the agents had to stay there. They'd show them what for, one more time.

When they were done at last, Licht thought he'd finally come to the moment he had so long dreamed about, the moment when he would cross the Spanish border, the moment that so many others longed for. Where was Judith? Would she ever succeed in coming to the place where he was? So much lay in her way. How could he help her? There was a kind of Chinese wall between them. Soon he'd be on the other side. He had left so much wreckage scattered behind: Germany, Luxembourg, Belgium, France, a business, friends, part of a family. In each he'd left part of his life, his person. Now there was no going back. There was no way of putting the old pieces together, to resurrect the past. Something new had to be built.

The train went through a tunnel, then three minutes later it stopped again: Port-Bou, Spanish customs.

—⁊⁊⁊—

The passengers, German, Belgian, French, Austrian, Polish, American, waited in a long line holding their passports. Licht and Lofe stood well back watching the document inspections in front of them. The Spanish official who took the passports handed them to a young man who carried them into a room across the platform. After about three minutes, he'd return with them and the official would stamp the visas.

"Without doubt," said Licht to Lofe, "there's a Nazi in that room. Of course he can't be seen. The Spanish can't so blatantly show that Gestapo agents are sitting at their borders."

Guides busily attended two groups in the line from Cook's and American Express. They reminded Licht of earlier times, when one traveled for altogether different reasons.

It was clear as Licht and Lofe approached that the Spanish passport agent had no say in anything. He was just a flunky for someone behind the scenes who made the real decisions. The elderly woman ahead of them had just handed over her passport. Licht imagined the guy inside would check it against his list and, not finding her name, hand it back to the runner to be returned to the passenger.

"Look straight ahead," Lofe said to Licht. "Right there is the jail." And so it was: they'd built a cage into the same room. It had an iron door surrounded by bars through which Licht saw a pale face. It was certainly possible, he thought, that he could end up in there. The Gestapo man behind the door could find his name on some list, decide his visa was forged, stand up and say: "Let's take a closer look at this guy. . . ." Then he was shaken from his reverie. "Your passport please," the Spanish agent said. Licht handed it to him. Through Licht's many travels it had lost its brown cover, making it hard to tell from a distance that it was a German passport, but the large "J" on the first page made it clear what the owner was.

Licht and Lofe's passports vanished behind the inner door at the same moment. Lofe was nervous, shifting from one foot to the other: anything that came down on Licht might taint him as well. They were dumb to have stood in the line together. Their Spanish visas looked so similar, had been issued the same day and signed by the same man. If the German doubted the validity of one he would certainly come to doubt the other.

Licht, who spoke a little Spanish, asked the passport agent when the next train left for Barcelona.

"In about an hour," the man replied.

"Then we should have plenty of time?"

"Most of those here won't catch it," the agent said, chuckling. "They'll have to spend the night in a hotel." But just as Licht began to think that the passport examination was taking a lot of time, the young man returned with the documents and the passport man stamped them. They had crossed the Spanish border; but the process was not over, and what followed was sheer theater.

They were directed to a large customs shed, which looked like all the customs sheds on earth. The bags sat on counters, which formed a large square. Inside the square were the customs men who wore the strangest headgear they'd ever seen. Were they hats or helmets? At a distance they resembled Napoleon's tricorne in the paintings of Waterloo. But they were of a different material. It had to be some sort of coated shiny black cardboard. Their uniforms had a similarly antiquated look, but on their hands they wore pure white gloves. Spanish law, Licht was told, did not allow them to reach bare-handed into foreigners' luggage.

A couple of Falangists also stood in the shed. They wore uniform caps shaped like those of the German SS, but red instead of black. And although it was already quite warm on that late winter day, they wore long capes, blue on the outside and red on the inside. As they observed the room, it was clear that they were the real lords of Spain. On their shoulders rested the guilt for a slowly starving nation. One day, in the final reckoning, their people would string them up.

One of the tricornes began to rummage through Licht's things, but it was obvious from his looks that it bored him.

"Nada, nada," Licht said.

"Habla español?"

"Un poco." Licht was proud that he'd been understood.

The luggage inspection was quickly finished. Now came the currency check as each person was called by a sort of servant in yet a different uniform and led to the next floor where the Spanish national bank had established an office.

"What you bring into Spain you may take out again. But no pesetas," the bank clerk told Licht.

Licht declared exactly what he had, bought enough pesetas for what he expected he needed for the remainder of the Spanish part of his trip, and returned to the platform where he found a nearly empty train. Most of the others, who had more luggage, still hadn't cleared customs, meaning they'd have to spend the night. Licht boarded the train nonetheless. He wanted to get to Barcelona soon. The further he was from the border, the better. Lofe's sister came to the train to tell him she and her brother wouldn't make it that day and would meet him at the station in Barcelona the next day.

The train pulled slowly out of the station. Across from Licht sat a Spanish officer. Licht wasn't sure whether the man was a party member or just a soldier. The man smiled at the others in the compartment, huddled back in his seat and soon fell asleep.

The train passed through mountainous country and through a string of sad-looking towns. Often it slowed at construction sites on the tracks, work done mostly, it seemed, by prisoners in tattered clothes—political prisoners, former republicans, communists, liberals, Licht thought—guarded by Falangists. The Falangists were the winners. They could watch the emaciated workers push carts of rock and swing their heavy picks at the side of the roadbed. What pleasure, to be the victors!

As it became darker outside, an official wearing an armband with the Spanish colors came to check passports. Licht showed him his visa.

"Where are you going?" he asked Licht in French.

"Today to Barcelona. Tomorrow to Madrid, and from there to Lisbon."

"Where are you staying in Barcelona?"

"I don't know yet."

"And in Madrid?"

"I don't yet have any idea."

"But you're leaving Spain within three days?"

Licht resisted the impulse to ask whether the man thought he'd stay an hour longer than he had to. "Absolutely," he answered instead.

In the darkening corridor outside stood a couple of people talking in French and watching the passing landscape. Their voices were altogether different from what they were when Licht had seen them at the customs check at the border. They were distinctly more cheerful. They discussed the names of the passing towns, the vegetation, the changing colors in the sky, as if they had once again become ordinary human beings who took pleasure in a train journey. Their shredded wartime existence had again become whole.

—⁂—

In Barcelona, the dimly lit streets swarmed with uniforms. Although most of the others on the ancient bus that took him to his hotel were emigrants like him, the ground under them was a little firmer than it was under him. They had received travel permits from the Germans, and so they could behave quite differently. He had not. He only knew that someone had bought his Spanish visa for him.

The first meal that evening was a remarkable affair. Aside from the fact that it was outrageously expensive and consisted in the main of an exotically named array of dishes, the meat portion was microscopic. Nor was he sure whether the bakery item they served him was supposed to be bread. It looked like a little yellow rock, maybe a brick, which couldn't be cut with a knife. With great force, he managed to break it. It tasted like sawdust. It seemed to him wholly improbable that a whole population could nourish itself with this "bread."

The hotel dining room, proudly decorated in the style of the early twentieth century, was full of foreigners speaking every language on earth other than Spanish, which was the only language the waiters spoke. But traditional courtesies hadn't been forgotten. Here fascism had apparently taken a deferential turn. There were no fascist salutes. The only reminder was a large oil painting of the Caudillo in full uniform hanging on the wall.

Licht would have liked to see the city by night. But he feared that he would be checked by one or another patrol, and so he went to bed.

—∞—

The next morning, on the way to the station to meet the Lofes, Licht stopped to buy their tickets to Madrid at Cook's, where he was told that nothing was available for the next five days. At best they could travel in a coach sitting up. He then showed the man a five-dollar bill and told him he was confident that he could find something for this evening.

"If not this evening," the man said, "then tomorrow morning."

"I'll be forever grateful," Licht said, and, with a friendly wink, handed him the bill.

As soon as he returned to the hotel, Cook's was on the phone.

"I have the honor," said the agent, "to tell you that you have reservations for tomorrow morning."

Licht was happy that they could continue on so soon. Because there were only two daily trains from Barcelona to Madrid, one in the morning and one in the evening, they were quickly booked, forcing many to spend up to a week in Barcelona. Seats for the twelve-hour trip between Spain's two largest cities were always hard to get.

There was no other way to go. There were virtually no cars. Taxis in Madrid and Barcelona were available only at certain hours. One saw none at all before eight in the morning or after specified times in the evening. And they were so expensive that only party bigwigs and big business people could afford them.

And, not surprisingly, the train to Madrid the next morning was badly overcrowded. But Cook's had reserved a compartment for Licht and the Lofes with enough space that they could travel in comfort.

—∞—

It was dark when they reached Madrid, a city that would be hard to describe to anyone used to a minimum of civilized life. Outside the station Licht and the Lofes were so engulfed by a horde of children that they could hardly go either forward or backward. All said the same thing: "Please give me a coin. I'm hungry." Their hands tugged coats, sleeves, whatever they could grab. In the weak light they looked like shadows from the underworld. Despite the cold, most wore almost nothing. Some had clothing made from sacks. Many were barefoot; their skin looked like yellow clay.

Not more than five meters away stood the Falangists. They seemed to see nothing of what was going on. There were still a few taxis, one of which took Licht and the Lofes to a quiet street where it stopped in front of a nondescript building.[1] Nobody came out, and they had to carry their own luggage inside. Inside a dark entryway they found a man who appeared to be the manager.

"If you don't have a reservation," he said, "we have no room."

For Licht, that began a familiar routine, but here he only needed a few pesetas, not five dollars, to get a set of lovely rooms.

When they walked around town the next morning, the impression of the previous night became even more powerful. Here the tinder was lying about in great heaps. Only a spark might start the shooting. It was hard to believe that even the heavily armed Falangists could long keep this poor, volatile mass fenced in. It was a mystery that people could tolerate these conditions for many days. Literally thousands of women and children stood, sat or lay begging on the cold streets. Many looked like they hadn't had anything decent to eat for weeks. Their eyes had become those of animals. Their scraggly hair hung down over their shoulders. They were blue with cold but they completely dominated the streets. Occasionally two or three Falangists, their rifles strapped to their backs, their faces closed, would step through them as if they didn't belong to this at all.

---

1. Who picked the place, or had the address, I never learned.

But what made the picture more terrible was the contrast. Now and then a grand car would pull up to a luxury shop—a jeweler, a dressmaker, a furrier—and an elegant woman, dressed in furs and covered with jewelry, would emerge from the car. She would glance neither left nor right as she walked into the store. As she stepped through, none of the begging children would dare ask for anything. It was foreigners they were beseeching. The Falangists protected the rich Spaniards. No beggar was allowed to approach them.

In a market hall, where everything the heart desired was on the shelves, but where there were few buyers, Licht, Lofe and his sister encountered a Spanish lawyer Licht had known before the war. How was it, he asked him, that almost everything was available but that there were so many hungry people?

"It's simple," he explained. "We ration things by letting them become so expensive that we need no ration cards and no regulations, and everything remains in good order. When ham costs twenty-five pesetas, only very few can afford it, and so for us the whole problem is solved."[2]

—⁂—

When they returned to the hotel, Lofe's sister, intending to buy a newspaper on the way in, found that her purse was gone. As she rummaged around in her pocketbook, she nearly fainted when she found that her passport was also missing.[3] The visas she had obtained with so much effort and expense were lost. She and her daughter were stuck in Madrid. Lofe had a fit of rage. "Haven't I told you a hundred times?" he shouted. "You should always keep your pocketbook under your arm. Instead you hang it over your shoulder because it looks smarter. Now everything is finished. I don't know what we're to do." He was on the verge of crying.

His sister was white as a sheet.

2. In 1941, the exchange rate was roughly ten or eleven pesetas to the dollar. Twenty-five pesetas must have been more than a tenth of a week's wages in a well-paying job.

3. This was an era when a parent and a minor normally traveled on a single passport. I only recently got confirmation of the story of the stolen passport when I discovered a little autobiographical sketch Liane Kayser Gutman, Lefo's sister's daughter, had written in 1990 for an unpublished "Collection of Memoirs by Jewish Survivors of Nazi Persecution from Mannheim, Germany." She was fourteen or fifteen when they were all in Madrid.

"Calm down" Licht said. "It's too late now to quarrel about it. The first thing to do is try to get the passports back. Let's go see the manager," who, since he got those pesetas the evening before, had treated them as valued guests.

"What nationality is the lady?" he asked when they told him the story. "She had a German passport."

"That's excellent. It gives her a ninety-five percent chance of getting it back. With an American passport it would be nearly impossible."

Licht asked for an explanation.

"As you may have seen, there's considerable poverty here. To make a little money people have devised all possible—shall we say—means. So, for example, they steal a passport—maybe better say, they borrow a passport. When you have a generous reward in the paper, they bring it back." The war made American and English passports much more valuable.

"What a nice racket," Licht said. "So how do we proceed?"

"You run a classified in the paper which says something like, "Lost passport. German lady, who during a walk on the lovely streets of Madrid lost her passport, kindly requests anyone who finds it to bring it back to hotel X for a generous reward.'"

"And then?"

"Then you wait."

Lofe went immediately to place the newspaper announcement and then to the German consulate to apply for a new passport.

"It's an old trick," the official at the consulate told him. "It happens here almost every week. But if you have a birth certificate and a certificate of home residency and we have nothing in our records that would prevent it, I can issue you a new one. Come back tomorrow morning with the necessary documents. Of course I can't do anything about the Portuguese and the American visas. But I imagine that their consulates here, if you tell them the situation, could handle it quickly."

The next morning, two hours after the ad appeared, a well-dressed man appeared at the hotel to say that he had found the passport at the entrance to his building. He assumed that this was the passport that was lost. He wasn't coming for the reward, he said.

The hotel manager conducted the negotiations.

"It's fortunate," the manager said, "that the document was found by someone as thoughtful as you who would make the effort to bring it back himself. It's lucky that these papers would fall into the hands of a person as honest as yourself."

"I regarded it as my civic duty," the man answered, "to hurry here this morning to return it to someone who must surely be most worried."

"I hardly know how in the name of my guests I can thank you. I hope I won't hurt your feelings if I offer you a ridiculously small gift for this great service."

"Nothing is further from my mind than to accept any kind of payment for such a service. But I don't want to offend your guests, who are also the guests of this country, by spurning what I would regard as a souvenir from such generous people."

With a bow, the manager handed the man a sealed envelope containing one hundred fifty pesetas. He could never have risked just handing the money over without a cover. Without opening the envelope, which would also have been a terrible breach of form, the man stuck it in his pocket.

"I would have liked," he said, "to have wished the lady all good fortune. Could I bid your grace to pass on to the lady my most sincere respects?"

They both bowed and, with that, the deal was done.

That evening Licht and the Lofes left for Lisbon. Cook's had gotten them a compartment that had been reserved for the police, and so under the protection of the two Spanish secret policemen with whom they shared the compartment, they rode into the night of Portugal.

15

Lisbon, Where the Lights Are On

Anyone who came to Lisbon from fascist prisons—or from Europe's pillaged, hungry occupied countries—was struck by so many powerful impressions that it became impossible to take them all in at once. Many little things were so striking that they immobilized those who saw them: the appetizing displays in the richly stocked food shop windows, the menus in the restaurants, the ability to openly buy dollars and other foreign currencies, the freedom to walk the streets and public squares with relatively little fear of the police, the brightly lit streets. In the midst of that, more ordinary things weren't as obvious and often went unnoticed. Many people were well dressed; they moved freely without lowering their heads between hunched shoulders. There were not as many uniforms on the streets. At first, many didn't even notice that.

When they arrived, it took some doing for Licht and the Lofes to find rooms. Everything was crowded. Lisbon was another catch-basin for European refugees. The hotels imposed their own terms: rooms were only available for those also agreeing to full board. And compared to France, they were expensive—extremely expensive compared to Spain. But with a room came real rest and a chance to begin to enjoy things.

Lisbon 1941, the Rossio at night, where hundreds of émigrés came to sit at the cafes.
Horácio Novais. FCG-Art library.

In Lisbon, even in late winter, the sun was shining, there was the dark sea; the things that had threatened to swallow them up lay behind them.

Licht and the Lofes put most of their bags in the left-luggage at the station so they could get out on the wide avenues as fast as possible, to be among real people, and at last walk around to show that they, too, were free people. "See? I did it! I'm one like you."

And they were almost speechless as they took their first evening walk. They stood before food shop windows and began to calculate the prices in French francs and found everything fearfully expensive. If they calculated the price in American dollars, however, it all appeared to be much cheaper. But what was most astounding was that it was available at all: that one could go into a store and say, "This cheese isn't ripe enough, that sausage not smoked enough; no, I want *milk* chocolate"—that was all so fantastic as to seem unreal. But for Licht, it was also the old Europe.

Slowly they wandered down toward the harbor. Even on this first evening, they encountered some familiar faces. A few former comrades from Saint-Cyprien greeted them. Some they hardly recognized. They had regained weight; their skin no longer sagged, their clothes fit. Sometimes their welcome for the new arrivals was a little condescending, as if they were experienced old-timers. Licht and Lofe's pockets were crammed with addresses. When some asked about their plans for the journey to America—what they were going to do about getting a ship—Licht shook them off.

"For now leave me be with all that," he said to one man. "Today I don't want to think about that. I want to have a good dinner. Then I want to sit outside a café, buy a nice bar of chocolate, get an English paper, and go to bed."

—⁓—

Licht went days without doing anything serious. He wanted to stay as long as possible, maybe long enough that Judith would catch up with him. He had time before his visa expired. Why should he make himself crazy these first weeks? Like many others, he would go at noon to the Rossio, Lisbon's great plaza, where hundreds of people, many of them refugees, came every day to sit at the cafés.

Nonetheless, many had visa troubles. The greatly insufficient number of available ship bookings jeopardized many whose visas were expiring, and so the consulates, the American consulate most of all, were besieged, as they were in most of Europe's other major cities. Many had come with forged visas and other invalid documents that they now had to try to replace with valid ones.

Licht had gone to the British embassy shortly after his arrival to honor his commitment to the French major in Marseille. He had tried to make clear how urgent it was for the British to do something to bring out the eight hundred French pilots waiting in and around Marseille, men who were ready to help. The consular official who met Licht had taken notes. He said he'd immediately pass the message on and would arrange to get someone to Marseille to organize transport for the French fliers. But when Licht went again later to follow up, nothing had happened. It was too complicated, he was told. Maybe, Licht thought, they'd tried and failed and just didn't want to admit it. Maybe they had bigger problems.[1]

1. As indeed they did, particularly in North Africa, where the British were being driven back by Gen. Erwin Rommel's tanks.

Licht was momentarily shaken out of his lethargy when rumors circulated that the Germans were on the verge of marching into Spain. It was said that Rudolf Hess, Hitler's deputy in the Nazi Party, had been to see Franco, that trains couldn't get through to Madrid, and that major troop movements were under way. And as Licht, accompanied by acquaintances, walked through the great Rossio square late one night, they encountered an anxious crowd that had heard the "news" that the Germans had crossed the Spanish frontier. Licht and his companions went to the offices of a Lisbon newspaper, where no one knew anything. That night he could hardly sleep. What would happen to Judith? What if the Germans caught up with him? For the first time since his arrival the need to plan his departure, something he'd driven to the back of his mind, became urgent.[2]

The next day the rumors turned out to be false, and the urgency faded with them. But the deadline for confirming the berths that Licht had reserved was fast approaching without any sign that Judith was on the way. Her last letter was discouraging. She pleaded with Licht to wait, that some travel possibilities had come to naught. And Peter had been sick. Between the lines Licht sensed how depressed Judith must be.

The Lofes sailed for America in April on the *Nyassa*, the same ship on which the Lichts were to sail in June. Licht had wished until the last moment that they might make this last trip together as well. He had even thought of abandoning the dream that Judith would arrive in Lisbon on time, and instead try to go with Lofe. But as he reread her letters, he knew he couldn't do that.

"Whatever else happens," he told Lofe as they parted at the ship, "I'm determined to wait for Judith. The only thing that would change that would be an imminent German invasion or my impending arrest here."[3]

---

2. There had in fact been a published report that Hess had flown to Madrid with an "urgent request" from Hitler asking Franco to join the Axis and let German troops march through Spain to attack Gibraltar. "Hitler Plea to Franco Reported," *New York Times*, April 21, 1941. On May 10, 1941, not long after the rumors that Licht apparently heard in Lisbon, Hess was flying to Scotland with his enigmatic offering of a peace deal with England.

3. According to ship manifests and US immigration records, Lefo, accompanied by his mother, sister, and her fifteen-year-old daughter, Liane, sailed in April on the *Nyassa*, the same ship on which we were to sail in June. They were briefly detained at Ellis Island

—⚌—

The days that followed ran along with an eerie sameness. Now and then Licht went to Estoril, lay in the sun in a deckchair, and drank port wine until the beach was spinning, the ocean one large blue wave. One day he didn't waken until evening. Later he'd go to the casino, play a little roulette, sit at the bar among Nazi agents, American consular officials, and Portuguese coquettes, drinking whiskey and soda, and then, together with friends, take a taxi back to Lisbon.

It was a letter from Judith, saying that she was preparing to leave and that he could count on her being in Lisbon between May 15 and May 30, that brought him back to reality and restored his sense of purpose. He had no idea how she intended to make the trip. Nor could he try to advise her. The mail was far too slow and insecure. No one knew whether a letter would take a week or three weeks, or whether it would arrive at all, or who might read it.

That same evening, when Licht returned to the room in the Rua Sta. Marta where he'd been living for a couple of weeks, he found a summons from the police. He had no idea what it was about, but it worried him.

When he went to inquire early the following morning, he was told that he had until May 20 to leave the country. Otherwise he would be jailed. Had he gotten such an ultimatum elsewhere he would have been frightened to death. Here in Lisbon, it was less serious. He would get an extension if necessary, and maybe Judith would arrive soon enough that he wouldn't need it.

But his equanimity was soon shaken.

"Have you heard?" asked an acquaintance at the café where he usually went for his morning aperitif. "They've arrested Duclos."

"For what?"

"His residence permit had expired. Despite his good connections, they refused him an extension. This morning two officers came and got him and took him off to jail."[4]

---

when they arrived on April 25 and within two weeks went on to Mexico, where Lefo had an export business after the war. My father's story says nothing about Lofe's mother.

4. Portugal's practices on visa extensions were always uncertain, teetering on the one hand between tight enforcement of deadlines, resulting from fear of communists and backlash against the thousands of refugees who had collected in Lisbon and neighboring

"Damn. That could happen to me on May 21."

"Take my advice, leave before then. I hear the *Guinea* sails on the twentieth. There's still space if you pay enough. Don't wait for your wife. What good would it be if she arrived and you were sitting in prison?"

At that moment Licht resolved that he would sail on that ship regardless of circumstances and went immediately to a ticket scalper to reserve passage for all three of them. He couldn't risk jail in Portugal. Judith would understand.

Now began the race between the ship's sailing date and Judith's arrival. His nerves would be severely tested; for days he heard nothing from Judith—no letter, no telegram, nothing. Sometimes he imagined that was a good sign. Sometimes he decided that her silence boded the worst: maybe her arrest in France, maybe something even worse. Lisbon began to irritate him. He came to hate the endless sun. People came to seem dirty: they spit; the women were fat; the food tasted of rancid oil. He was sick of Portugal.[5]

Relief came one morning in a telegram from Marseille. "Arrived safely. Please telephone or telegraph Hotel Terminus Marseille."

The next day another telegram arrived asking him to get her and Peter a Portuguese visa as fast as possible and to wire the Portuguese consul in Marseille when he got clearance for it. Fortunately, among his many acquaintances in Portugal, Licht had met a woman who had some contacts at the police.

"I can get it for you within eight days," she said.

---

coastal communities, and on the other hand exhibiting the flexibility demanded by the British, who were funneling escaped war prisoners and downed fliers through Lisbon and back to England. Lisbon, in Arthur Koestler's words, had become "the bottle-neck on Europe." Many of those refugees were described in a *New York Times* report as destitute, "one chapter in [the] human tragedy that has been brought about by the new political regimes on the European continent." "Lisbon's Refugees Now Put at 8,000," *NYT*, Dec. 15, 1940. The reporter of the *Times* story was James B. Reston, who, as managing editor thirty years later, would interview me for a job at the *Times*, which I foolishly declined.

5. Perhaps the best portrait of Lisbon was Erich Maria Remarque's novel *The Night in Lisbon* (New York: Harcourt Brace, 1961). Lisbon, he wrote, "was the gate to America. If you couldn't reach it you were lost, condemned to bleed away in a jungle of consulates, police stations and government offices, where visas were refused and work and residence permits unobtainable, a jungle of internment camps, bureaucratic red tape, loneliness, homesickness, and withering universal indifference."

"That won't help," Licht said. "I can probably get it myself in five days. I come to you because I know that you are able to do it so that a telegram can go off to the consul in Marseille this evening."

"The police here these days are completely crazy. I'll do what I can."

"I know your fee," he replied. "I'll pay twice what you usually ask if you meet me this evening, say at six, and tell me it's all settled."

"Okay," she said. "I'll try."

—⁓—

She arrived promptly at six at the café where Licht was waiting. He tried to discern from her face what she would have to say, but couldn't tell. On the way in she stopped to talk excitedly to another woman. Then she stood alone in the middle of the room for a moment. At last she approached Licht.

"The telegram," she said, "has just gone out."

"Really?" Licht asked. He was incredulous. "It all worked?"

"I myself accompanied the official who took it to the post office. I stood next to him at the window from where he dispatched it. But it was no easy thing. I think the chief himself signed the clearance without knowing what it really was. It was in a stack of papers. My friend shoved this into the stack he was signing. I watched from the next room. I was scared to death when he started reading, but finally everything went well. Your wife can travel tomorrow or the day after."[6]

She looked at Licht. "I really have a great job," she said. "I can make money and make other people happy. I see more disappointed faces than happy ones. Still, one happy face compensates for a hundred others. You're happy?"

"I don't know what to say. It all still seems so improbable. Now Judith and Peter will be here on time so we can sail together on the twentieth."

"Actually, I have another good piece of news. The sailing date of that ship has been delayed. I just heard it. I assume that pleases you." Licht then immediately sent Judith a telegram to give her the news.

---

6. As in the case of Hans Licht's residence permit for Les Martys, shoving papers into stacks of other documents before bored bureaucrats in those years was probably a common way of getting something stamped or signed that might have caused difficulty had it been properly examined.

16

Crossing the Lines Again

A s soon as my mother returned from southern France she began to
make the rounds in Belgium for the documents we would need
for our trip to America—the American consulate, the Portuguese, the
German commission, in hopes of getting a travel permit to let us get
into northern France—even as my father was in pursuit of documents
in southern France. The American quotas made it virtually impossible
for anyone from Germany to immigrate directly to the United States,
even with the help of my American grandmother. Instead we got immigration visas to Mexico, obtained by circuitous routes I've long
forgotten, if I ever knew. Those visas, after struggles with a sequence
of US consular bureaucracies—and probably a hefty dose of the pervasive State Department anti-Semitism of that era—were ultimately
sufficient to secure US transit visas (changed to visitor's visas after we
got to the United States; by 1947, six years after we arrived, our number
finally came up and we were able to formally "immigrate"—by way of
Montreal—and start the clock on the naturalization process).

We had planned to travel with Piccard (Pellmans) in February, but I got the flu and the trip was postponed. Eventually we left early in May, almost a year to the day after the beginning of our first attempt to escape from the Germans, and just six months (as I learned much later) before the Nazis ordered all Jewish children in Belgium barred from the public schools. I knew that, other than the American transit visa, we would be setting out without documents. We were to travel with "Harry," a man that Jean Piccard, who for some reason couldn't take us, had recommended. Piccard, the smuggler who had found the organization that got my mother to southern France the year before, was a man whose urbanity and charm, when I met him later in his villa on the French coast near Bordeaux, earned him something better than such a scruffy description. But within hours after we left the station in Brussels everything went badly wrong.

My grandmother refused to go with us. She said she was too old, tired, and infirm for the journey and would stay (as I understood it) in the apartment in Brussels, a decision that can hardly be said to have displeased me. Had she gone, it seemed to me, she would have made us even more vulnerable to the hazards of a trip that even I knew would be risky enough. By then I had stricken my mother from my list of women whose competence I distrusted—she had gained a great deal of new authority in my eyes. I had seen her cope so well, first through the disasters at Boulogne, then through a whole year of occupation— and through the perils of her trip to get my father out of Saint-Cyprien, about which I still knew little—that she had, both through necessity and merit, become both father and mother.

But not long into the trip, my confidence was shaken by her decision once again to bring along another anchor of vulnerability, a young woman my mother was to call *"Die Kleine Reinemann,"* the little Reinemann (much later I learned her first name, Marianne). The woman, whose husband, Heinz, was also a prisoner at Saint-Cyprien, seemed so flustered, nervous, and seemingly incompetent that I resented her from the first moment—with, it turned out, good intuitive reasons. Against all warnings of the danger and unbeknownst to anyone else in Harry's group, the little Reinemann had crammed the corners of her suitcase with every piece of jewelry and silver imaginable, all of it subject to heavy customs controls, German and French. But her Bavarian accent charmed my mother. And Reinemann's very nervousness seemed to give my mother confidence.

I didn't understand the plans for the trip, but since they collapsed almost immediately it didn't make much difference. Our group, Harry's group, was scattered through the train to Paris. But in Lille, the very first baggage checkpoint on the trip, the French customs people, accompanied by Gestapo, found Reinemann's valuables—it was hard not to find the stuff. And, since my mother and I shared a compartment with her, they yanked us all off the train, which, as they strip-searched the women and went through every bag and every pocket, and while we sat anxiously hoping they'd hurry, left Lille without us. It was the realization of every traveler's nightmare of that time.

I recall sitting in a little office off the platform and, through the window, watching the train, with the rest of our group, with the smugglers, with God knows what hopes, slowly beginning to move down the track and, as it moved ever faster, disappear out of view. There had probably never been a time in my life, nor, I think, would there ever be another, when I felt as forlorn.

Eventually they detained only Reinemann. I don't recall ever seeing her again. How my mother and I managed to be allowed to continue— escaped what, with hindsight, now appears to have been almost inevitable—neither of us ever fully understood. They had a matron strip-search the women, and then they not only searched but prepared to cut open my mother's enormous yellow leather handbag into the bottom of which she had sewn those American dollars. She later said that it was at that point that she panicked and, though I don't recall it, began to scream at them to cut it open, something which they then didn't bother to do. But it was a near thing. How many thousands of others were hauled off trains by men in uniform and never reached their intended destinations?

We got another train and spent that night in a little pension in the town of Albert, a place some twenty miles northeast of Amiens. Since I knew we had to get to Paris—and then far beyond to an unspecified

place I only understood as being in southern France—the Midi—
Albert, which then struck me as a forlorn, godforsaken place, was a
dreadful letdown, somehow symbolizing our failing journey.

My mother, who had traveled to southern France and back in the
year before, both times by less than legal means, seemed to have discovered by some means that there was a German checkpoint outside
Amiens for which we had no papers and which must somehow be cir-
cumvented. Albert was the last or next-to-last stop short of it. Whether
she also knew that in Albert she might get help I've never learned, but
as soon as we arrived, she went out for what she said was "information." After the failed flight that ended in Boulogne the year before,
I was used to unexpected stops in unlikely places, but that hardly as-
suaged my anxiety and confusion about voluntarily leaving a train that
was going on, and instead stopping in a place totally devoid of interest
or romance. On trips since, waiting in a service station somewhere
for a car to be repaired or sitting on the tarmac in some airport until a
spare part was brought to an airliner, I've had the same sense of frus-
tration and inadequacy—the world going on, while one waited in an
absurd place on the side of the road.

The next day we boarded a train again, this time in the company—
indeed, apparently in the charge—of an elderly man, what the French
call a *passeur*, who as soon as the train began to move from the station
asked my mother for what I think was two hundred French francs,
but may have been more, and after she gave it to him left the two of
us alone in the compartment. I have no idea how she found him in
Albert—maybe through the landlady of the pension where we stayed.
Being close to the German checkpoint in Amiens, Albert had probably
grown a small cottage industry of smugglers, but I doubt my mother
knew precisely how it was all supposed to work. There wasn't much
conversation between us about such things, sometimes because there
wasn't time—often, I suppose, because it was safer not to talk. One
quickly became habituated to restricted conversation and communica-
tion by the fewest and briefest signals.

As the train slowed on the outskirts of Amiens, the man returned.
When it came to a stop in the railroad yard outside the station, he
opened the compartment door, got down with our two suitcases,

handed us off the train, and hustled us behind some freight cars on an adjacent track. I still recall the anxiety I felt that, once again, a train was slowing, actually stopping where it had no business stopping. Then I realized that the train had been stopped momentarily for our benefit, with the help of the francs and a cooperative engineer who, like the elderly man from Albert, seemed to combine a little patriotism—a tweaking of the Nazis' noses—with a little commerce. I think the smuggler asked for five hundred or maybe a thousand francs for his services. My mother gave him a little more.

As soon as we were down, the train proceeded on its way to the station, to the platform checkpoint for which we had no documents. Meanwhile, my mother, our smuggler, and I tripped over the tracks through the train yard, through a hole in a fence, and into the city whence, now safely past the checkpoint, we doubled back to the station and on to another train. I didn't realize until many years later what a lovely city Amiens, with its great cathedral, really was. In 1941, it was just another place to get through.

—⁂—

Paris, where we spent a day or two, was a confusing blur, a place to which I had desperately wanted to get the year before, but which turned out to be superbly indifferent, if not hostile, to our arrival. That the Germans now occupied it had not totally deflated the importance it had gained in my mind in 1940, when we never reached it. It's hard to imagine what I now expected—a stay in some grand hotel, elegant food served in covered silver dishes, bright lights, a welcome commensurate with the desire and effort to get there (here again, I missed my father's cosmopolitan, seigniorial presence). After a year in Nazi-occupied Brussels, we had become accustomed to the German uniforms, the swastika on the public buildings, the enforced darkness of the blackout, the cautious silences. For us there were no grand hotels, just another cheap room and some fiddling with money to get served in restaurants without French ration stamps.

To get to our hotel from the station we rode the Métro—my first ride on a subway—where I promptly got the rucksack on my back caught in the closing automatic doors of the crowded train. We must have looked like foreigners from a mile away. Although it took only a moment for someone to force the doors back and free me, I panicked trying to free myself. Somehow, I later realized, that brief moment encapsulated all the terrors of the whole year; the fear of being found out, the fear of again being hauled off a train, the shadow of the camps. The fear of the consequences of calling attention to myself in a strange place remained with me for the rest of the trip. In a thousand different ways you learned to make yourself inconspicuous. When you had no documents, you worked at it even harder.

There were, as I recall, further inquiries at consulates in Paris about papers—visas for Spain, for Portugal, an exit permit from France— though apparently with only limited success, since we would have to do much of it again in Marseille. (Recently I learned that we had re- ceived our US transit visa from the consulate in Brussels in March, but with the exception of the Portuguese visas that my father bought for us in Lisbon, I never learned what my mother did to get the rest. Nor did I ever learn whether my mother's passport, left behind by Lisieux on her trip south the previous year, was returned or, more likely, with what it was replaced).[1]

In Paris one night there was a brief Allied air raid, the warning si- rens, some distant explosions, during the course of which I recall peo- ple leaning out of their darkened second- and third-story windows and applauding. But maybe that was only a dream or my imagination. If it did happen, it was the only sign for me at that time that this city and I had anything in common or that I in any way had any claim upon it.

—⁂—

One of the lasting images of that journey was something altogether trivial: the dim greenish glow of the phosphorescent numerals on our little folding alarm clock in Verdelais during the night before our planned attempt at crossing the Line of Demarcation. The clock said 2:45. We were to rise at three, but I had been awake most of the

1. My father was obviously traveling on his original German passport. His immigra- tion listing on our arrival in the United States was "Israel Otto Schrag." But my mother was Judith Haas Schrag, no "Sara," which the Nazis added to all documents issued to Jewish women.

night—perhaps my mother had been too—looking at the dial of the clock that stood on the nightstand between our beds in the house where another *passeur*, also an elderly man, had put us up. At one point we talked and I sensed her anxiety. That morning, before dawn, we were to cross on foot from occupied into Vichy France. We knew it would be the most dangerous part of this trip.

"Everything will be all right," I said, although I couldn't have known more than a part of what might befall us and certainly had no idea of whether or not we'd make it. I knew about the patrolling German soldiers and about the dogs they were supposed to have; and I had heard about the concentration camps, but no one could have imagined everything that meant or would eventually come to mean.[2] My mother and I had, by then, grown quite close, probably not altogether as parent and child but as fellow travelers through a common danger and sharers of a common set of experiences that, by now, dated back a year. Were the women's disabilities I had disdained in her—her inability to drive, what had seemed her unworldliness and studied impracticality—were those disabilities a stock part played by, or maybe imposed on, bourgeois women of that time and culture for the men around them? At that moment probably more than any other I respected, loved, and trusted her.

There had been a brief stop a day earlier at the seaside town of Arcachon near Bordeaux. This time there was even a taxi ride—to a magnificent house overlooking the beach and the Atlantic, where we found Jean Piccard, the smuggler in whose company we might under other circumstances have made this journey. He had obviously been doing well in the smuggling trade—or did he have other sources of income? My mother must have had an address, though how she had ever found him in the first place, or how she found the man in Albert, I never learned. But that knowledge also raised my mother's stature in my eyes. She, too, possessed mysteries I knew little of.

Piccard said he couldn't take us on; they were watching him, he said—after the war I heard somewhere that he'd been caught and ex-

---

2. It was at the Wannsee Conference in January 1942, some eight months later, that the Nazis formally adopted their policy of mass murder in the gas chambers.

Sign, in German and French, warning that anyone crossing the
Line of Demarcation who ignores an order to stop would be shot.
We never saw any such sign, but I'm certain my mother
knew the risks when we crossed it in 1941.

Etcomp.

ecuted[3]—but he had a name and an address of someone in Verdelais,
a town maybe fifty kilometers from Bordeaux and quite near the Line
of Demarcation. It was from there that the crucial crossing would have
to be made. Theoretically, in those first two and a half years after the
French defeat, everything south of that line was still controlled by the
French, though that would be further compromised after the American landings in North Africa in 1942, when the Germans occupied
the rest of France. But from early on, Vichy had collaborated with the
Germans, turning over people on the Nazi wanted lists, using its own
police to meet the Nazis' execution quotas, and delivering tens of thousands of Jews for shipment to the camps of the East. Long before the
defeat in 1940, France had been suffused with its own deep streak of
anti-Semitism and xenophobia.

3. My father's story suggested that Piccard was a member of the French resistance, and
not just a smuggler.

We had no papers to cross the line. It was only in the hours after we arrived in Arcachon that I learned that we would be crossing at night, on foot. And so that afternoon, after we had seen Piccard, we took a taxi back to Bordeaux, boarded a bus, and arrived in what was, at best, a hamlet at the end of the road. The Michelin now says that Verdelais, on the AutoRoute up the Garonne toward Toulouse, has some eight hundred inhabitants, but in those days it seemed not to have half that number. There was no highway then, only the narrow paved road that turned to dirt in the middle of town.

At four-thirty the next morning we were at the end of the street, waiting in the shadow of a building with a half dozen others, listening for sounds, looking for motion between the houses in the half-moonlight.

Our smuggler marched us single file through the plowed fields beyond the town, usually along rows of trees and hedges, and then into the woods. In summer camp a few years later we would be taken by some older boys on what was called a snipe hunt and left on a narrow strip of ground in the middle of a swamp through most of a long and terrifying night. The two sensations, probably never very different, have long since fused in my mind, though probably the night in the swamp was the more terrible for lack of a guide. Our emotional repertoire is really not that great.

It was sometimes difficult to keep up, especially across the open fields, where we were urged to hurry. In addition to my knapsack I carried the same black leather suitcase I had carried through northern France the year before. The suitcase had become part of us; we had sat on it in waiting rooms and had pushed it in and out of countless train compartments. But it was still large and heavy for me, and sometimes someone, to hurry me along, would help me carry it through the fields.

Despite the pace, for most of the walk the damp chill seemed to be more pronounced than the fear. When at last we left the narrow trail and marched, still single file, into the wood, I knew what was causing me to shiver. The pace had become more deliberate—sometimes the figure who led us would stop to listen. Once, not too far in the distance, I heard the yapping of dogs and we were signaled to lie flat on the damp ground. Much later my mother recalled the sound of voices speaking in German. I only recall the dogs and the moon that moved behind the broken clouds above us, and then the first amber light of dawn before us.

At last we reached a high cyclone fence topped, I think, with barbed wire and, as we moved alongside it through the shrubbery, we came to a gap where two sections of the fence did not quite meet. It was through that gap that we crossed from occupied into unoccupied France—a short step, single file, that seemed to have no more significance than it had drama. I had expected a fence that looked precisely like that fence, and so, when I saw it, I assumed it wasn't the place I had waited for so long. Real places never looked like one imagined them. The event seemed unworthy of the fear I had felt that whole night. Now that we had reached and crossed it, it was a letdown.

Our guide led us through a wood to another road, where he left us. From there, a few kilometers further on, we would come to the town of Saint-Pierre (probably Saint-Pierre d'Aurillac, which is about five kilometers from Verdelais)—I only remember Pierre, my name then, without the Saint—and to a little whistle-stop station where we would get a slow, rickety train later that morning that took us to another train that would take us, after a very long day's journey, to Marseille. We were all worried that someone would stop and question us as we walked into Saint-Pierre, but apparently strangers with luggage walked out of the woods into Saint-Pierre almost every day. By the time we got there, I was an illegal immigrant at least three times over.

—⁓—

I recall almost nothing about Marseille, or how long we were there, or whether we also shuttled to Perpignan in our chase for documents. Maybe Piccard had given my mother the name of another hotel or pension where, using his name, we could stay without questions being asked or *fiches* of registration being delivered to the police. Maybe, as I thought about it much later, he had connected us with a whole network of smugglers, but I knew nothing of that. We did know that my father had gotten to Lisbon many weeks before and that we had to get to him before the clock on his various documents ran out.

We made the rounds of consulates and probably some visits to people who could provide less legitimate documents. My father had managed to get us the Portuguese visa, which was a requirement for the Spanish visa. And then we required the exit visa from France. Whether we got those from the consulates and prefectures—and if so by what means or where—or whether we traveled with complete forgeries I probably never knew. And always, of course, whenever one sought papers by less than official means there was the risk that the seller was either a scammer or an informer. If one got cheated, there was nowhere to go to get justice or compensation, nor could one be sure that the document one bought, real or forged, or sometimes maybe real and then forged, looked genuine enough. Neither the Vichy government nor the Gestapo nor the Falange took complaints from Jews who'd been defrauded.

But other than the rounds we made in Marseille, I recall little until we got to the train station in Madrid. There we were suddenly engulfed by a sea of aggressive beggars, some of them wretched women in ragged clothes, but mostly children, many of them barefoot, one hand grabbing our arms, our clothes, our legs, the other reaching up in supplication. It was then two years since the end of the Spanish Civil War, and the damage—in the places we had passed on the train, in the ruined buildings, and in the human wreckage around us—was staggering. But this mass of miserable people was both the most frightening and the most moving of all. And of course all appeasing gestures for the beggars engulfing us in the station, the gift of a coin or a piece of chocolate, only fired others' desperate aggression.

When we had finally waded through that mass of humanity and my mother went to buy some pesetas, she discovered that her purse was gone from her big handbag. In the ensuing panic, we found a secure bench somewhere to survey the damage. Did she still have her documents? If they were gone we would be stranded. What about the dollars in the bottom of the handbag? I immediately noticed the long slit that had been cut, probably with a razor, in the end of her bag—which was obviously how her purse was taken. But the documents and the dollars were still there.

Even to my untrained young eyes, the contrasts in Madrid were astonishing. For anyone with money, everything could be had in Madrid, for those without, as we had already seen, there was very little. The police, the Guardia Civil in their shiny black tricorne hats, the uniformed Falangists, who seemed to be everywhere, had blatantly divided the two worlds: some places swarmed with mendicants; in others there were none. But for those like us, who had come from countries where everything was scarce and rationed, it was a chance to fill up—as my mother had promised me in Boulogne just a year before. I didn't much like the food, wasn't used to the taste of olive oil in everything they cooked, but it was still a joy to get it.

—m—

I can only imagine the mix of thoughts and emotions that engulfed my parents when they first saw each other on that train platform in the Estação Central in Lisbon: joy, love, relief, dreams (or maybe anxiety?) about the future, wondering whether they still knew the person they hadn't seen for so many months. Everything they had struggled for in that year of maydays had now been accomplished. Now what? What did each know about the other that I knew nothing about? What had my father been doing beside trying to get travel documents and hanging out with friends in Lisbon or lying on the beach and playing a few escudos in the casino in Estoril? When our war began, on that May morning the year before, I somehow knew that a world was coming to an end. But no one could guess what would replace it.

Yet it was in Lisbon that we all finally felt free—free, for me, in the joy of seeing my father for the first time in more than a year, free in the security that his presence restored, free in the abundance of everything, in the food especially—cheese, bread, butter, meat and cold cuts, chocolate, pastry—free from the intimidating presence of the troops and police who seemed to be everywhere in the places we'd been for the previous year.[4] Free in the nighttime brightness on the streets. For much of the prior year we had lived in blacked-out towns and cities, and by the end of it we were hardly aware of it any more;

4. In 2013 I learned, almost by accident, that Marc and Bella Chagall, who had been aided by Fry, and might never have made it without Fry's audacious help, arrived in Lisbon on May 11, 1941, which must have been almost the same day that we got there. But, of course, we knew nothing of any of this.

now all was light. Free in freedom. Probably no one who's lived all his or her life in America can understand that sense of liberation.

Portugal, wrote Erich Maria Remarque many years later, "was the gate to America. If you couldn't reach it, you were lost, condemned to bleed away in a jungle of consulates, police stations and government offices where visas were refused, work and residence permits unobtainable, a jungle of internment camps, bureaucratic red tape, loneliness, homesickness and withering universal indifference."[5] That was the jungle we had come from.

Most of all, however, Lisbon brought relief and the joy of reunion for my mother, freedom now from the dreadful burdens she had been carrying for us all. At my age then, I couldn't begin to understand the enormity of those burdens. After their first long hug on that train platform, my father asked my mother, "Where's the rest of your luggage?" In reply she gently put her hand on my head and said, "This is it. This is all I bring you." What a heavy load that must have been.

But now that I think about it, I also realize how much had changed. The grand tour trailer-load of luggage that we began with in Brussels the year before was now down to two small suitcases, a large handbag, and a backpack.

Even now I'm not sure I can imagine the difference women like my mother made for their men, and how much stronger they so often were. Is that something that no one realized in that era? Had it not been for her strength and resolve, I doubt that any of us would have survived; more likely than not, for many thousands, women like her were the difference between survival and the Holocaust. Many of the men who remained at Saint-Cyprien would be transferred to Gurs when Saint-Cyprien was destroyed in the floods of October 1940, and then shipped to the notorious Drancy "transit camp" and subsequently to the death camps in Germany and Poland. For many, staying put and playing it safe, either in Brussels or at Saint-Cyprien, as many did, was the most dangerous decision of all.

—∿∿—

5. Remarque, *The Night in Lisbon* (New York: Harcourt, Brace, 1964), 1.

My father had booked rooms in a grand hotel for our stay—was it just a few days, or was it a week or two? Until our ship sailed, I played endlessly with the red Schuco toy car he had gotten me as a sort of welcoming present. After all that we went through, I was still a kid. At first he talked about the possibility of taking the "Clipper"—it took me a while to understand that it was an airplane, the Pan American Airways flying boat, the newest thing in travel across the ocean. But ultimately we settled for the *Nyassa,* the Portuguese ship that seemed to specialize in transporting refugees, sailing early in June. On arrival in the United States, the ship's "Manifest of Alien Passengers," the official list of the Immigration and Naturalization Service, classified our "race or people" as "Hebrew"—others were listed as "English" or "French" or "Slav," but on our trip that June there seemed to be many more in the first category than in all the others combined. Those "classifications" dated back to the American national origins immigration quota laws of the 1920s. My father's first name, courtesy of the Nazis, was listed as "Israel Otto." My mother's occupation was "housewife."

On the deck before landing on June 13, a sign informed the passengers that we would dock in Brooklyn, which worried me as yet another unscheduled event in our travels. I thought we were supposed to land in New York.[6] But we were not detained at Ellis Island, as my father had feared and as some others were.

On June 22 of that year, nine days after we arrived in New York, Hitler invaded the Soviet Union, thereby making the fatal mistake that my father's generation hoped he'd made when he invaded Luxembourg, Holland, and Belgium on that fateful day in May the year before.

6. Judging from news reports of that year, the *Nyassa* was not an entirely happy ship. On a trip in August, her mast was bent when it hit the Brooklyn Bridge on the approach to her pier. On a prior trip, in April, she carried hundreds of people, most of them European refugees, jammed into "abominable" dormitory-like conditions in the hold that were reported to be similar to conditions in steerage in the nineteenth century. "Ship Snaps Her Mast on Brooklyn Bridge," *New York Times,* August 10, 1941; "Tiny Liner Brings 816 From Europe," *NYT,* April 26, 1941. The Lefos were on that April voyage. We had a cabin on our trip in June—not large, but comfortable.

Epilogue

Wartime always leaves great trails of irony, and 1940–41 was no exception. The "Pure Germans" were released from the camps, while the Jews and the other refugees from the Nazis, who desperately desired Hitler's defeat and often were willing to enlist in the fight, remained imprisoned—and in thousands of cases were later delivered to the death camps in the East. Those who, wanting to be free of the camps, enlisted in the Foreign Legion were often treated as badly in the North African camps where they were assigned, and subject to conditions as marginal and humiliating as those they had escaped.

My mother, for all her survival skills, her determination, her energy, and her courage during the year beginning May 10, 1940, never really managed to cope again after it ended. Within four or five years after our arrival in America, which she came quickly to dislike, she fell apart, sank into a deep depression, tried two or three times to commit suicide, or pretended to, and lived the last years of her life in London, where she was institutionalized for a time and where she died in 1990. I visited her occasionally in her flat in the very Jewish neighborhood of Golders Green, where she lived in the last years of her life and where she occasionally got to see her American grandchildren. Who is to say she wasn't a Holocaust victim, like countless other "survivors"?

The ultimate irony in her story—in this case in more senses than one—was that it took some doing to persuade two rabbis that she was really Jewish so that she could be buried next to her father, Ludwig Haas, in the Jewish cemetery in Karlsruhe, as she wished. She had idolized him. Before her death she researched and wrote a long essay about him and his distinguished career as a statesman in the Weimar period, published by the Leo Baeck Institute.[1] In New York during the war, as my father and I lampooned everything German, she kept talking about Goethe, Schiller, and Heine. I think the piece about her father may have been another way of demonstrating that not everything German was evil.

My half-American father, who became a great booster of everything American in the years after we arrived in this country, couldn't make a living as a fiction writer, despite the three novels that were published here; he returned to Germany in 1950 to reclaim and rebuild the family malt-processing business, which had been Aryanized by the Nazis in the 1930s. Because it was easier to compromise, he became the senior partner of the sons of the Aryans who got his business from the Nazis fifteen years before.

Later he divorced my mother, remarried, and did well enough in the business so that he and my stepmother could become knowledgeable collectors of German Expressionist art. As he was going through the legal negotiations to regain the business he wrote another novel, published in Germany, and he translated James Jones's huge novel *From Here to Eternity* into German. By the time he died in Baden-Baden in 1971, he had again become the complete German. During one of my post-war trips to Germany he told me how offensive he found it when one of his old New York friends visited him and wanted to be taken to Dachau. He remained interested in American culture, but often with an undercurrent of disdain, even contempt, that, after the all-American phase in

1. Judith Schrag-Haas, "Ludwig Haas: Erinnerungen an meinen Vater, 1875–1930," *Bulletin des Leo Baeck Instituts* 4 (1961): 73–93. As a boy I knew nothing about him. He died before I was born, though I recollect pictures of him in a spiked German helmet in World War I, during which he served as an officer and the German army's representative to the Jewish community in Poland.

which he once seemed so comfortable during our years in New York, seemed quite shocking.

I don't know what happened to Brust or Veilchenfeld or the other pseudonymous Jewish émigrés about whom my father wrote and with whom he was interned, or even, with the exception of Lofe (Lefo) and Löwe (Baer), what their real names were. Nor do I know anything about the fates of the Jewish refugees in Brussels who told my mother she was crazy for trying to get out without documents.

Hirsch (German for stag), my father's pseudonymous business partner, whose real name was Cerf, the French equivalent, vanishes from my father's story. According to that story, he went his own *sauve qui peut* way, despite his promises to help us, leaving my mother and me on our own as the Germans were invading Belgium. But in 2013, when I found my father's records in the French archives from Saint-Cyprien, I learned that in July 1940, a few months after my father's internment, Léon Cerf, a citizen of Luxembourg, was living in Aix-en-Provence in southern France and had hired a lawyer named Pellegrin to get my father and his friend Lefo (Lofe) out of Saint-Cyprien. I'm not sure my father ever knew that. And he probably never learned that, despite the extensive supportive documentation Cerf provided, including a long list of the French and American clients of my father's malt business and a year-old affidavit in which my father pledged his loyalty to France, the request was refused. The reason, according to a note on his dossier: the German authorities denied the travel permit he needed, as they did for all German and Austrian Jews.[2] But the file makes clear that while "Hirsch," according to my father's story, had abandoned my mother and run to save himself during the flight from Brussels, Léon Cerf had made diligent efforts to secure his colleagues' release when he got to Aix. Could he have done both?

I said above that we never saw the "little Reinemann" again after we were hauled off the train in Lille, just as we lost track of our other fellow

2. Camp de Saint-Cyprien: "Notice Individuelle" for "Othon Schrag," I 54 in the archives of the Département des Pyrénées-Atlantiques in Pau. Copy in the archives of the US Holocaust Museum in Washington. With the help of Catherine Bertrand, an archivist in the Département des Pyrénées-Atlantiques in Pau, I found the lawyer's letter in my father's file with the camp documents. The lawyer's letter also said that if my father or Lefo were returned to Brussels or Luxemburg, they would be subject to reprisals.

travelers in the various legs of our journeys. But many decades later I learned that Marianne Reinemann had made it to Marseille. There she joined her husband, Heinz (later Henry)—he had also been interned at Saint-Cyprien and, after the floods there, at the camps at Gurs and Les Milles—at almost the same time we got there, and a year later got to America.[3] She died in Vermont in 2011, just short of her hundredth birthday. In a videotaped interview she did with the USC Shoah Foundation, she told only that the Nazis took every valuable she had when they hauled us off the train in Lille, leaving only money she had hidden in a sock. But she gave no hint in the interview of what prompted the search or how she made the rest of the journey.[4] Nor, apparently, did she ever talk about the journey to her son, whom I interviewed after her death.

Reading the accounts of others among the many thousands who were my father's contemporaries in the camps of southern France, even a few from Saint-Cyprien, I'm struck by how different their experiences were— a few better, some much worse—and yet how similar. More than one of those German Jews confessed that, like my father, he had obediently reported to the police as ordered in May 1940 because, as Marianne's husband, Heinz Reinemann, put it, he had been too much influenced by "the Prussian idea to do what we were told," to which he had been trained in his German education.[5] For others, the same obedience led to even more terrible results. Rudolf Breitscheid and Rudolf Hilferding, leading Social Democrats during the Weimar Republic, refused to travel illegally to escape from France, as Fry urged them to do—because of their prominence, Hitler wouldn't dare harm them, they thought—and were later arrested by the Vichy French and delivered to the Gestapo.

3. Henry Reinemann, the husband of Marianne, my mother's "little Reinemann," would say in his taped interview for the USC Shoah Foundation, that the camp at Les Milles was more civilized than Saint-Cyprien or Gurs. But he also talked about "the beautiful view" of the Pyrenees beyond the barbed wire of Saint-Cyprien (which was true, at least on clear days without sandstorms). Oral history interview with the USC Shoah Foundation Institute, VHA interview code 15620. (Video interview).

4. Marianne Reinemann, testimony for the USC Shoah Foundation Institute: VHA interview code 15622. (Video interview). She did say that she had been traveling with another woman and her little boy who had since become a "well-known" journalist.

5. Henry Reinemann, op. cit.

As I reread the story of Hans Licht and his companions in Barracks 25 of Ilot I, it seems, if anything, to have greatly understated their grim privations and humiliations. On September 16, 1940, a few weeks after my father and his friends escaped—and some three months after France had surrendered and the Aryans (the "Nazis") in the camp had long been repatriated—René Kapel, a rabbi from Toulouse and not long before a French Army chaplain, who had visited Saint-Cyprien, sent a letter to the chief rabbi of France, describing the conditions:

> The despair is great; they don't understand why they continue to be interned. They asked themselves in anguish if they'll ever be liberated. They have neither plates nor forks or spoons or cups. They have no blankets; a thin layer of straw serves as their bed. Because of poor hygienic conditions, diseases have ravaged the camp. For several weeks, typhoid fever has claimed a number of victims. The physicians asked urgently for medicines, for bandages, for disinfectants. Some of the internees have visas to go abroad, some of them on the verge of expiring. Since France can't keep and doesn't want to keep these aliens, why doesn't she facilitate their emigration?[6]

What still puzzles me, as it confounds many historians of that era, is France itself: its divided sensibilities, cosmopolitan, tolerant, nativist, vengeful, with a strong streak of anti-Semitism threading through its democratic, egalitarian, and civic ideals. Why did the French (in 1938 and 1939) and the Belgians (in 1940) reflexively imprison people who had long been the greatest enemies of fascism—Spanish, German, Austrian—and were eager to join the fight again, and did so when they could? Why, beginning in 1942, did the Belgians, like the French, deliver tens of thousands of Jews, foreign Jews especially, to the Nazis to be shipped to the death camps? Why was there not more resistance? As a number of scholars have pointed out, the occupiers couldn't have done

6. René Kapel, letter to the chief rabbi of France, September 16, 1940, Mémorial de Shoah, accessed March 2013, http://bdi.memorialdelashoah.org/internet/jsp/media /MmsMediaDetailPopup.jsp?mediaid=109665. Kapel's letter also stressed the great number of professionals—artists, lawyers, government leaders in Weimar Germany, academics, physicians, engineers, scientists—who were among the Saint-Cyprien prisoners.

it without the collaboration of the local authorities.[7] The whys pile up, one on the next. It wasn't always the Nazi occupiers who spurred the anti-Semitic legislation and the subsequent roundup and internment of Jews in France. In 1940 the French were at times ahead of the Nazis.[8] At the same time, countless people, often at great personal risk, shielded refugees, among them thousands of children, in their homes and villages.

The French and Belgian smugglers were often older men and sometimes teenagers—not surprising at a time when most young adult men were either injured, with the free French overseas, or in German prison camps. Some, like the man who walked us through the train yard in Amiens and our leader across the Line of Demarcation, were aging *ancien combattants* who got safely through the carnage of World War I. For them, smuggling refugees, escaped war prisoners, Allied fliers who'd been shot down (and who knows what other contraband?) must have been both a patriotic act of resistance, a way to indulge a little nostalgia, and, at times, a means to make a little money. In 2013, I spoke to a woman in Michigan named Liddy Weinberg, then eighty-six. In July 1942 the French arrested her, her sister, and their parents, German Jews from Frankfurt, also via Brussels, in the town of Palavas-les-Flots where they were hiding. After they were interned in the camp at Rivesaltes in 1942, a Red Cross worker rescued them from the train in which they were to be shipped east. Somehow, using falsified identity cards, they found their way to Les Martys a year or fifteen months after my father and his friends had stayed there and lived in a house very similar to the one they had occupied. They pretended to be Alsatians and posed as Catholics; the French believed them, or pretended to. As a teenager Liddy worked on nearby farms—among other things stuffing geese for their pâté—in return for milk, butter, and other food. The family lived there until the first American troops arrived in 1945.[9]

7. See, e.g. Fraser, *The Fragility of Law: Constitutional Patriotism and the Jews of Belgium* (Abingdon, UK: Routledge, 2008).
8. See, e.g., Michael Marrus and Robert Paxton, *Vichy France and the Jews* (New York: Basic Books, 1981).
9. Liddy Weinberg, telephone interview with author, March 5, 2013. USC Shoah Foundation Institute testimony. VHA interview code 43553. (Video interview). Liddy Weinberg died in August 2013, a few months after our interview.

It's understandable that French tolerance and hospitality were severely tested by the millions of foreign refugees, Dutch, Belgian, German, Polish, Czech, Romanian, who found their way—or were driven
by the Nazis—into France at the start of the war, and in the years just
before. At a time when the German occupiers hauled off French workers,
industrial equipment, and food for their own consumption, the French
economy was stressed to the breaking point. But that makes the unwillingness of French authorities to issue exit visas even more puzzling. It
also underlines the questions raised by Marcel Bervoets: Why were the
French willing to receive and intern the thousands of foreigners, not all
of them Jews, who, like my father, were arrested by the Belgians on May
10 and the days immediately after and shipped to the camps in southern
France, most of them to Saint-Cyprien?

What understandings did the French and Belgians have? Was it true
that the French ambassador in Brussels had agreed before the invasion
that the French would take thousands of internees from Belgium? Who
funded the deportations, arranged for the collaboration of the Belgian
and French railroad systems, paid for the guards, the train engineers?
An exhaustive Belgian study of Belgium's persecution of Jews before and
during the German occupation concluded that many documents on the
French–Belgian understandings regarding the internment of German
and other aliens were destroyed when the French burned their Belgian
embassy files before the Germans arrived in Brussels.[10] So the questions
may never be answered: How much did Belgium pay the French for the
detention of those thousands of deportees? Out of whose budget did it
come and under whose authority? Marcel Bervoets searched everywhere
but still couldn't find an answer to the question: How could France detain thousands of people without any administrative document justify-
ing their arrest, their deportation, and above all, their imprisonment?[11]
And how, and by whom, were the designated camps chosen? Whatever
documents once might have existed about any of those arrangements

10. Rudi Van Doorslaer et al., *La Belgique docile: Les autorités belges et la persécution
des Juifs en Belgique pendant la Seconde Guerre mondiale*. SOMA-CEGES (2004–2007),
accessed July 2014, http://www.senate.be/event/20070213-jews/doc/rapport_final.pdf,
note, p. 176.

11. Bervoets, *La liste de Saint-Cyprien* (Brussels: Alice, 2006), 150–153.

have long since vanished. Here, too, it seems, a set of war criminals escaped any chance to hold them accountable.

I was also puzzled, as I'm sure many others were, by the inconsistencies in the treatment of the inmates at Saint-Cyprien: the harsh and dangerous conditions on the one hand, including the threat that anyone caught outside the barbed wire enclosure would be shot and, on the other, the subsequent willingness of camp commandants to grant their prisoners furloughs in Perpignan, and maybe elsewhere, to get medical help and secure visas and other documents to emigrate. (At the camp at San Nicola, where prisoners were officially warned that if they slipped out they'd be shot, the demoralized guards encouraged internees to crawl under the barbed wire fence and enjoy themselves in the nearby city of Nîmes.)

Getting much further without documents was always hard. It was France, as Feuchtwanger said, that was the prison camp.[12] Did those inconsistencies, at least in the case of Saint-Cyprien, merely reflect personnel changes in camp administration or the vicissitudes of the war, or were they another example of the deeper French ambivalence? Prisoners like Rabbi Leo Ansbacher, who was also interned at Saint-Cyprien, and later in Gurs, believed that the military authorities were always more decent than the civilian police. The Germans played a large role in Vichy France—or more accurately, different roles at different times—but we'll probably never know how much influence they exercised at different times in the management of the camps.

For generations, the most common line of defense of France's wartime behavior—including the delivery of tens of thousands of people to Nazi extermination camps—was that the Germans made France do it, and that indeed France succeeded in saving tens of thousands of others. But as Marrus and Paxton, among others, make clear, the "legislative assault upon Jews living in France"—among them the notorious *Statut des Juifs* of October 1940, which excluded Jews from high positions in the civil service, from the officer corps and from the press, from teaching and from other professions—began well before the German occupiers in

12. Feuchtwanger, *The Devil in France,* 184

Paris had time to unpack their bags and without any sign of German pressure.[13]

Nor did the French have great compunctions about the inhumane conditions in their camps, which, in the years before the Nazis turned to genocide, were sometimes compared sardonically to the Nazi camps by those who had been unlucky enough to have been imprisoned in both. "The Nazi," said Arthur Koestler, who had been interned both in a Spanish prison during the Civil War and at Le Vernet in southern France, "had taught us to comfort ourselves with comparisons."

> In Liberal-Centigrade, Vernet was the zero-point of infamy; measured in Dachau-Fahrenheit it was still 32 degrees above zero. In Vernet beating-up was a daily occurrence; in Dachau it was prolonged until death ensued. In Vernet people were killed for lack of medical attention; in Dachau they were killed on purpose. In Vernet half of the prisoners had to sleep without blankets in 20 degrees of frost; in Dachau they were put in irons and exposed to the frost.[14]

In July 1940, prisoners at Saint-Cyprien sent a letter to the International Committee of the Red Cross, unmentioned in my father's story, complaining about drinking water polluted by fecal matter from the open latrines, and about the rats, flies, fleas, lice, and other vermin, the malnutrition, and the total absence of medicine and disinfectants. As it was sent, hundreds came down with dysentery—another hundred fifty had malaria, and then came the typhus that was only conclusively diagnosed when a courageous doctor—my father's Löwe—slipped out of the camp to get blood samples tested. When the first prisoners arrived from Belgium, the barracks had no floors—they slept on damp sand and flea-infested straw—no windows, and no furniture of any kind. Within three weeks, seventeen died.[15]

---

13. Marrus and Paxton, *Vichy France and the Jews*, 3–5.

14. Arthur Koestler, *Scum of the Earth* (London: Eland, 2006), 68, 94.

15. Denis Peschanski, *Les camps français d'internement (1938–1946)*, Doctorat d'Etat, Université Panthéon-Sorbonne, 2000, accesssed May 2014, https://tel.archives-ouvertes.fr /tel-00362523/document, 395–396.

The inhumanity was not directed particularly at Jews. Saint-Cyprien and the other places in southern France where German and Austrian refugees found themselves had first been thrown up for the hundreds of thousands of refugees who fled Franco's Spain after the end of Spanish Civil War; they were treated no better than the Jews who replaced them in the camps. And it wasn't anti-Semitism that motivated the wholesale plunder of prisoners' possessions by French and Belgian guards—cash, watches, bracelets and other jewelry, silver photo frames.

The maltreatment of prisoners in the French camps would soon be overshadowed by the alphabet of butchery of the Nazi concentration camps, from Auschwitz-Birkenau, Majdanek, Sobibor, and Treblinka to Zyklon B—the whole lexicon of industrialized murder—and the monsters, Eichmann, Mengele, Heydrich, associated with it. That's what the world mostly remembers, when it remembers at all. Without Hitler and the Nazis, there would have been no flood of refugees to the West. There would have been no Vichy. There probably wouldn't even have been a Franco in Spain and thus no exodus into southern France. Mussolini would have been even more of a footnote to history than he became.

The French tried to exonerate themselves with the argument that they saved thousands of Jews even as they betrayed others. And yes, after 1940 they were both beaten by invaders and overwhelmed by refugees. And yes, thousands of French citizens often risked much and gave a great deal of their scarce resources to help refugees. In towns like Le Chambon-sur-Lignon in the Haute-Loire region of south-central France, Protestant pastors like André Trocmé and Edouard Theis, in defiance of Vichy, led whole communities in harboring children and other refugees and helping some escape to Switzerland.[16] We ourselves—my mother, my

16. That story was movingly told in Philip Hallie's *Lest Innocent Blood Be Shed: The Story of the Village of Le Chambon and How Goodness Happened There* (New York: Harper, 1979), and more broadly and with more context by Caroline Moorehead in her *Village of Secrets: Defying the Nazis in Vichy France* (New York: HarperCollins, 2014). Among those who survived there was young Peter Feigl, son of Ernst Feigl, who had been interned at Saint-Cyprien and was later gassed at Auschwitz. But against those triumphs there is the terrible story of Izieu, a village in central France, where Klaus Barbie, the notorious "butcher of Lyon," accompanied by some Gestapo thugs, raided a children's home where forty-four Jewish children were hidden, one as young as four, dragged them off, threw them into trucks like so many sacks of grain, and sent them on their way to the death camps of the East. One child, hidden by an aide at the children's home, survived.

grandmother, and I—found safety and peace with the nuns on the Rue Butor in war-ravaged Boulogne. My father and his friends found refuge in Les Martys. And yes, the United States government interned 120,000 Japanese, two thirds of them native-born American citizens, at almost the same time that the French were beginning to ship their interned Jews to Nazi death camps in the East.

And yet none of that makes the callousness, indifference, and brutality of the French and the Belgian authorities any more justifiable. Hitler did not create French anti-Semitism (and his defeat did not end it). His propagandists fueled the defeatism of a French Right that seemed to prefer fascism to its own domestic Left, but he did not create it either. He did not write the American immigration quota laws that kept hundreds of thousands of European refugees—Jews and others—out of the United States in the 1930s, '40s, and '50s. He was not the one who reneged in 1939 on the British promise of 1917 to support creation of a Jewish homeland, a decision that shut millions of Jews out of Palestine. He was not responsible for the refusal of the thirty-two nations at the Evian Conference in 1938, notwithstanding the pious declarations of sympathy for Europe's Jews, to admit any more refugees. He did not turn the SS *St. Louis* away from American ports when the Cubans refused to allow her nine-hundred-some refugee passengers to come ashore. Some of those passengers would later also find themselves in the French camps—an estimated fifty would be interned at Saint-Cyprien—and later at Auschwitz and Buchenwald.[17] He did not erect or run Argelès, Saint-Cyprien, Gurs, Rivesaltes, Le Vernet, or any of the scores of other *camps de concentration* in southern France. As Lion Feuchtwanger would remind us, what the French call *je m'en foutisme*, the condition of not giving a damn, applied not only to the French, but in this story to the French most of all.

—⁂—

In 1943, Hannah Arendt, who had herself been interned in Gurs and had, like us, arrived in the United States in 1941, published a piece in

17. Of the ship's 937 passengers, most of them German Jews who had embarked at Hamburg in May 1939 hoping eventually to get to the United States, some were admitted by the British, some by Belgium, some by the Dutch, some by the French. But many were caught again in the German invasion in 1940 and interned by the Belgians or French, and/or eventually by the Nazis.

the *Menorah Journal*, an American periodical dedicated to the encouragement of "Jewish humanism" and identity, that may have defined the dilemmas of a generation of Hitler refugees as well as anything ever written. It certainly defined my dilemma. Central to that dilemma is that we never wanted to be known as refugees in any of the places where we came to rest: not in Belgium, not in France, not in America. In part it was pride—we didn't want to be seen as victims or supplicants. We didn't want to be seen as anything but masters of our own destiny. And we didn't want to bore people with stories that sounded like a thousand other stories, or maybe like something lifted from *Casablanca*. For many years I thought it was just me, a young boy. But it was true of most of us. We were immigrants, exiles maybe: "We declared," Arendt wrote, "we had departed of our own free will to countries of our choice, and we denied that our situation had anything to do with 'so-called Jewish problems.'" As German Jews, most of us hardly thought of ourselves as Jews at all. The mad pursuit from consulate to consulate in Marseille and elsewhere for a visa for any place that would take us put the lie to that pretense. But Arendt said more:

> We were expelled from Germany because we were Jews. But having hardly crossed the French borderline, we were changed into "Boches." We were even told that we had to accept this designation if we really were against Hitler's racial theories. During seven years we played the ridiculous role of trying to be Frenchmen—at least prospective citizens; but at the beginning of the war we were interned as "Boches" all the same. In the meantime, however, most of us had become such loyal Frenchmen that we could not even criticize a French governmental order; thus we decided it was all right to be interned. We were the first *"prisonniers volontaires"* history has ever seen. After the Germans invaded the country, the French government had only to change the name of the firm; having been jailed because we were Germans, we were not free because we were Jews.[18]

18. Hannah Arendt, "We Refugees," *Menorah Journal* 31 (1943): 69–67, reprinted in Marc Robinson, ed., *Altogether Elsewhere: Writers in Exile* (Boston: Faber and Faber, 1994), 110–117.

The last is perfectly encapsulated in "Othon" Schrag's *Notice Individuelle* from Saint-Cyprien and the accompanying document from his former partner Léon Cerf's lawyer in Aix-en-Provence listing all the evidence testifying to his loyalty to France—the sworn affidavits, the witness statements, the names of his long-time French business connections—and thus the argument for his release, as if this were just a rational everyday legal proceeding. But along with that there was the cramped handwritten phrase, interlineated on the dossier in the sentence about the prisoner's hope to get his release so he can get his visa for America: the clincher, *"refus de l'autorité Allemande"* (blocked by the German authorities). His story indicates that he feared as much, but it's unlikely that he ever saw those words.

—⁂—

There is an old adage that in war, the first casualty is truth. But it is surely just as correct that in the fog of war, little can be seen very clearly. Even the count of those interned at Saint-Cyprien at any given time varied widely—the best guess is about 7,500 at the end of May, of whom 2,500 were repatriated to Belgium or elsewhere in June or July. And of course there was even more uncertainty about how many were German nationals or Austrians or Jews, or about the number from Saint-Cyprien who were hospitalized in Perpignan with malaria or with what was called typhus but may in some cases have been typhoid fever.[19]

And there's uncertainty in some of the stories in this book as well. Some of my father's narrative about me and my mother struck me as absolutely accurate, evoking memories long forgotten; much corresponds uncannily with accounts and reports from other witnesses, and much is corroborated by the documents from the camps. A few things I found hard to believe, contrary to my own memory, and I have edited some out—he could have gotten it wrong or he might have been writing fiction.[20] Where it seemed true, or was corroborated by other sources, I left

19. There were probably 150 cases of malaria and 112 hospitalizations for typhus, of whom 17 died within three weeks.

20. I was also surprised that my father did not make more of the appeal that prisoners at Saint-Cyprien sent in July 1940 to CICR, the International Committee of the Red Cross,

it in. I am often reminded that at the time I was only eight or nine. As I indicated above, I also left in his story about the children who lived with us in Brussels in 1940–41, although I recall none of it, because it was so integral to his story. Did I just forget?

And there is a lot that this story can't tell. It tells almost nothing about the women, many of them wives of the internees at Saint-Cyprien, often accompanied by children, who were interned at Gurs or elsewhere, or about the countless other camps in Vichy France. It tells little about the hazards and conditions of life for the spouses and families in Perpignan and the other cities near the camps where they struggled—and waited— to get their husbands and brothers released. It's hard to imagine that the cheerful, easy-going, sunny Perpignan of today—as Catalonian as it is French, where you see the orange and yellow Catalan colors as often as you see the tricolor of France—was such a place. I almost called this story *Fidelio*, after the Beethoven opera about a woman who dresses as a man and goes to work in the prison where her husband is unjustly locked up by the tyrant who plans to murder him—and at last gets him freed. There must have been hundreds like her in southern France.

In the early 1940s, the coast north and east from the Spanish border, much of it now a chain of beach resorts—Saint-Cyprien Plage, Le Barcarès, Argelès-Plage, as well as some spots a few miles inland—was a gulag archipelago. Today's residents of the pink and yellow apartment buildings along the shore seem to know nothing of what occupied the beaches where they now swim and sail and sun themselves and where they ride their bicycles by the cafés on the beachfront. Many of those places had been what Christian Eggers called the "antechambers to Auschwitz." Saint-Cyprien was closed in October 1940 after a week of devastating floods, the prisoners moved to Gurs. But with a few exceptions—the memorials at Gurs,[21] in the old brickworks at Les Milles near Aix-en-Provence, the memorial being developed at Rivesaltes, and the

---

cataloguing the horrendous conditions—the rats, the lice, the open toilets, the lack of medications and disinfectants, the unfiltered, polluted water, and all the rest.

21. The memorial is now maintained by Jewish groups and by German cities in Baden— Karlsruhe, Freiburg, Mannheim, among others—from which the Nazis drove thousands of the Jews who were interned, and many of whom died, at Gurs. Thousands of the Gurs prisoners were later delivered to the Nazis and shipped to the death camps in the East.

evocative paintings and drawings of Felix Nussbaum, Osias Hofstät-
ter, Carl Rabus, and Karl Schleswig, all interned at one time at Saint-
Cyprien—there's little trace left of most of the other camps, not on the
ground or in the memory of those who live nearby.

And although there are countless Spanish and North African faces—
in Argelès there's also FFREEE, the association of descendants of Spanish Republican exiles—little remains of the thousands of spouses and
children of the Jewish internees in that gulag archipelago who waited
for them in Perpignan. Only the old landmarks remain—the park in
Perpignan where some felt safe from police roundups, the historic Hôtel
de France, the Castillet, the snow-capped Pyrenees to the west, the wind
called the *tramontane.*

One of the things I was hardly aware of before I worked on this story
is how many people had been interned not in one camp but in three or
four. Heinz Reinemann said the old brick factory at Les Milles, one of
three camps in which he was interned, was "more civilized" than Saint-
Cyprien or Gurs: it wasn't dangerous for healthy young people. Those
who survived could have written comparative guides to the centers of
starvation, disease, misery, and humiliation in which they were confined,
and Koestler nearly did. One, Kurt Baum, born Kurt Feigenbaum, was
interned in ten camps, French and German, from Saint-Cyprien to Buchenwald, from which he was finally liberated by US troops.

Nor does this story tell about the half million refugees from Franco's
Spain, often entire families, the *Retirada,* who, having been offered asylum, had overwhelmed the French in their numbers and needs and had
then been the first to be interned there. They built the jerry-rigged barracks inside the barbed wire fences in which "Hans Licht" and his friends
were imprisoned. Many died in those camps. Some eventually emigrated
to Mexico and other countries willing to take them; some were shipped
to North Africa and reinterned there, some forty thousand were impressed into French labor camps, the "Groupes de Travailleurs Etrang-
ers" (GTE). Many were returned to the tender mercies of Franco's Spain.

I briefly mention Varian Fry and the New York–based Emergency
Rescue Committee, and Harry Bingham and Myles Standish, the vice
consuls in Marseille, who, though they played small parts in this story,
were major players in getting people out of southern France in 1940–41

and were soon recalled by a State Department that was thoroughly opposed to their efforts. In October 2000, the financier Felix Rohatyn, then the US ambassador to France, came to Marseille to honor Fry. As a child—Rohatyn came from a family of Polish Jews living in Paris—he narrowly escaped with his family by way of Marseille. Rohatyn told about Breckenridge Long's State Department memo of 1940 "advising our consuls to put every obstacle in the way—to require additional evidence and to resort to various administrative devices to postpone and postpone and postpone the granting of the visas." The man in Hans Licht's story who blocked access at the Marseille consulate was one little cog in that effort.

But neither my story nor my father's tells much, if anything, about the many others, individuals like Lisa and Hans Fittko and Karl Frucht, who guided refugees in the tough climb over the Pyrenees—did my father know anything about them when he shuttled around Marseille?[22] Nor can one story do justice to the many relief groups, the Jewish organizations that amalgamated as HICEM; the American Jewish Joint Distribution Committee; the Quakers, the Unitarians, the Red Cross, the American Federation of Labor, and many others who tried to help, provided some supplementary food, clothing, and medicine in the camps, and sent paper, pencils, and paint, needles and thread, and sometimes even musical instruments to relieve the boredom, depression, and misery.

22. It's possible that my father later met Frucht when, like Frucht, he was one of the émigré writers and intellectuals who were paying guests in the 1940s at Jimmy and Blanche Cooney's Morning Star Farm in West Whately, Massachusetts. I spent some summer weeks as a young teenager there pitching hay, pulling weeds, picking tomatoes, herding and milking cows, and learning about the grueling work of family farming. Among the other guests were the journalist Hertha Pauli and her friend the German author Walter Mehring, who had also been interned (briefly) at Saint-Cyprien, and from whose poem "Odyssey at Midnight" I quote two lines at the beginning of this book. The poem was published in a small collection, *No Road Back* (New York: Samuel Curl, 1944), which was in fact a portrayal in verse of an odyssey through France, through the camps, very similar to my father's at the same time. But I recall few of the guests. In those days I wasn't interested in refugees. For more about the Cooneys and that unique place, see Deirdre Bonifaz, "A Haven in Whately," in Peter I. Rose, *The Dispossessed: An Anatomy of Exile* (Amherst: University of Massachusetts Press, 2005), 203–230.

It's a long list. At the Maternité Suisse d'Elne, set up in an abandoned château near Elne, not far from where my father and thousands of others were unloaded from the cattle cars and taken to Saint-Cyprien, the Swiss nurse Elisabeth Eidenbenz and a group of others were delivering and caring for the babies of the pregnant women they'd somehow rescued from the surrounding camps. There was Aristides De Sousa Mendes, the Portuguese consul in Bordeaux, a good Catholic, who, in defiance of his government's orders, in June 1940 issued some fifteen hundred visas to the desperate refugees, nearly all Jews, trying to escape the Germans. He would pay a high personal price for it.[23] And, as I indicated above, there were the church people in small towns and villages, Protestant and Catholic, who took in Jews, children especially, listed them under new names, and hid them until the end of the war. One of the measures of the banality of evil in those years is how much courage it took for ordinary people just to treat their fellow humans with a measure of decency.

I never had the presumption to describe myself as a "Holocaust survivor" until I was chastised by an old friend in New York who is married to a Hungarian Jew—now an American-Hungarian Jew—who narrowly escaped both the Nazis and the Russians. Yes, she reprimanded me, you certainly are a Holocaust survivor: no, you never were in a camp and, as you say, you have no tattoo on your arm. But you lived in, and escaped from, Nazi-occupied Europe. You came within a hair of being hauled off that train in Lille, you could have been shot on your walk through the woods at the Line of Demarcation from occupied into Vichy France.

My mother, I've come to realize, could have been arrested countless times at the various checkpoints on her undocumented trips from Brussels to southern France and back—and then back again. If it hadn't been for her courage, her determination to get my father away from Saint-

---

23. De Sousa Mendes was immediately recalled by the Portuguese dictator Antonio Salazar, who had issued the orders; stripped of his job and his livelihood (he had thirteen children), he died penniless. Salazar's attempts to protect his country's neutrality—and profit richly from it—by catering to both sides in World War II is itself a long and fascinating story. And so was the scene in Lisbon, famously a nest of spies, where thousands of refugees collected desperately waiting for visas and passage anywhere out of Europe. And alongside them the spies, and the waiters, chambermaids, hotel clerks, and others in their pay, and the PVDE, Salazar's secret police, watching them all.

Cyprien, and her success in finding him a hiding place at Les Martys (along with the risks that Mayor Ilhe and many others took), he might well have ended on the same forced march through the concentration camps—from Saint-Cyprien to Gurs or Rivesaltes to Drancy—that took thousands of others to the gas chambers of Auschwitz. Those of the German exiles who "had in various adventurous ways reached the south of unoccupied France," in Koestler's words, "were hiding in little villages in the Pyrenees... and on the Mediterranean coast. Their fate depended on the local gendarmes, mayors, and prefects. Any of these had the power to throw them back into a jail or in a concentration camp, without legal proceedings."[24]

No one will ever know how many of the people who advised my mother not to take the risks she took, choosing instead the apparent comfort and safety of their lives in the Brussels of the 1941, ended in the death camps of 1942, 1943, and 1944. For many millions, the difference, despite their courage and determination, often was no more than a roll of the dice, a flip of the coin, pure chance. Courage was essential, but for many it wasn't enough. Nor will we ever know how many thousands of "survivors" were, like my mother, permanently injured, even when they had no brands, no tattoos, and no visible scars.

24. Koestler, *Scum of the Earth*, 243.

SOURCES AND ACKNOWLEDGMENTS

AS INDICATED IN THE INTRODUCTION, MY FATHER'S STORY HAD
been lying around in one or another drawer for more than seventy years.
It might have been lying around forever had it not been for the urging of
friends and relatives, chief among them my wife, Patricia Ternahan; my
son Ben; and my cousin, also named Peter Schrag. Nor is it likely that I
would have gone through with it had I not found confirmation in Marcel
Bervoets's monumental book, *La liste de Saint-Cyprien,* which has the
names, birthdates, and other details of some four thousand of the men
who were interned at Saint-Cyprien, my father's among them. I use the
word "monumental" not only because of the enormous amount of work
it must have taken Bervoets to produce it from the individual archival
files on each prisoner and from other documents, Belgian and French,
and from the great amount of other painstaking research involved, but
also because he would probably never have undertaken it except as a
sort of monument to his father and uncle, both of whom were interned
there and later died at Auschwitz. In the years since I began my work,
Bervoets has also provided other background and constant encouragement mixed with wise caution about the project. Ultimately he read the
whole manuscript made many valuable suggestions and, in the process,
became a warm friend. I owe him a lot.

But I also needed help from many others. Since my father fictionalized parts of his story, often changing the names of people and places,
including his own, and since my own childhood memories were often
incomplete and not always trustworthy, much had to be corroborated
or, in my case, filled in, by research in independent sources. Many of

the sources are cited in the footnotes, some not, and many are not fully credited for the help they provided: archivists and chroniclers both in this country and in Belgium, France, Germany, and Israel: scholars and French nuns in Paris; government officials, children of camp internees, those still living, among them the late Liddy Weinberg, who, with her parents, had been rescued from a deportation train and lived and worked as a teenager in Les Martys in the years immediately after my father hid there, very possibly in the same ramshackle house. I also relied on the rich collections of Holocaust documents at the Center for Jewish History and the Leo Baeck Institute in New York, at the United States Holocaust Memorial Museum in Washington, at the Tauber Holocaust Library in San Francisco, at the Mémorial de la Shoah in Paris, and in the voluminous trove of videotaped interviews of survivors at the USC Shoah Foundation at the University of Southern California in Los Angeles, where I found, among others, a taped interview with Marianne Reinemann, who had briefly traveled with my mother and me during our escape from Nazi-occupied Belgium in 1941—the first I had heard of her since we were separated at the train station in Lille some seventy years before.

Never has a major historical event been documented as painstakingly, extensively, wisely, with more devotion, or in more institutions, nor have many archives been maintained so well, or for so noble a purpose, as those pertaining to the Holocaust. Given the vast range of material and people involved, I can't possibly name all the individuals who helped and sometimes guided me at those institutions or elsewhere. In the United States, I owe a special debt of gratitude to Vincent Slatt, librarian at the US Holocaust museum, who not only arranged my viewing of the microfilm of key French records but often got me back on the trail when I'd lost it; to his USHMM colleague Caroline Waddell, who helped me search out and provided copies of the rare photos that were taken at Saint-Cyprien; to the exemplary Michael Simonson and his colleague David Rosenberg for their invaluable help at the Leo Baeck Institute in providing both documents and artwork, and in helping me to contact other sources; to Tara Craig of the Columbia University Rare Book and Manuscript Library; and to Devon Maeve Nevola of the Columbia Preservation Reformatting Department. I'm also indebted to Misha Mitsel of the American Jewish Joint Distribution Committee in New York for digging out an old report that I never hoped to find; to archivist Glenn Worthey and his colleagues Anna Levia and Zachary Baker at the Cecil H. Green Library at Stanford University for securing and helping me negotiate the tapes of the oral interviews from the USC Shoah Foundation; and to countless staff members and archivists at the State Department in Washington and the US consulate in Marseille in my search for records and photos bearing on my father's pursuit of and eventual success in getting his US visa. What surprised me in that search is that while there are countless pictures of his colleague Hiram Bingham in the visa section of the Marseille consulate, nowhere—not in the State Department archives nor in other archives—could I find a single picture of Myles Standish, the vice consul (Stanwick in my father's story) who most probably issued his visa.

Among those overseas who were of particular help, I owe special thanks to Anne Goulet and Catherine Bertrand of the Office of the General Counsel in the Département des Pyrenées-Atlantiques in Pau, who first located and sent me copies of my father's and his friend Fritz Lefo's dossiers from the camp at Saint-Cyprien. Those dossiers conclusively confirmed that I was on the right track and that my father's narrative was much more memoir than novel. I also owe thanks to Sylvie Vander Elst and her colleague Gert De Prins of the Service Archives et Documentation of the Social Security Administration in Brussels for providing copies of other official documents from the time of the Nazi occupation of Belgium; to the archivists at the Département de l'Aude in Carcassonne; to Prof. Anne Grynberg of the Universités à l'Institut National des Langues et Civilisations Orientales, Paris, author of *Les camps de la honte,* a comprehensive study of the French camps, who provided important leads and much encouragement; to her former student Johanna Linsler, of the Centre de Documentation at the Shoah Memorial in Paris; to Bronislawa Sarnowski of the International Tracing Service; to Patricia Domps at the mayor's office in Les Martys and Patrick Claret, the grandnephew of Paul Ilhe, the one-time mayor of Les Martys, who helped me confirm his great-uncle's identity and identify the now beautifully restored home that was probably the derelict house Mayor Ilhe provided for my father and his friends, and which served as their hideout in 1940–41. I also owe thanks to Sœur Annie of the Service des Archives of the Filles de la Charité and Sœur Fromaget of the Service des Archives of the Compagnie des Filles de la Charité de Saint Vincent de Paul, both in Paris, who helped me pin down the location of the convent, now long gone, where their predecessor sisters housed and sheltered my mother, my grandmother, and me in the weeks after the battle of Boulogne.

Many of the books, articles, and witness statements that I especially relied on are cited in the text. Among the most significant on a long list: Lion Feuchtwanger's *The Devil in France*; Arthur Koestler's *Scum of the Earth*; Varian Fry's *Surrender on Demand*; Monique-Lise Cohen and Eric Malo's *Les camps du sud-ouest de la France, 1939–1944*; Max Lagarrigue's *La France du repli, L'Europe de la defaite*; Ruth Schwertfeger's, *In Transit: Narratives of German Jews in Exile, Flight and Internment during the "Dark Years" in France*; Michael R. Marrus and Robert O. Paxton's *Vichy France and the Jews* and Dan Michman's *Belgium and the Holocaust: Jews, Belgians, Germans*. I also relied on the exhaustive document produced by Rudi Van Doorslaer and his collaborators, *La Belgique docile* (a thousand-plus-page commission report on Belgium's behavior toward Jews and aliens before and during the war); on Maxime Steinberg, *La persecution des Juifs en Belgique*; Joël Rochoy, *Le Boulonnais dans la guerre, 1939–1945*; Susan Zuccotti, *The Holocaust, the French and the Jews*; Lisa Fittko, *Escape Through the Pyrenees*; Ronald Weber, *The Lisbon Route: Entry and Escape in Nazi Europe*, plus a considerable list of exhibition catalogs, *catalogues raisonés*, and other books on the major concentration camp artists.

In my search for artwork from Saint-Cyprien, especially the works of Felix Nussbaum, Karl Schwesig, and Carl Rabus, and for maps and other illustrative material I got special help and warm encouragement from Dr. Pnina Rosenberg of the Technion in Haifa, an expert on the art produced by inmates in the French internment camps, and author of the comprehensive *L'Art des indésirables*. I also appreciate the help of Anat Bratman-Elhalel, director of archives at the Ghetto Fighters House Museum in Western Galilee, Israel; of Sheryl Ochayon of the Yad Vashem Museum in Jerusalem; of Roland Krüppel of Herrsching, Germany, and the Buchheim Museum in Bernried, Germany, which has many of Carl Rabus's works; and of Anne Sibylle Schwetter, research assistant at the Felix-Nussbaum-Haus in Osnabrück, Germany. I must also express my gratitude to cartographer Darin Jensen of the University of California at Berkeley for his careful work on the map of the various journeys described in these stories.

Finally, I owe more than I can say to the many people who encouraged this project, read parts or all of the draft, made helpful suggestions, sometimes accepted, sometimes not. During much of the time I was working on this book they seemed to have more confidence in it than I had. That list includes my daughter, Mitzi Schrag, a wise reader of literature; my sons, Ben and David; my cousin Anthony Haas; and my long-time friends and former colleagues at the *Sacramento Bee* Claire Cooper and Rhea Wilson, who made wise suggestions on early drafts of this story. It must also include my friend and agent Ellen Levine of the Trident Media Group, who worked hard on this project, mostly for friendship's sake, since there was little hope that it would ever become a big commercial success in a market with ever less room for Holocaust memoirs, or maybe, given our time and culture, for any book of this kind. I'm also grateful to the people at Indiana University Press, among them my editor Robert Sloan, to David Miller and to Candace McNulty, who did as smart and thoughtful a piece of copy-editing as any I've ever benefited from in a long career as a writer.

Finally, in the category of last but most, I owe much more than I can say to my wife, Patricia Ternahan, not just for her constant encouragement and belief in this project and in many others, but for much practical help. As a talented photographer who works with and knows Photoshop, she devoted countless hours tweaking and testing any number of possible illustrations, many of which would never have seen print without her skillful help.

And now I must deliver the ultimate acknowledgement. This book is dedicated to my late mother, something that authors do for their mothers every day, but which had never occurred to me with any of the ten or so books I'd published before. As I said in the epilogue, my mother had a breakdown soon after the war and was never in good emotional shape thereafter. As a teenager, I sometimes served as a sort of surrogate parent and counselor to her, and for many years afterward we had only occasional contact. It was not until I read my father's story and recalled my own that I realized how courageous and strong she had been during the war. She had almost certainly saved my life, maybe more than once, had rescued my father from his internment camp and found him and others their place to hide. For none of that did she ever get much recognition. My father's title for his draft memoir, *Heroes Without Courage*, is thus doubly ironic. The title had it almost exactly backward. My great regret is that my acknowledgement had to come so late.

OTTO SCHRAG was born into a middle-class Jewish family in Karlsruhe, Germany. His father was a lawyer; his mother, the former Bella Sulzberger, was born in New York. As he was finishing his university studies at Heidelberg before the war, he entered his grandfather's malt (for beer) processing business. In 1935, two years after the Nazis came to power, he moved his family to Luxembourg and, in 1939, as war loomed, to Brussels. With the German invasion of Belgium, Luxembourg, and Holland in 1941, the Belgians arrested him and thousands of other German expatriate refugees, most of them Jewish, as enemy aliens and shipped them to southern France, where they were interned in concentration camps. Schrag, with help from his courageous wife, Judith, eventually escaped. It is the story of that imprisonment and escape, ultimately to New York, that he tells here. In the 1940s, he was the author of three well-regarded novels, *The Locusts, Sons of the Morning,* and *Bedrock.* He was also among the writers, many well known, associated with a literary magazine called *'47.* In 1950, he returned to Germany to reclaim the business the Nazis had seized and rebuilt it again into a successful enterprise. In Germany he also wrote another novel and translated James Jones's *From Here to Eternity* into German. He died in Baden Baden in 1971.

PETER SCHRAG, former editorial page editor of the *Sacramento Bee* and former executive editor of *Saturday Review* magazine, is a lifelong journalist. He is the author of articles and reviews in *Atlantic, Harper's, Nation, New Republic, Playboy, American Prospect, New York Times, Los Angeles Times, Washington Post,* and other publications. His book *Paradise Lost: California's Experience, America's Future* (New York: New Press, 1998), was chosen as a *New York Times* Notable Book and issued as a paperback by the University of California Press in 1999. Among his other recent books are *Final Test: The Battle for Adequacy in America's Schools* (New York: New Press, 2003) and *California: America's High-Stakes Experiment* (Berkeley: University of California Press 2006). His latest book is *Not Fit for our Society: Immigration and Nativism in America* (Berkeley: University of California Press, 2010). He has taught at Amherst College, the University of Massachusetts at Amherst, the Bread Loaf Writers Conference, and the Graduate School of Journalism and the Graduate School of Public Policy at the University of California at Berkeley.